V. Dark Visions

CONVERSATIONS WITH THE MASTERS OF THE HORROR FILM

Other Interview Collections by
Stanley Wiater
from Avon Books

DARK DREAMERS:
CONVERSATIONS WITH THE MASTERS OF HORROR

V. Dark Visions

Conversations with the Masters of the Horror Film

STANLEY WIATER

AVON BOOKS ◆ NEW YORK

DARK VISIONS is an original publication of Avon Books. This work has never before
appeared in book form.

AVON BOOKS
A division of
The Hearst Corporation
1350 Avenue of the Americas
New York, New York 10019

First Avon Books Trade Printing: February 1992

AVON TRADEMARK REG. U.S. PAT. OFF. AND IN OTHER COUNTRIES, MARCA REGISTRADA,
HECHO EN U.S.A.

Printed in the U.S.A.

OPM   10   9   8   7   6   5   4   3   2   1

To my parents—
who once crazily believed these films would warp my mind

and

To my godmother Audrey—
who always encouraged me to play in the twilight zone

and

To Iris—
who keeps me from getting lost in the darkness

Acknowledgments

An endeavor of this size cannot be done alone. My deepest thanks go first to the talented people interviewed, for this book, who took time away from their busy schedules to deal with my never-ending questions. My gratitude as well (and you know what you did!) to G. Michael Dobbs, Stephen R. Bissette, Chas. Balun, Christopher Golden, Anthony Timpone, Dennis Daniel, Philip Nutman, Steve Swires, and John Gilbert. Without their help, this project could have never been started, let alone completed. Thanks also to Eric Caidin of Hollywood Book and Poster Co.

A special tip of the hat to my Avon editor, John Douglas, for his patience, and to my agent, Catherine Mahar, for her persistence along the way.

Contents

CONTENTS

Dark Visions

CONVERSATIONS WITH THE MASTERS OF THE HORROR FILM

A Conversation with the Interviewer

by G. Michael Dobbs

The Eisenhower years of status quo, white-bread Americanism seemed hardly appropriate to be the time in which two culturally subversive forces rose full grown to stalk through the country's imagination. One was rock 'n' roll, the music that not only dared to cater to the growing numbers of teenagers, but also helped break down walls between white and black America.

The other was a new and intense interest in horror, specifically horror films. Certainly, there had been several times when the moviegoing public was treated to cycles in which such films were in vogue, but something was different in the midfifties. These horror films were aimed at the teens who were now making up a vital part of the movie audience. Adults were staying home more to watch television and were only lured to the theaters out of habit or when a spectacular, such as *Ben Hur*, gave them what free television couldn't.

Theater owners were elated when independent producers started giving them movies that teens enjoyed—rock 'n' roll musicals, lurid tales of kids-gone-bad, and horror and science fiction films. At the same time, Universal Pictures sold packages of their classic horror movies to television stations around the country. The now-legendary "Shock Theatre" included such favorites as Bela Lugosi's *Dracula*, Boris Karloff's *Frankenstein*, and Lon Chaney, Jr.'s *The Wolfman*.

Many stations even hired hosts to introduce the films. Personalities such as John Zacherle who were not content just to tell people what they were about to see but gave many viewers their first taste of dark humor. As a kid, I vividly remember an appearance by Zacherle on "The Today Show" that both scared and delighted me. Zach was chortling maniacally as he was showing Jack Lescoulie his giant "amoeba," in actuality a stitched-together cheesecloth bag of Jell-O—a delightfully odd image for 7:45 in the morning!

There was a new esthetic being born, although scarcely anyone would have called it that back then (and I shudder to sound so pompous now). Young people were discovering a darker kind of entertainment. A celluloid roller coaster that in moments could whisk them from nervous laughter to sheer terror. The images of death and the supernatural were no longer taboo. They were (gasp) (shudder) *cool.*

Certainly there was plenty of resistance to horror. After all, Dr. Fredric Wertham's infamous *Seduction of the Innocent* was fresh in the collective American memory, and this book practically killed the horror comic industry all by itself. Many people were concerned by the more overt sexuality and the increased bloodletting in contemporary horror films (Hammer's 1957 production *The Curse of Frankenstein* was considered "revolting" by many critics).

One could imagine why the Wiaters of placid Hadley, Massachusetts, became concerned about their son Stanley's viewing and reading habits. Hadley was known as a rural community populated by salt-of-the-earth Yankee and Polish farmers. Its broad green fields of corn, squash, and asparagus were not the appropriate backdrops for vampires, zombies, and werewolves. Young Stanley's interests may have been viewed as an exception to the norm by his parents, who couldn't possibly realize just how many kids were being thrilled by the things-that-go-bump on the television or movie screen all across the country.

Like rock 'n' roll, horror films seemed to be the near exclusive province of the postwar generation. Rock 'n' roll had token adult Dick Clark to promote it, and monster movies had Forrest J. Ackerman, a kindly uncle sort whose publication *Famous Monsters of Filmland* gave horror fans a voice and meeting place. For Stanley Wiater, discovering *FM* proved to be a turning point in his life, just as it was for film directors Steven Spielberg, John Landis, and Joe Dante. (Not to mention an entire generation of horror writers, including Stephen King.)

Ultimately, Stanley's parents were so concerned that they told him he could have a subscription to any magazine he wanted so long as he gave up reading monster movie publications. He chose *Playboy*, believing they would never let their fifteen-year-old son actually receive it, but they were sincere. Stanley of course did not live up to his part of the bargain and started sneaking *Famous Monsters* into the house under his shirt and reading late into the night with his flashlight.

Stanley has come a considerable distance since his flashlight days. He has not only met and interviewed many of the people responsible for his interests, passions, and career, but they view him as a colleague. This is partly because, besides being an accomplished journalist and "cineteratologist," he is also a considerable writer of horror fiction. (Short stories for now, with novels and screenplays on the way.) Put another way, he knows this territory of fear from both inside and out. Now, to set the tone for the fascinating conversations that follow, let's interview the interviewer.

DOBBS: What is your earliest fantasy film memory?
WIATER: It would have to be the original *Godzilla*, as that is the first movie I ever convinced my parents to let me stay up and watch on the late, late show. I was about six or seven years old, and completely hooked on dinosaurs. And after that movie, I found myself sneaking downstairs after my parents had gone to bed to stay up for "Shock Theatre" and see the great old Universal horror films. Basically, it was *Godzilla* that eventually led me to sleeping by day and living by night.
DOBBS: What did your parents think about all this?
WIATER: My interest in the fantastic was pretty innocent at first. Dinosaurs seem harmless enough, but then it was the idea that my folks didn't really know what was going on. You see dinosaurs were also *monsters*, and I craved anything that might have to do with that subject. I was begging, as all children beg their parents, to stay up late at night to watch these shows. This was around 1959, 1960, and there were great horror shows on like "Thriller," "Way Out," "The Twilight Zone" . . . even "Alfred Hitchcock Presents" could scare the hell of out you back then.

All my parents could figure out was that it didn't seem like the best thing for their son to be hooked on. Back then, articles were being published in the newspapers and general interest magazines by so-called experts saying, "Hey, horror movies might be giving your kids nightmares. This might lead to permanent brain damage someday, or maybe just rabid juvenile delinquency. So watch out!"
DOBBS: For me, an interest in horror has a subversive quality to it. I

mean, you're not outside tossing the football with Dad, you're spending a lot of time in dark theaters or glued in front of the television
with these ugly monsters. Did you ever feel that?

WIATER: I did. I knew it didn't please my parents, and none of my
relatives—with the exception of my wonderful godmother—understood it, and I guess that was part of the unconscious attraction to it.
With horror, I could say "This is mine. You don't understand how
important it is, and that's great."

DOBBS: When did horror become something you purposely sought for
entertainment?

WIATER: I'd say between ten and twelve, that magical period when
you're not quite a child and not yet a teenager, and you're still trying
to figure out what you're supposed to be doing in the world. But in
1964 I was actively reading horror and science fiction comic books
and paperbacks, which my parents really didn't mind because at that
point they were just happy to see I had an interest in reading. Anyway,
the day came when I saw *Famous Monsters of Filmland* at the newsstand—issue 30 I believe, with Bela Lugosi on the cover—and that
cemented it all for me.

It was the idea that horror was not just a weird interest for a little
kid in a one-horse town, but that people took it seriously enough to
actually publish magazines on the subject.

DOBBS: I think that's the whole reason all the other horror fanzines
sprang up. People wanted to communicate with others their interest
in horror, and *FM* was the catalyst.

WIATER: Exactly. There was also *Castle of Frankenstein*, which
remains my favorite. The point is, you could find these magazines at
nearly every newsstand, and it made you realize, Well, I'm not very
good at science. I'm not very good at Little League, and I'm not very
good with my hands in terms of being a plumber or a carpenter. But
so what—these people are happy talking and writing about monsters
and death and the dark.

As I was growing up, and began hanging around with guys my
own age, we had our own monster club for a while where we put on
makeup and pretended to be famous monsters and swapped issues of
assorted horror comics and magazines. This club was something that
brought me into the world of lasting friendships and imagination. It
wasn't Little League—my parents forced me into that stupidity for
two summers and I hated every minute of it.

But *Famous Monsters* gave me my first clue by saying that people
write about this for a living, make horror movies for a living, and
maybe—just maybe—somehow I can fit into this special world. It was
a light saying, "Come, come this way. We'll get you going in life

on this path." And the path was monsters. You had to be very brave or very naïve to think that's where your destiny was. But I always did.

DOBBS: Do you recall your first fright in a movie theater?

WIATER: Sure. My dad would drop my two older sisters and me off for the Saturday or Sunday matinee almost every weekend. We saw everything, from Disney to Elvis Presley. But this time it was the *House of Usher*, and I was all of seven years old. It scared the hell out of me. [Laughs.] Yet it was a wonderful feeling finally seeing a horror movie on the big screen because at that point I had only seen them on television, and of course on a black-and-white set. It was very memorable to finally see blood in color, if you know what I mean.

DOBBS: You started your career as an interviewer while still an undergraduate at the University of Massachusetts?

WIATER: Yes, I won a scholarship to study moviemaking at Warner Brothers Studios in the summer of 1974. That experience gave me the opportunity to interview several authors and filmmakers, including my literary idol Ray Bradbury and the late George Pal. I sold the interviews to a local newspaper upon my return, and I thought, Hey, this is something I can do with my life after college. I may never be as famous as a Bradbury or a Pal, but at least I can interview famous people until my own writing career takes off. I'm still trying to have my cake and eat it, too.

DOBBS: You've already done a volume of interviews with horror authors in *Dark Dreamers*, many of whom you'd admired since childhood. In this collection, you speak with both Vincent Price and Roger Corman, the star and director respectively of *House of Usher*. It must have been a thrill for you to talk with the two people who gave you your first movie theater scare.

WIATER: It was wonderful! It's one thing reading about the idols of your childhood, or seeing documentaries about them, but to be able to meet these people and tell them directly: "You know, you changed my life forever thirty years ago" or "Because of you I discovered what I wanted to become in life" is something else again.

As far as I'm concerned, there's so much inherent sadness in the world and so much grim reality that to find any happiness is a long shot. So it's great if you're able to thank that person who made you happy at a time when you didn't fully understand what was supposed to make you happy. One of the reasons I did these books is because I wanted to go and meet those people who so favorably upset my life—and become another link in that chain of helping people learn more about what brings them joy.

DOBBS: You cover a wide territory of talents, from directors to actors to screenwriters to producers in this book. Why not just stick with directors?

WIATER: I wanted to look at the horror film industry from more than one aspect for the simple reason that filmmaking is a collaborative art. With the exception of a very few, such as John Carpenter for example, directors rarely write the screenplay and compose the score as well as direct the picture. I thought that in this particular genre, the special makeup effects people, such as Dick Smith, have as much creative input as does the screenwriter or the actor. Then again, what would *Psycho* have been like if Joseph Stefano hadn't written such a brilliant screenplay? And what would *A Nightmare on Elm Street* have been like if Robert Englund hadn't done such a great interpretation of Freddy Krueger? Or how successful would *Aliens* have been without an incredibly creative producer like Gale Ann Hurd?

I wanted to get as many different voices, as many different visions as I could. And I wanted to keep it as contemporary as possible, not a trip down nostalgia lane, with the obvious exception of Vincent Price of course!

DOBBS: Any of the interviews for which you have a particular fondness?

WIATER: That's difficult to say. As I stated before, growing up in a small town, you often felt everyone was right and you were wrong when folks said horror was bad for you, and that playing sports and looking forward to a nine-to-five job was supposed to be the only normal way to act.

What I found most memorable in these interviews is how these people were able to put out sensible, logical, and persuasive arguments about why horror is, in a word, good for you. I grew up trying to explain my beliefs to my peers and probably did a poor job of it— why there's nothing strange in liking monster movies and collecting monsters models and the like, while still enjoying every other "normal" aspect of life.

Yet when I interviewed the gifted personalities who make up *Dark Visions*, what was most fascinating to me was how, on many different levels, they could articulate that the "strange" people who write, produce, and direct horror movies are helping keep us "normal" people all sane. That if we didn't see the release of violence and death on the screen or in some fictional form, then we'd all be a lot more screwed up as human beings than we already are.

As I stated at the beginning of *Dark Dreamers*, the people who best enjoy the light are those who willingly explore the darkness.

DOBBS: Do you get any overall sense of what the future of horror in the cinema will be like from these "conversations with the masters of the horror film?"

WIATER: Just that the endless series of *Friday the 13th* sequels and *Halloween* clones seem to be on the wane. The so-called "splatter films" have pretty much run their course. It seems that horror films are continuing to follow in the tradition of horror literature, and the current trend in horror fiction is away from the explicit description of gore and mayhem and is now moving into deeper psychological and metaphysical themes. Although since the fifties most horror films have been geared primarily with an adolescent audience in mind, I think we're seeing a change toward some truly adult horrors. Technically and esthetically, we've gone to the limit of bloodletting and exploding heads. I believe what the people involved in *Dark Visions* are saying is "We know already that we can do all that, so now let's investigate more primal fears."

DOBBS: What's next on your agenda in the horror field or as an interviewer?

WIATER: I'd like to do a book of interviews with the top comic book artists and writers in the world, as I've always had a great affection and respect for comic books that has never left me. As the saying goes, "It's never too late to have a happy childhood." Until then, I hope I've done my job by exploring these dark visions.*

---

*Author's note: G. Michael Dobbs is a college instructor, film historian, and writer who has interviewed dozens of people in the motion picture industry, as diverse as Lillian Gish, Rick Moranis, Dave Thomas, and Elvira. He is currently working on a book on the life and career of pioneer animator Max Fleischer and has written *The Year in Fear,* a calendar for horror fans with artist Stephen R. Bissette. He lives in Springfield, Massachusetts, with his wife Mary and daughter Chau.

Geoff Shields

Clive Barker

I f there's anyone who deserves to be in both *Dark Visions* and its already published companion volume, *Dark Dreamers: Conversations with the Masters of Horror*, it would have to be Clive Barker.

This multitalented horror superstar is acclaimed as an award-winning writer of fiction (*Books of Blood, Weaveworld, Damnation Game, The Great and Secret Show, Imajica*), screenwriter (*Underworld, Rawhead Rex*), and director (*Hellraiser, Nightbreed*). He was also executive producer on *Nightbreed* and the sequels to *Hellraiser*, the first being *Hellbound: Hellraiser II*, with the third film in the series about to go into production. He has a two-picture deal in the works with Universal as writer-director, and has several other film deals in various stages of development, primarily stories from his six-volume *Books of Blood*. Like that of his good friend Stephen King, virtually all of his published work, whether in

novel or short story form, is under option. Among the topics
not mentioned in this interview are the comic book adaptations of his stories or the forthcoming books of his fantastic
and grotesque artwork.

Clearly, Barker has already sold his soul to the devil to
keep all these projects going simultaneously without having
his brain explode.

In person, Barker does project himself as a individual of
seemingly boundless energy, who just happens to be doing what
he loves best: taking us past the borderlands to even stranger
worlds just beyond this reality. Born in Liverpool, on October
5, 1952, Barker is most revered by his fans because he makes
no apologies for being a person consumed with "dark visions."
Like many of the great dark dreamers of our time, Barker was
enthralled with horror from a very early age and even built the
Aurora kits of the Wolfman and the Mummy.

His enthusiasm on any subject he cares to discuss is infec-
tious, and he clearly enjoys being identified as someone who
prefers to be making horror films rather than musical comedies.

I interviewed Clive Barker as he was working on the treatment for his next project as writer-director, an original retell-
ing of one his favorite childhood horror themes: the ancient
legend of the Mummy.

SELECTED FILMOGRAPHY

Underworld (1985) (screenplay only)

Rawhead Rex (1987) (screenplay only)

Hellraiser (1987) (screenplay, director)

Hellbound: Hellraiser II (1988) (story, executive producer)

Nightbreed (1990) (screenplay, director, executive producer)

WIATER: Oliver Stone, who directed two mediocre horror films early in his career, once said that to be a truly successful director of horror you "have to be a sadist with a camera."

BARKER: There are two levels in which there's an element of truth in that statement. First, you've got to communicate something very intense to an audience who is being pushed beyond the limits of their taste or what they feel is acceptable. I think that's part of your duty as a director; people are coming to horror movies for a very different kind of experience than they would in a thriller or suspense movie. They're there to be *terrified*.

That's got to be at least part of what their response to the movie is. Maybe the movie is going to make them feel repulsed, distressed, uneasy. Full of dread. If the inducing of those feelings in an audience is "sadistic," then Stone is correct. But to be a true sadist, you've got to be doing this to *somebody who really doesn't want to have this done to them*. [Laughs.]

But the experience is really an act of pseudosadism: the audience *knows* what they're coming to see, they've paid their six bucks. They're saying, "Okay, Mr. Barker . . . or okay, Mr. Cronenberg, okay, Mr. Lynch, or whoever the director is, *horrify me*." So true sadism may be *not* horrifying them!

WIATER: However, for those who regularly attend this kind of movie, it seems that every generation has new heights—or depths—of what it takes to be satisfied as a collective audience. Perhaps there's almost no way to truly scare an audience anymore—they simply want gory special effects brought in as quickly as you can kill the characters off?

BARKER: There is *absolutely* a problem with the attention span of today's younger audiences. Which is certainly a consequence of the way television programs and MTV and advertising presents images. Young audiences are much less willing to sit through the conversation and character-building scenes. In testing *Nightbreed*, for instance, if a scene of two people talking went on for more than three minutes, the audience got restless! There really is the constant seeking for the new sensation, the new special effect. And a filmmaker who wants to work in a populist area like a horror movie—rather than making an art house movie—then you've to be aware that you're going to have this problem with an audience. And you've got to find some way around it.

I tried it one way with *Hellraiser*. I tried it another way with *Nightbreed*. One of the ways I did it in *Hellraiser* was presenting some pretty threatening material; it would silence them for the next ten minutes . . . sort of tamed the audience temporarily. I will continue to find other ways with my next film.

WIATER: One of the most eagerly anticipated films of 1990 was your *Nightbreed*. Unfortunately, the studio literally dumped the movie on the market, with almost no publicity. Frankly, it was as if they just wanted to throw your effort—and their money—away.

BARKER: I remember how the studio executives saw the finished film and said, "How do we sell this thing—the monsters are the good guys!" [Groans.] The problems started to appear then. But these people have such a low opinion of you and me—the audiences for these kind of movies—that they are intellectually (and I use the term loosely) condescending to us. That somehow we just *don't care* if a horror film is good or bad; we don't have any critical facilities one way or the other.

More than one person of the upper echelons at 20th Century Fox and Morgan Creek, the production company, said to me: "You're an intelligent man, you can make movies. Why do you make *these* kind of movies? Why do you do it?"

WIATER: In other words, you have some taste and talent, why are you jumping into the sewer with this unworthy genre?

BARKER: That's exactly right! In their eyes, it's one step up from making hard-core porno movies. Their attitude as far as horror movies are concerned is much the way the critics' attitudes towards horror and fantasy literature was twenty, twenty-five years ago. Movie companies do not like to risk anything—they want to be the second to do it. They never want to originate. They're fearful of originators—they love people who make wonderful pastiches of something else.

But using your analogy of "going into the sewer" in terms of how studio executives feel about horror films, the fact is, if that's where your personal vision takes you, then *that's where your personal vision takes you*. So you cannot be bothered by the way the world treats you. Any more than Francis Bacon could be bothered about it when he was painting his extraordinary flayed bodies, while the art community thought he was a wretched and disgusting voyeur!

But you get on with it and you paint. You get on with it and you make movies. And you take the consequences, no matter what those consequences are.

WIATER: Speaking of working in a populist arena, you obviously don't object to having sequels made of your work, including the possibility of a *Nightbreed II*. How can you claim to be offering original visions when doing these sequels?

BARKER: There's a long and not dishonorable tradition of sequels in the movies, and I'm not as "antisequel" as some people are. For example, I prefer *Bride of Frankenstein* to *Frankenstein*, and I prefer *The Godfather II* to *The Godfather*. I think John Carpenter's version of *The Thing* is better than Howard Hawks's. There's a lot to be said for movies that are sequels or follow-ups or remakes—which are actually vast improvements over the originals. David Cronenberg's *The Fly* is a *vast* improvement over the original. So I'm not against that in principle.

What I think is important is that new ideas be brought to the project. Now in the case of *Hellraiser II*, there were some new ideas in there (I didn't quite like the way they'd been dealt with), and I certainly don't think the movie is a complete botch by any means. I'm hoping that *Hellraiser III* will also move into fresh territory. That's what counts.

WIATER: It's interesting to note that you have such an affection toward monsters, and that your primary monsters in those films, the Cenobites, have since been transformed into a plastic model.

BARKER: I am delighted by the fact that Screamin' Products has put out the *Hellraiser* model. And Pinhead is far and away their most successful model. I think Pinhead is a class act. The fact that he holds people's attention, and he doesn't do that with witticisms and doesn't attack people in showers, makes me hope that in the movies I plan to make in the future, people will find something interesting and poetic and strange in the creatures I create, and will want more than just bloodletting and naked girls in the showers.

WIATER: Of course, everything in the arts goes through cycles. It would appear that the "slasher" movies of the past fifteen years have finally begun to lose their effectiveness—and their popularity.

BARKER: I tend to agree that it has seen its day. I would like to see horror movies taking a move toward the fantastical. I have always believed that the whole area of imaginative moviemaking and imaginative fiction on the page is in fact *one* territory. It isn't divided up neatly into science fiction and horror fiction and fantasy fiction. *Alien*, for example, is very clearly a horror movie. And it's very clearly a science fiction movie. They are *not* mutually exclusive genres.

I would like to see more cross-fertilization between these areas than we've seen in the eighties, when horror movies had only one thing on their minds: to make people jump and accomplish very little else. Where there was the occasional *frisson* because the soundtrack went quiet for a while, and then a loud sound came in and a guy with a

machete appeared, I would like to see the movies embrace a more
fantastical and more imaginative attitude to horror fiction. Any genre
is the sum of the people who want to work in it; there's always been
an audience for this kind of picture. There always will be.

WIATER: So how is Clive Barker going to make his mark on the
cutting edge of the fantastic cinema? How do you stay ahead?

BARKER: Well, part of the problem of course is that you can never
know what the enemy is thinking. And by "enemy" I mean the
corporate mind. You can never know what they're going to get worried about this season. Are they going to be worried about sex? Are
they going to be worried about religion? Are they going to be worried
about violence? What are they going to try and persuade you *not* to
do in your film?

   You just have to be prepared to speak to your vision, even if it
does not suit certain individuals, and know that when you make movies, you have to work with other people. You have to share your
vision with others and say, "Listen, come with me on this adventure." You hope to find producers sympathetic to that. You hope to
find marketing people who will understand that vision. You hope to
find actors and special effects people who will give their life's blood
to make that happen. Most of the time you're disappointed.

WIATER: But when you write a novel or short story, you have no
compromises to make with anyone then, do you?

BARKER: You fight battles in movies in ways you don't in books.
There's only one real enemy in writing books, and that is your own
entropy. Your own laziness. In movies, there are all kinds of enemies:
lawyers, accountants, list makers, the upper echelon of the studio
sometimes, people who don't want to risk their jobs, people who
don't want to support an original vision. There are compromises and
intellectual mediocrities. There are a lot of these enemies in the studios—but there are a lot of them in every walk of life.

   You are also constantly working with people who don't fall into
any of those categories; you align yourself with these imaginative,
creative people. That's got to be the way forward for me, to try and
do that. Hopefully, I will get lucky and end up working with people
who share my vision and want to preserve its purity, and fight a
reasonable battle.

WIATER: But more often than not, the corporations who hold the purse
strings ultimately decide the fate of your film, as witness *Nightbreed*.

BARKER: I *know* I'm going to lose some of those battles. [Pauses.] I
guess if you can't stand the heat, you get out of the kitchen.

WIATER: Whitley Strieber, author of *The Wolfen* and *The Hunger*,
among his many best-sellers, once told me that he doesn't consider

his vision complete unless it's been published *and* filmed. Do you feel that same way?

BARKER: No—if no other movie was ever made of my work, it would not break my heart. The book is the ultimate statement that I can make; it's the most intimate, the most confessional. Movies are fun because you can remake the story. But the book is not the movie, and the movie is not the book. The book is God—in the beginning was the Word, and the Word means the author. I've been driven more crazy by more people directing two movies than I have writing eleven books.

WIATER: Then why do you claim to enjoy making movies?

BARKER: Because I'm a moviegoer. I love the sensation of movies, and I love to be among audiences experiencing them. I even love movies that date badly. By that I mean there are sections of *King Kong* that don't look so great anymore, or *Bride of Frankenstein*. But the fact is, between those creaky performances, there are moments that after nearly sixty years—in spite of technical advances—are still moments of magic that are extraordinary and unsurpassed.

So, for me, my career is a whole mishmash of possibilities and activities. I'm drawing a lot, I'm painting, I'm making movies, I'm writing books. And at the end of my three score years and ten, I'm hoping people will say, "He was a good, professional imaginer. He expounded his philosophies and processes of imagination in a variety of media, with care for his craft and respect for his audience."

WIATER: That's a long epitaph, Clive. [Laughs.]

BARKER: I'm planning on a *big* tomb. [Laughs.]

WIATER: What advice do you have for someone who wishes to be a screenwriter, or is interested in writing horror fiction?

BARKER: For anyone who wants to be a writer, I simply say, "To thine own self be true." The major gift that anyone has to give is not a technical gift but the gift of their own personal vision. We all know authors who are not great stylists but whose vision is compulsive reading. And we also know great prose stylists whom we fall asleep in front of. I've always told young writers to find that part of themselves that is uniquely them—find those visions that everyone else has said they should have nothing to do with, that forbidden part, and write them. Tell the world about the dark stuff, and do it without embarrassment.

WIATER: You make it sound so natural, almost effortless.

BARKER: You've got to want the process of writing more than the achievement. The pleasure has got to be in the business of the writing, not the business of the publishing. If you spend the six months of writing a novel thinking about what it's going to look like on the bookshelves, you're not doing it right.

A lot of fledgling writers that I've spoken to, if there's one pitfall they weren't aware of, it's that the writing life was great—except for the bit about actually doing the writing. [Laughs.] They loved the idea of being published, they loved the idea of going on TV talk shows, but if they could just get over this fucking business of actually doing the writing; if they could just get that bit over!

WIATER: How differently do you approach writing screenplays compared to writing fiction? Is there a different mind-set?

BARKER: For me, totally. You know how movies are rewritten and rewritten and rewritten. *Everything* in a screenplay is conditional. Anything you write down is subject to almost infinite change. A screenplay is a blueprint for another activity—that activity will happen on the floor when you actually start to shoot the picture. At that point, another set of voices—quite different from the producers' and the executive producers' voices you've already heard—enters the scenario.

There's the actor who feels a line could be improved or turned, the cameraman who has a different view of how the scene should be shot—it's a long list. Then, when the shooting is done, the voice of the editor, who can literally reorder the lines you've written on the page and can make completely new sense of them. Or make complete nonsense of them. So a screenplay is a very tentative article.

With *Hellraiser II*, for example, when Peter Atkins and I had originally beaten the story out, it made sense. But by the time it went through all those voices, by the time it actually reached the screen, it didn't make anything like as much sense as it should have done.

WIATER: How about the two motion pictures that first brought your work to the screen: *Underworld* and *Rawhead Rex*? You've pretty much disowned the films; do you have any good memories of the original screenplays?

BARKER: Oh, sure! They're primitive work compared with some of my later scripts, but I like the screenplays a lot. One of these days, I wouldn't mind seeing the screenplays published. Because it would in some way validate that while the movies are not great, what was on the page in the first instance—while not *Citizen Kane*—certainly made more sense than the movies that emerged from them! Particularly in the case of *Underworld*—which potentially could have made a very nice picture—it just didn't come off.

WIATER: Then how do you do craft horror for a movie, versus the manner in which you devise a horrific situation for a book?

BARKER: Let me try to explain my situation, which is that now I'm writing screenplays in the certain knowledge that I'm going to direct them. I don't write screenplays for other people. So I'm writing screenplays now in a kind of shorthand, and working on a film that way. The process of generating the horror on the page in a novel or a short story is going to be one of completely involving the reader with the full range of sensations that are necessary to evoke that feeling. In a screenplay, that's just not the case.

You're offering the bare bones of the activity, knowing that it's going to be filled in by the special effects men, by the actors, the designers, and so on. A screenplay is a very quick read; takes an hour to read. So it takes a lot of colors to be filled in to make it all work. I think reading screenplays is actually quite difficult, because a large amount of imaginative commitment must be made to get past the words on the page and to what those words are going to mean when they're finally on the screen, transferred into images.

WIATER: Do you ever restrict your vision for the screen, simply because of the economics of moviemaking?

BARKER: I'm pretty much aware that movies cost a lot of money. [Laughs.] I love special effects movies. I love big, fantastic pictures. But I have to continue to earn the right to make them. I think the way I earn the right to make them is by making movies that *work*, by spending other people's money intelligently. I admit there's a big ego satisfaction from directing movies. I get a big high from it; there's no two ways about it. You write something on the page, or you describe something in a sketch, and the next thing you know, money is being spent to make that idea flesh—or at least latex.

But somewhere within this incredible high of having this happen, you've got to be aware that this is a *large* amount of money, and it has to be used intelligently. I was also the executive producer on *Nightbreed*, so it was like looking at the production from both sides of the fence, as it were. Moviemaking is not a cheap art form.

WIATER: But in terms of censorship, do you ever "precensor" your cinematic vision, figuring that the Motion Picture Ratings board may brand you with an X rating if you don't?

BARKER: Well, you certainly can't shoot a film thinking about the censors. That's no way to run any creative endeavor. But, it's equally no use for me to spend a day shooting a piece of special effects, if I know full well it's not going to find its way onto the screen. So what I try to do is find ways of making the material work so that the MPAA will look at the material and realize that *all* the material is dramatically justified.

WIATER: But because you do make horror films, won't the MPAA be looking at your film closer than they would, say, a cop movie?

BARKER: Of course they're going to find some tough material in my pictures and in my choice of subject matter. There's no way that they're not going to find stuff they're going to choke over! What I'm saying is that when I go on the floor in the morning to shoot a scene, I'm not thinking of the MPAA—it's a useless endeavor. What they may be believing in today, they may disbelieve tomorrow. As I stated previously, certain areas of censorship come in and out of vogue. There are all kinds of areas that are subject to change, and I think they are a reflection of social pressures, and to some extent, political pressures.

WIATER: But in terms of ever influencing culture, wouldn't you say that more people will see your most poorly distributed film than will ever read your most accomplished work of fiction?

BARKER: That's probably true, if you're counting heads. But I'm not sure if that's the only way you can assess these influences, and I'm not sure it's even a particularly useful way to assess them. You could go one step further and say that *The National Enquirer* is read by a lot more people than, say, *War and Peace*. But whether the material contained in *The National Enquirer* has any significant influence on the minds that it touches is a different issue. There are clearly cultural phenomena that come into fashion, like Hoola Hoops and yo-yos, and next year are completely forgotten. The same thing applies to movies and books.

What's important is not whether a movie or a book or a television show is in fashion or whether it's going to sell for a short time very intensively. What matters is whether it will *last*. Whether the images in the book or the movie have any staying power; that's far more important than the success over a six-month period that a movie or video may do. Movies date badly. Books date very well. Imagine if *Great Expectations* had first been a movie rather than a book. Or *Les Miserables*, which now has found a new and extraordinary life as a musical, of all things.

WIATER: To go right back to the very beginning as we end our conversation, why do you think people have always been fascinated by horror in the arts, no matter what the medium?

BARKER: I don't think there's a simple answer, Stanley. We both know there's been an enthusiasm for this kind of material since a group of higher primates sat around a fire together and told each other ghost stories.

WIATER: As if it's always been human nature to look at the dark side, no matter how safe and secure your life may apparently seem?

BARKER: Right. I can imagine that the first conversation was something like, "Gee, I'm glad we've got fire. But doesn't it make the darkness even darker?" I think we've answered the question right there.

John Carpenter

Ome of the most popular and celebrated directors of dark visions, John Carpenter has been responsible for some of the most entertaining and thought-provoking genre films ever made. If anyone can be considered to have achieved mainstream success as a director of commercially successful horror, fantasy, and science fiction films, it would probably have to be Carpenter.

Born in Carthage, New York, in 1947, Carpenter is one of those special individuals who knew very early on in life what he wanted out of it: to be a filmmaker. Fate had him seeing the 1953 3-D release *It Came from Outer Space*, and at that point, Carpenter's interest in motion pictures would forever be geared toward the fantastic and grotesque.

In terms of his career, it was by writing and directing the 1978 film *Halloween* that Carpenter made his initial breakthrough, since two previous films—a science fiction movie and a contemporary action-thriller—appeared and disappeared almost without a trace. His *Halloween* was a hit, however, and at the time of its release was the most successful independent feature ever made. Produced for $300,000, it has since earned over $75 million worldwide. (It has so far spawned no less than four sequels.)

Refreshingly, Carpenter doesn't try to disguise what kind of films he is making; he doesn't have the pretentions to say that what he is doing is something other than providing good, solid thrills and chills for a receptive audience. But because Carpenter is himself such an unabashed fan, he brings an added edge to his work. In other words, he knows *we* know it's all been done before—which is why he is constantly able to surprise us with his next movie. At the very least, his *Halloween* and *The Thing* are already considered classics.

Extremely friendly and surprisingly humble about his impact on the history of horror films, I spoke with John Carpenter as he was doing research for his next, as yet unnamed, film project.

SELECTED FILMOGRAPHY

Dark Star (1974)

Halloween (1978)

The Fog (1980)

Escape from New York (1981)

The Thing (1982)

Christine (1983)

Starman (1984)

Big Trouble in Little China (1986)

Prince of Darkness (1988)

They Live (1989)

WIATER: A fairly obvious question to begin with: Why do you continue to make only horror and science fiction films?

CARPENTER: I'll give you my philosophy, which I developed in film school. When I was at USC, I decided I was going to be a professional film director and that I was going to do whatever it took to accomplish that goal. I made a low-budget science fiction picture called *Dark Star*. But it didn't really work; I didn't get any offers to direct. So I started writing—straight, commercial movies. Westerns. Love stories. Action pictures. I wrote *Eyes of Laura Mars. Black Moon Rising.* I wrote a Western they're finally shooting now for television called *Blood River*, and another Western that's going to be on HBO called *El Diablo*.

Now in 1978, I made a television thriller called *Someone Is Watching Me*, I made a movie for television called *Elvis*, and I made a theatrical film called *Halloween*. And *Elvis* was the most successful made-for-television movie, *ever*. And *Halloween* was this huge horror hit, but that happened to be in the area I most wanted to work in—feature films. So I naturally got offered all those kind of films once I broke into features.

WIATER: But don't you feel trapped to some degree, now that you've spent practically your entire career in genre films? I know that your colleague Wes Craven, for example, would love to do a romantic comedy.

CARPENTER: Well, I got to do my romantic comedy with *Starman*. And I got to do my kung fu movie with *Big Trouble in Little China*. You see what I'm saying? I feel real lucky that, in the context of the horror-fantasy–science fiction genre, I've gotten to do so many things. But when I really look at it deeply, I *love* those kinds of movies! I grew up with those kinds of movies. I have the lobby cards of those movies on my wall. I love horror and science fiction: It's a deep, deep part of me. It's something I have a real feeling for. [Pauses.] I don't have a choice for some of it; it just comes naturally.

I'd love to be able to make Westerns, because that's as deep a part of me as horror and science fiction. But I'm here to make movies, and I suppose I would have made Elvis Presley movies if that had worked first for me. [Laughs.] It just happened that *Halloween* got me known as a filmmaker—*Assault on Precinct 13* didn't do it, *Dark Star* didn't do it. But that film did, and for that, I'm enormously thankful.

WIATER: I know you read *Famous Monsters of Filmland* as a child in the 1950s. Did you ever get exposed to the equally great E.C. horror and science fiction comics, which Stephen King and George Romero have said were a major influence on them?

CARPENTER: Well, you see, I got hooked on *Weird Science* and *Weird Fantasy*, and that was just straight science fiction. Time travel, flying saucers were all major subjects in these. I had a older cousin who collected them, and then I started getting into them. I couldn't get enough of them! I know somebody else who was hooked on them, and that was Dan O'Bannon, whom I did *Dark Star* with. In *Weird Science*, I believe, there's a story called "Seeds of Jupiter," which is *really* the inspiration for *Alien*.

The movie that really did it for me, that got me cranked, was Ray Bradbury's *It Came from Outer Space* because of the 3-D effects, and the meteor blowing up in my face. Then there's just a series of highlights: *Forbidden Planet* had an enormous effect. *The Thing* had an enormous effect, as did *King Kong*. Then "Shock Theatre" was on on Saturday nights at ten o'clock, and I watched all the old Universal monster movies, which was fun. The British *Quatermass* had a tremendous effect on me, and by that time, I was hooked. But Westerns, and romantic comedies . . . I was just hooked on movies.

Still, that meteor looms large in my mind.

WIATER: Modesty aside, you're one of the rare breed of people who seemingly knew from day one what you were destined to do in life.

CARPENTER: Yes, I did. I knew it because when I went to the movies, it was a magic land that gave me a great deal of happiness. It was a fantastic illusion, and I wanted to be the maestro behind the scenes, creating that illusion. *I* wanted to put on the show. I didn't want to be on the screen as an actor necessarily, but I wanted to produce the emotional effects that I myself was feeling as a child. [Pauses.] So, it happened.

WIATER: But there are so few people who have careers as motion picture directors, and fewer still who make their reputations in this genre. Is there some special kind of talent required to make horror or fantasy movies?

CARPENTER: I would say there is definitely some kind of psychological or emotional engine that propels one to do this. Clearly. I think of that when I read Stephen King and he writes some particularly vicious action scene and I think, Wow! The engine that drives his imagination is one that runs down that track. But I could say that about Edgar Allan Poe, or H. P. Lovecraft. I could say that Franz Kafka's engine of imagination was really pretty grim! [Laughs.] I don't know if I would have ever imagined a story where I woke up one morning and turned into a bug.

But in making movies, I think you have to be attracted to the visualization of terror. You have to repeat to yourself a little litany that goes something like this: The strongest emotion is fear. The oldest emotion is fear. We all have it, and it is a very deep pool inside every human on the planet. So there are some of us who dive into that pool because we are both repelled and attracted by it.

But I think a lot of directors who make horror films sleep pretty well at night, because they're able to express through their movies very hateful and vengeful feelings. We're kind of engaged in this ongoing life therapy.

WIATER: I've done another volume of interviews with horror authors, and I discovered that's a popular form of therapy for them as well. As human beings go, they appear extremely well adjusted, considering their supposedly grim and morbid area of interest.

CARPENTER: Well, the most well-adjusted person I know is Roger Corman. [Chuckles.] He's just the most fabulous person I know. I was with him and Clive Barker over in London, and we were doing this little round table discussion for the BBC, and I realized then that some of my favorite movies of all time were made by Roger Corman! *It Conquered the World* for instance. I really love that movie—remember the cucumber monster from Venus? But Roger Corman is so well adjusted about his path, and about who he is!

I'm a lobby card collector, and so I went over to his house. I acted like a fan—I brought a bunch of lobby cards for him to sign. He was so embarrassed about it, but he wrote these incredibly funny lines, captioning each one of the posters. There's one from the *Viking Women and the Sea Serpent* where they're carrying this Viking woman over a burning pit, and Roger wrote on it, "Lunch was a little late that day!" [Laughs.] He's unbelievable. I wish I could deal with movies with the same sort of light enthusiasm he has. He always has a smile on his face, and he always says, "I won't pay for that."

And George Romero is one of the nicest, straightest, most innocent and fun-loving people I know of. Very relaxed, very conservative! He's like a bebop hipster from the fifties. I mean, he's created this entire myth in American cinema, and I don't think people realize how profound it is. George Romero invented the Attack of the Third World; that is what *Night of the Living Dead* is all about. The Dead are the Third World—and they *are* going to eat our flesh. I can't tell you the influence that movie had on horror movies afterward.

WIATER: True enough, but I think the same could be said for your *Halloween*. After its release, horror in the cinema was again irrevocably altered. Many critics believe that film will stand the test of time just as well as *Night of the Living Dead*.

CARPENTER: [Hesitantly.] It may. We'll see. You never know.

WIATER: In general, films are more explicitly violent than ever; how does a director ever hope to shock an audience that by now is pretty much numb to any sort of sensation?

CARPENTER: There are a couple of easy things that you can do; it's just a matter of timing. You can break the rules, because all the rules have now been set up. One of the aspects about any film that is incredibly powerful, like a thriller or a horror picture, is that everything you've come to expect *turns on you.* So it's a matter of sitting back and looking at what the rules are, and then bending them on the audience. I think that situation will come about as more directors figure out how to do it and have the opportunity to do it.

But the only way to approach making a picture is just to figure out what your story is, and serve it. We have one god in movies, and that's our story. You have to stay true to it. If it's a realistic story, the violence should be realistic, and the scares should be realistic. If it's a fantasy, then the opposite is appropriate. If those of us who make movies stick by that rule, then I think we'll be okay. Maybe I'm being too optimistic. . . .

WIATER: You've had your share of successes. Yet one notable critical and box-office dud was your remake of *The Thing.* Why didn't it do as well with the general public, even though horror fans everywhere certainly thought it was wonderful?

CARPENTER: I was *completely* savaged by the critics on *The Thing.* But slowly, over the years, people seem to creep up secretly to me and say, "Boy, did I love that movie!" I don't know—it's impossible to say that you can't take it seriously or that you're not hurt by the negative reviews. We're all human beings! But I think you have to have an enormous sense of humor about how things go, and I often don't have that. I get very angry when these things happen. But, it's show bizzzzz! [Laughs.]

And at the time *The Thing* was released, the public needed a film like *E.T.* They needed it! *The Thing* was *exactly* the opposite. *E.T.* was uplifting, and life reaffirming, and *The Thing* gave you the bleakest of all messages. You have to be prepared, if you say something that's bleak, then not everybody's going to want to see it!

I felt it was a powerful statement about our doubting if we're human. You can see the Thing as being cancer or AIDS or whatever you want to say, but it's about the disintegration of humanity and people's lack of trust. But it was not a message that a general audience wanted to embrace and carry home with them. And I can understand that; that's part of the risk of making a film that doesn't compromise.

WIATER: An interesting aspect of many of your movies is that you've also composed the scores; especially notable being your score for *Halloween.* Just how important is music to your creative drive?

CARPENTER: Music has always been an *enormous* influence in my life. I listen to music a lot and fantasize listening to music while I'm not. I was an only child, and my dad has a Ph.D. in music and was a music teacher. He had an enormous collection of records, all classical. I got very much into listening, and fantasizing movies and moods based on music. Then I became a big rock 'n' roll fan and played in a rock 'n' roll band. I remain a fan of rock 'n' roll and pop music.

My own music—my own scores—I really haven't used much as a source of inspiration because the scores that I compose are utilitarian. And by that I mean they are part of setting a mood for something that already exists. The way I score films is to edit the movie, and then put it on tape and bring it over to a recording studio and start playing opposite the scenes. With my music supporting the scenes where they need it and getting the audience into a mood. If the scene is working without music, then I leave it alone.

But because I've done so many scores for so many movies, it's kind of burned me out of using my own music for inspiration. I can still go back and put on some classical music and work out a plot problem that I'm having or a character problem I'm having in a screenplay or an idea that I want to flesh out. I'll put on the music and often fantasize my way into some solution.

WIATER: You also write the screenplays for most of your movies. How much do you enjoy this process?

CARPENTER: I live in the Hollywood Hills overlooking Los Angeles, and I have this job-robbing view. When I go out and look at this view, I can't write a word! You just become mesmerized. I have to go downstairs, to what looks like a closet, and be very uncomfortable. I have my typewriter facing a wall, with a light over my shoulder and a calendar that shows when my deadline is. It's like cramming for a final, because writing is not fun. Stephen King must love it— he must love to play with words. I *hate* playing with words. I'd much rather direct: "Let's get a scene here! You come in that door, we'll drop the fire on you, and we'll do this next!"

No, I have a totally different approach to writing. I have to get into such a state, mentally, because it really takes such an enormous amount of commitment and dedication. You just can't indulge yourself when you write. And I really am lazy. And I really enjoy being lazy. [Laughs.] So that's my confession about writing.

WIATER: How do you explain what it takes for some directors to be able to declare this is an "Alfred Hitchcock film" or this is a "Howard Hawks film" and get it above the title of the movie? How do you explain what a "John Carpenter film" is?

CARPENTER: Style. That's all it means. It's not anything else but style. Alfred Hitchcock, John Ford, Howard Hawks, Orson Welles, Sam Peckinpah—they were great directors because of their style. Whatever the style is, whatever the influences are, whatever it is we're trying to say, that's what we're selling with those words on the credits. I think it became *the* thing to do after that *auteur* theory book by Andrew Sarris came out, with the idea that the director was an artist, which was an idea he imported from the French critics. So every director is Hollywood decided he was an *auteur*. [Laughs derisively.] Everybody was! Now we all have "a film by . . ." Aren't we cool? Jesus Christ, it's embarrassing. We embarrassed ourselves.

WIATER: But considering that in most instances you wrote, scored, as well as directed the picture, the credit line with your name above the title has more validity being there than others, don't you feel?

CARPENTER: Yeah, it's somewhat valid. They *are* my version of this story is what it really comes down to. "This is the way I view this story." But I don't know. I remember the height of my own awful ego is what happened on *Christine*. I saw this billboard that had my name on it so many times . . . ! I thought to myself, How can I go and show my face around anymore? Who do I think I am? This is Stephen King's *Christine*, not mine. It belongs to *him*. Then I realized what I had done and had never thought of it before. But I had these super agents and lawyers reminding me, "Hey, on the last movie you got 'John Carpenter's . . .' and you don't want to give that up." Well, of course I don't, but only later after it was all over did I realize what an asshole I was!

The strange thing is *Christine* is my weakest movie, with no doubt. I shouldn't have done it. I probably should have put a corpse in the backseat, but by God, I didn't want to do any more corpses in the backseat!

WIATER: Then why did you choose that particular project, knowing it was so closely identified as a best-selling novel by a very popular author?

CARPENTER: I wanted to do something with people, and that was the opportunity to do it. But it just wasn't scary. If I had put that rotting corpse in the backseat, I guarantee you it would have been better. I can't say anything in my defense except I had just come off *The Thing*, and I don't know if you know anything about professional wrestling, but I just had about five body slams in a row! From the critics, from everybody. I had a lot of people in Hollywood advise me, "John, you've just got to do this movie." [Pauses.] So I did.

WIATER: What do you think about the current state of censorship in the film industry? Especially in terms of the Motion Pictures rating board?

CARPENTER: I'll tell you what, there's a very simple rule. If you're an independent filmmaker, you'd better watch out. If you have a major studio behind you, don't worry too much. I had an experience where I made a film for a major studio, and the MPAA called up this major studio and said, "We want to give this film an X." The major studio said, "No." And the MPAA didn't! I didn't cut a frame. But if you're an independent, then they're on you like stink on shit!

I'll tell you what's happening all across the country that has resulted in all this. In the early seventies and late eighties, religion began to creep back into politics. All over the world, including the United States. Now, ten years later, you're seeing the return of the puritan. And censorship is being directed at whatever is not in the mainstream. In other words, if you're a big corporation that supports the system, then you'll get by. If you are an independent, and you come up with this evil moral tone, then you will get censored.

Listen, it would be real easy for the MPAA to solve the problem if they wanted to. They created PG-13, they can create R-21. They don't have to just stick with X. Any moral offense, they can put "Restricted—under 21 not admitted." They know the difference between pornography and a serious film. You do. And I do.

I hate censorship, in all forms. I think everything ought to be allowed. I think it's only how much freedom we really do want as a society that's reflected in our culture. Right now we don't want so much freedom. We're all scared. Isn't it weird? We seem to be frightened of everything. *Everything*. That's why you won't see too many successful horror movies for a while. It's scary enough out there anyway; everybody thinks the world is going to end. Just wait for the millennium, man. It's just starting. Soon it's going to be the turn of the century, and everybody's going to go a little crazy.

WIATER: A society too afraid to see who controls it is a lot of what you seem to be saying in your most recent film, *They Live*. A major theme running through many of your films is that of individuals in society fighting to retain control of their lives, isn't it?

CARPENTER: I believe that's pretty accurate. In the case of *They Live*, I can be even more specific. It's Republicans controlling us! [Laughs.] The Reagan revolution is controlled by aliens from another world, and we'd better wake up and realize it. I made *They Live* as my version of *Invasion of the Body Snatchers* for the eighties. Not that I think my film is as good as *Invasion of the Body Snatchers*, but its message is the same. I remember thinking about it a great deal because I have a lot of Yuppie friends, and when I got a good look at what the whole country was doing, it was really terrifying. It depressed me and made me angry. I'm really glad I made the film.

It was a story that was really unpopular with Universal Pictures. (It's also a film about Hollywood; that's wrapped up in there, too.) The first thing they told after I started making it was, "Can't you make these characters middle-class, so the audience can identify with them?'' I said, "But that's the whole point: the aliens are controlling the middle-class. You're only pure if you're poor. You haven't been touched by this incredible greed." Then one of the Universal executives said, "Then what's the point of this? We all sell out every day. Might as well be on the winning team." And I wrote that down and used it in the movie! Can you believe it? He didn't know what we were talking about.

We tried to do it so that people would walk out of the theater and laugh and say, "Yeah, but that wasn't *me*!" Maybe we weren't that successful, because people don't like to be preached to. But the film got some of the best reviews I've gotten since *Halloween*. Amazing.

WIATER: John, you are one of the few people working in this industry who can actually say "I always wanted to be a movie director, and so I became one." What advice do you have for someone who shares a similar dream?

CARPENTER: Oh, man . . . ! Well, I think that everybody who has a dream of being a film director—or just making it in Hollywood—they already know in their hearts that it takes persistence. That they have to be tough. But there's one thing that nobody wants to hear, but it's so true: you just need a lot of luck. If you don't have a relative in the movie business, you need a *lot* of luck. And there's nothing you can do about it; you either have it or you don't.

I know a guy I went to film school with, who I think is one of the most talented filmmakers I've ever known, and who has a lot more talent than I do and has never made a feature movie. A lot of it is because of luck. Everybody has dreams, but you have to be realistic so you don't get destroyed if it doesn't work out. There are very few directors who last. And just look at the odds of somebody becoming a film director and making a career out it. How many people are there in the Directors Guild—three hundred?

All of us look at a movie and think it isn't that hard to do. But it ain't necessarily so! Moviemaking is hard, especially the politics, and especially the business end of it. To keep your integrity and your beliefs intact, to keep your family and your emotions intact—and your sanity—it's very tricky.

WIATER: Do you think you've come through the industry intact?

CARPENTER: I'm surprised at myself, I've survived pretty well. I'm real proud of my work in movies, and I'm relatively happy. It's been difficult, and continues to be quite a war, but no, I feel pretty good about it all. I don't regret too much. I have made my share of mistakes—it's the only way you learn. But I guess my only regret is that I wasn't born Roger Corman. If I only could have been Roger . . . ! [Laughs.] He's this glowing symbol of happiness. He's the happiest man on earth.

LarCo Productions

Larry Cohen

Although prolific writer-producer-director Larry Cohen will never deny that he is deeply involved in the horror and science fiction genres, he prefers to think of his basic body of work as black comedies. This may well be the case, but his considerable body of work is usually first identified by the size and diversity of the monsters it contains. From his first major success with *It's Alive!* (mutant babies) to *God Told Me To* (extraterrestrial-influenced killers) to *Q* (giant prehistoric flying reptile), Cohen usually manages to get his satirical message across, but not at the expense of delivering an exciting and entertaining movie first.

Cohen began his career as a writer for television in the 1960s, most notably as the creator of the popular science fiction series, *The Invaders*. Although he has worked in other genres, including "blacksploitation" films such as *Black Caesar* (1973) and *Hell Up in Harlem* (1973), Cohen has for the

most part remained in the genres that best allow him the freedom to explore his consistently dark and paranoid visions.

And freedom is the cornerstone of the way Cohen works
as a filmmaker. Although his movies have not yet received
the critical recognition of a Cronenberg or a Romero, Cohen
at least has the right to say he always remains the total *auteur*
of his films. Through his own Larco production company,
Cohen has managed to write, produce, and direct an enviable
number of fascinating movies, from Hitchcockian thrillers
such as *Special Effects* (1984) to grisly satires of the food
industry with *The Stuff* (1985) to two sequels to his most successful film to date, *It Lives Again* (1978) and *It's Alive III:
Island of the Alive* (1987).

A full-length critical study of Cohen is long overdue, since not
only is he worthy of examination as a filmmaker, but also writes
enough material annually to keep several more filmmakers and
television production companies in business.

I spoke with Larry Cohen from his home in Coldwater
Canyon, California, shortly after he had finished the screenplay for the sequel to *Maniac Cop* for fellow independent director William Lustig.

SELECTED FILMOGRAPHY

It's Alive! (1974)

God Told Me To (1977)

A Return to 'Salem's Lot (1977)

Q (1981)

Special Effects (1984)

Wicked Stepmother (1988)

WIATER: You've done very well as a screenwriter in Hollywood; what
was your motivation to become a director? You could just as easily
be writing novels at this point in your career, if the answer is you
wanted control over your material.

COHEN: Someday I expect to do novels. But directing takes a lot of energy, and this is a job to do while you're still young. I'll do novels later on, when I don't want to get up at four o'clock in the morning, work with a cast and crew, or travel as much. But I became a screen-writer first because I was movie crazy.

WIATER: You're one of the few writers in the industry who is apparently capable of producing enough material that you can direct yourself or sell to other producers, as you did with *Maniac Cop* and *Bestseller* and *I, the Jury*. How do you chose?

COHEN: When it's a particular piece that I'm really in love with, that I'll direct. But I write so much; I write every day. When I have nothing to do, or am waiting for something to happen, I'll write. So by the end of the week, I've accumulated a stack of pages. And by the end of year, I have more scripts than I could ever possibly do myself. There are scripts I write that nobody likes, but eventually, sooner or later, most of them find a home.

WIATER: I have this image of a man who, like novelist Dean R. Koontz, is happily chained to a word processor sixty or seventy hours a week.

COHEN: Surprisingly, I have a very leisurely life, with a lot of free time. I don't work that hard. I do write every day, but I limit that to two or three hours. I have more leisure time than a lot of my friends. [Chuckles.] Sometimes I'll write my two or three hours late at night— I'll slip out of bed, go downstairs, and write from about two in the morning, and go to bed at about four. But I don't let the writing interfere with my leisure time, with my personal life. I'm always there to go out and have a good time or take a trip. I'm fortunate in that I can turn it on any time of the day or night and the material flows.

If I don't write one day, then I don't feel quite as good. I don't feel terrible, but I just don't feel quite as happy.

WIATER: Your *It's Alive!* films continue in a developing saga and are not merely remakes of each other. It's obvious that, as the writer for all three films, you consciously tried not to repeat yourself.

COHEN: I wouldn't want to make another *It's Alive!* picture if there wasn't anything new to say. In each film, the story is more about the characters and less about the monster babies. It's about the unusual and bizarre things that happen to us, that we don't *want* to happen to us. But they do. Peoples' lives can be shattered, no matter how happy they may be. Your kids leave for school, and in the back of your mind, you're wondering if they will make it back in one piece. No matter how beautiful or sweet life is, there are always shadows lurking around the corner. And you're always saying, "It's not going to happen to us, it'll happen to somebody else's family." And my characters are basically nice people who find themselves in the middle of one of those awful situations.

WIATER: Complex religious and political issues turn up repeatedly in your films, such as *Q* or *God Told Me To*, to name only two. Clearly you're using the horror genre to explore a lot of serious issues beyond the "Let's find and kill the deadly monster!"

COHEN: That's exactly what I'm trying to do. I'm taking the genre of the monster picture and making it a legitimate thematic format. A lot of people have come up to me and said, "Oh, I saw your film on cable the other night and really enjoyed it. But I never would have paid to see it in a theater, since I usually don't like *that* kind of movie. But I just happened to see it on cable and it was really a very good film." What often happens is the advertising campaigns on a lot of these pictures turn away the very people who would enjoy them the most.

WIATER: Many critics automatically assume a genre film is not important or "relevant." Needless to say, only a "mainstream" movie with big-name stars or a huge budget are worthy of their time to examine or recommend.

COHEN: Most mainstream pictures are hardly relevant at all! They're mostly buddy-cop films that have no relation to reality. Or they're just a lot of stunts strung together with a lot of dirty language and dirty jokes. The top stars may play in them, but there's really no substance to them. They're usually something that's been done before—only on a bigger budget.

The world seems to operate today on volume. The music has to be *loud*. The soundtracks have to be kept *loud*. So you have to have as much destruction and violence as possible. You just keep hitting the audience with larger and larger explosions, and they're not going to realize, when the picture is over, that they didn't really see anything!

The philosophy seems to be, give audiences a lot of volume—not substance—for their money. "Oh well, we blew up fifty cars in our last picture—how 'bout we blow up a hundred cars in this one? I don't have any new ideas: let's just do we what we did before, and do it louder." It's the same reason why we have so many sequels being made today: "Let's take what we did before and do it again, only instead of spending $25 million, let's spend $40 million. Give the audience the same thing, but more."

WIATER: Then why did you do a *Maniac Cop 2*?

COHEN: I wrote it, but I didn't direct it. But it's a continuation of the original story, with a development of the characters. It's *not* a repeat of what's been done in the first film—or what's been done in any other film. I wouldn't have been able to write it if there hadn't been anything new to say. If it was going to be a rehash of the first film, I would have passed on the deal.

WIATER: How do you respond to the charge by some critics that the violence in movies carries over to the level of violence in real life?

COHEN: Well, I can tell you that in *my* pictures the violence is usually committed by a monster baby or a killer ice cream or a dragon—it's hardly relevant to the kind of violence you find in real life. I don't see how anybody could be affected by it; the violence in my films is so extreme—so beyond the norm. I don't make these films to portray intensely realistic beatings or intensely realistic tortures. I think films that do are basically sick, because they are catering to the basest elements in human nature. I couldn't make that kind of film. I know I couldn't make a *Friday the 13th*.

Unless there's a reason for the violence—to explore it seriously. But to have it gratuitously put there, simply to parade one vicious act following another, trying to outdo yourself with more blood in each scene, that's just sadism. I don't enjoy those films.

Even so, I don't think movie violence has too much of a relationship with reality. Because we've all seen a million movie fights. You see them on every television show, night after night. And once in a great while, you'll actually see a real fight, in a restaurant or in the street. And people don't fight in real life the way they do in the movies. It's not like that *at all*. It's a different world—it's a different reality. What I'm saying is that people are not numbed out by the violence they see in the movies or on television. They know the difference.

I don't like to look at films that are trying to be more graphic, more violent than the last picture. But I realize there is a certain element of the audience, especially young teenagers, who go to these films because they're interested in the special effects and the makeup. Who want to know ''How'd that guy's head come off'' or ''How did they drive that nail through a guy's forehead?'' This curiosity is nothing new—the Grand Guignol did this in France for years. It was a major attraction for this theater group to perform these horrific acts onstage. People would go to see it just to ask, ''How did they do that? How could they chop somebody's head off right on the stage?'' So I can understand how there's always been a certain market for that sort of thing.

It's just never been my idea of show business.

WIATER: I'm wondering if you've had any encounters with the MPAA, the motion picture ratings board, with any of your films? As an independent filmmaker, aren't your films treated differently from those produced by a major studio?

COHEN: I think they are less likely to give a harsh rating to a film that has a major star performing the questionable act. If Gregory Peck is doing it, as he did in *The Omen*, you'd have a lesser chance of it getting an X rating than if it were an unknown actor. I mean, here you have Gregory Peck putting his son on an altar and trying to stab him to death with a knife. But if it was a low-budget "exploitation" film with a man trying to kill his son in a church, on an altar . . . I mean . . . wow! But because it's Gregory Peck in a big-budget picture, that's *different*.

The ratings board can't help but be affected by who's doing the film: how expensive it is, how glossy it looks. Sometimes it's different when the picture is based on a best-selling book. *The Exorcist* was a best-selling book, so it's acceptable for a girl to masturbate with a crucifix. But if I wrote that in a script for a low-budget picture, the MPAA would be having a fit, and giving me an X rating. But, again, it's a big-budget film with major stars, so it has an air of respectability to it. But you still can't forget that one of the scenes in the film is of a girl masturbating with a crucifix.

WIATER: But do the ratings affect how you make a motion picture? Do you ever pre-censor your dark visions even before you start the production?

COHEN: No, because I usually expect to get an R rating. I'm not making motion pictures for a teenage audience or for kids. I'm making them for adults. Actually, *It's Alive!* was rated PG. The MPAA couldn't find any reason *not* to give it a PG. For *It's Alive, Part II*, they gave it an R rating. So I appealed it. I asked them, "How could you give the second film such a rating, when it was identical to the first film in terms of degree of horror or violence or monsters or whatever you want to call it—how come it's getting an R rating now? There are no dirty words or nudity." They said, "Larry, there's nothing in the picture that warrants an R rating, but we're giving it one because we think parents will want it to have one."

And I said, "I think you should rate a picture by what it *is*, not by what people *think* it's going to be." I went before them with evidence from Warner Brothers, the distributors of *It's Alive!*, that they had never received complaints from anyone on the first picture being PG rated. But still they maintained the R rating. And I still have never figured out why. Maybe because the second picture was a sequel to a big hit and had more visibility, maybe that worked against me. I don't know why—it should have worked more in my favor! So that was the only occasion that I went before the board in that capacity.

WIATER: How did you get involved with a sequel to *'Salem's Lot* for Warner Brothers?

COHEN: I was talking to them about making another *It's Alive!* picture.

And they proposed that they had the rights to Stephen King's novel, and they were interested in making a sequel to *that*. So we made a two-picture deal, done out of the Warner Brothers video division, to do *It's Alive III: Island of the Alive* and *A Return to 'Salem's Lot*. We made the two pictures back to back, using many of the same actors in both pictures.

WIATER: But since most of your films are from your original concepts, what interested you in devising a sequel to an already well-known novel?

COHEN: It was a sequel they *wanted* made. Warner Brothers said, "Well, as long as you use the title, you can do anything else to it you want." And since they said I could do anything with it that I want. . . . I also didn't want to redo what Tobe Hooper had done in the first one. Curiously enough, I had been hired years before to write a screenplay of *'Salem's Lot* for Warner Brothers. I wrote the screenplay, but they didn't like it. They didn't make it as a motion picture, but subsequently started from scratch and eventually made it into a four-hour television picture. And that was apparently cut down to a two-hour version for videocassette, and that did okay as a foreign release. So that's why they wanted their home video division to distribute a sequel.

And that's really why I did it—it seemed to me that everything had come full circle—so I got to do my *'Salem's Lot* for Warner Brothers. And they made quite a lot of money on each picture. They had made a profit already on cable and videocassette sales alone.

WIATER: Is that also why your films apparently always make a profit, even though they seem to have almost no theatrical release?

COHEN: Even if my pictures had done very well in a theatrical run, they still would have lost money. Because theatrical costs are so high—the advertising costs are so tremendous they eat up all the revenue. That's why if a picture is a moderate success at the theaters, it loses money. In our system, such as it is, if it's low-budget it will automatically make a profit if it goes into the cable and cassette markets and the worldwide theatrical ancillary markets. And you also have the television packages that will be sold to stations and play forever. So these films will all make money. Playing in theaters, you might not make money. It's just a question if you want your picture playing in that mall or multiplex, or you want to make money.

If you play theatrically and it's a hit, you may make more money. But there's a good chance you won't make any. A film that's been made for $30 or $40 million *has* to play theatrically—you have to try and get your investment back immediately. A picture that's made for $3 million can make that back even without a theatrical release. But if you go theatrically, you have to put in $6 or $7 million for advertising. And that may mean you're ultimately not going to make *any* money.

WIATER: The logical question to ask: Do you prefer genre films because they are almost guaranteed to return a profit?

COHEN: That may be. But the reason I go back to these kinds of films is that those are the ideas that pop into my head. I get those ideas, what can I do? If that's what I'm thinking up, then that's what I've got to write. There's no conscious effort to come up with those specific kinds of ideas at the expense of anything else. My mind just works in those channels.

WIATER: Some of your films are not well known to the public at all. What do you consider your most successful film?

COHEN: *It's Alive!* is definitely the most successful in terms of box office; it's grossed some $40 million, and that's in 1974 dollars. It's on the list of the twenty-five top-grossing horror, fantasy, or science fiction films ever made.

WIATER: To put the question another way: Do you have a favorite film?

COHEN: Well, I liked *Q* with Michael Moriarty. The experience of making the film, actually shooting there on the top of the Chrysler Building, dangling off the skyscraper to shoot the movie—that was literally a once-in-a-lifetime experience. And I was very pleased with *The Private Files of J. Edgar Hoover* with Broderick Crawford. Once again, we shot it right on location, in Washington D. C., in front of the FBI building. We shot it in 1974, when everybody said we just couldn't make such a picture. I made the picture, and nothing bad happened. It's a fair picture of the man. So I'm pretty happy with that.

I love it when I get to work with the actors that I like. We did *Wicked Stepmother* with Bette Davis, and that was a great experience. It was her last film. She managed to get through most of it, but she couldn't finish the picture. But her being in it brought a lot of joy and inspiration to everyone else working on the film.

WIATER: One of the noticeable aspects of all your movies is that they're so well cast. The actors working in your movies obviously aren't doing it for a paycheck, but because they believe in your project.

COHEN: Well, thank you. I try to get people who will be fantastic in a particular part, and I'vc been lucky to get a lot of big-name actors to appear in my films. People who I get a big charge out of working with. Like director Sam Fuller in *A Return to 'Salem's Lot*: I wrote the part for him, and he agreed to do the picture. Same with Bette

Davis. I wrote the part for her, she agreed to it. And she did it. Unfortunately, she couldn't do all of it, but she did enough of it that I'm very happy to have had the chance to work with her.

WIATER: You once said that the difference between you and studio filmmakers was like the difference for an author being published in hardcover or in paperback.

COHEN: Yes—in the big world of movies, the theatrical release of a picture was like the hardcover release of a book, and the videocassette release was like the paperback. A lot of times, a publisher loses money on the hardcover edition; they just don't sell that many copies. What I was saying was that if a picture doesn't come out theatrically, there's no shame to it. It's just a different way of doing business. If you can make more money putting a book out in a mass market paperback, what's wrong with that? So what's the difference of seeing a movie on the screen or watching it at home?

Sometimes a picture is better when seen at home; at least you have control over the sound, over the focus. In some theaters today, the movie is just not shown very well. The theaters are small, and the screens aren't very large anymore, anyway. You're knee deep in old popcorn and other people's spilled Coke, and it's not a very pleasant environment. And you're paying seven dollars a ticket, not to mention parking besides.

WIATER: So you feel that the prestige of a hit movie at the downtown theaters is not the only way to gauge a movie's eventual success, overall?

COHEN: You always hope to have another big hit like *It's Alive!*, where you go to the theater and there's a line around the block. I've had that happen a few times myself, and you always hope to have it again. A lot of that depends on how the film is going to be advertised and promoted. In order to get that kind of money at the end, you have to spend a lot on advertising and promotion. So that when a picture opens—whether you like it or not—there is so much hype that you *have* to see the picture. So the times I've had a reasonable advertising budget, the film has always made a profit.

You have to promote the picture—that's as important as the picture itself. The audience knows right way when a production company or a distributor is not confident about their film. They can sense it. If you want to do some business theatrically, you have to go out there and promote it like it's the greatest picture ever made. Otherwise you might as well go directly to videocassette.

WIATER: Which is one of the reasons you are becoming increasingly known to the public—your movies are all available on videocassette or play frequently on cable television.

COHEN: Thank God that there are those new marketplaces for me! I have a whole new audience that has discovered my films in the video stores and on cable. It's nice—some video stores around the country even have whole sections devoted to my pictures. That's very flattering. And I've gotten calls and letters from all across the country, with people telling me they've seen my films and how much they liked them. So it's nice to know that somewhere every night there's somebody out there watching one of my pictures.

WIATER: And as low-budgeted as your films may be, they always have something to say other than serving as showcases for gory special effects and car explosions.

COHEN: Hopefully a large portion of my audience can discern the difference between content and just a big budget. Hopefully they can see that I make my pictures with a serious intent and a lot of thought behind them.

WIATER: You seemingly have been able to do it all in Hollywood as an independent filmmaker: produce, write, and direct. What advice do you have for someone who wants to try and be a success in at least one of those areas?

COHEN: Anybody who wants to do what I'm doing—that is, write and direct motion pictures—first they've got to *write*. They've got to write continually, like I do. All the time. They've got to turn out some scripts. The easiest thing to do—of all the challenges to overcome—the easiest one is writing. If you can write something and someone reads it, they might very well make the picture. A director has a harder job: he has to have film, equipment; he's got to have a crew, got to have actors, got to have a script, locations. He's got to have a budget. A writer only needs a piece of paper. All it costs him is 120 sheets of paper. You can turn out a product at a negligible cost.

So I would say if you have writing talent, then you should utilize it. If you don't have writing talent, then you have a problem. Then you've got to find somebody *else* who can write, team up with them, and hope to come up with something.

If you're a producer, you find somebody who's written a script, and try and find a home for that script. You might try and tie them up with a director . . . there's a lot of ways to do it. Writing is still the easiest way—*if* you have the talent. But if you don't have the talent, what's the difference? You know, "That's a good suggestion, but I don't have any talent." That's why some people become producers or studio executives. They still want to be in show business whether or not they have any talent at all.

Roger Corman

If there's anyone for whom the term "living legend" is applicable in the genres of the fantasy, horror, and science fiction films, it would have to be Roger Corman.

In a sense, Corman is a one-man film industry unto himself. Since the 1950s he not only directed more than 50 feature films, he has produced more than 200 and distributed who knows how many more. Rather than working for a major studio, Corman has instead primarily produced his own films independently, many for American International Pictures in the 1950s and 1960s, then for his own company—New World—in the 1970s. After selling that company, Corman choose not to sit back on his laurels, but started up yet another company, called Concorde. As he mentions in the interview, Concorde is the last of its kind—the only complete production and distribution company for low-budget films in the United States.

The fact that most of the films Corman has been associated with over the past four decades are most commonly referred to—and dismissed by critics—as "exploitation flicks" doesn't really do justice to his accomplishments. Not only has Corman been responsible for many of the most enjoyable horror and science fiction movies of the 1950s and 1960s, he also brought into the industry several of today's most important filmmakers. These include such luminaries as Francis Ford Coppola, Martin Scorcese, and Ron Howard, to name only a very few.

In spite of his film classics having such titles as *Not of This Earth*, *Attack of the Crab Monsters*, *It Conquered the World*, *The Last Woman on Earth* (which was written by a then unknown Robert Towne), and *The Pit and the Pendulum*, Corman has always been secure in his ability to entertain. It is one thing to realize that his films are shot on a low budget, usually without any name stars, and are often advertised in the most lurid manner possible. Then again, if Stephen King believes his books are the "literary equivalent of a Big Mac and fries," then certainly Corman has been satisfying millions of people around the world with his own particular recipe of cinematic "junk food."

Born on April 6, 1926, in Detroit, Corman, for all his past successes, just keeps adding to the legend. Several books have already been written on him, and even a selected filmography would fill pages. Trust me: Almost anyone who has ever enjoyed a drive-in B movie—or more recently gone to the exploitation shelves of their local video store—has probably seen a movie that was in some way influenced by Roger Corman.

Busy as ever, Corman spoke with me after he had just completed work as a director—his first project in this capacity in some twenty years—on *Roger Corman's Frankenstein Unbound*.

SELECTED FILMOGRAPHY

The Day the World Ended (1955)
The Little Shop of Horrors (1960)

House of Usher (1960)

The Intruder (1962)

Tales of Terror (1962)

The Terror (1963)

X-The Man With the X-Ray Eyes (1963)

Tomb of Ligeia (1964)

WIATER: I understand you recently wrote your autobiography?

CORMAN: Yes, I've written an autobiography, but it's primarily about my work in film. There's very little about my personal life in it. It was done for Random House.

WIATER: Why did you wait nearly twenty years before going back to directing?

CORMAN: I had never really planned to stop directing at all. I just felt in 1970, when I finished *Von Richthofen and Brown*, that I had directed so many pictures I wanted to take a little time off. I thought I would just take a year off. What happened was I started New World Pictures during that time, and the company became successful faster than I thought it would and I just stayed with the company. Every couple of years I would say, "Well, maybe I'll direct a film now," and I just never got around to it until finally, nineteen years later, I did it last year.

WIATER: Why did you specifically choose *Frankenstein Unbound* as the project to make your return to directing with?

CORMAN: Strangely enough, it wasn't my choice. Universal Pictures a few years ago had done some market research. As part of that research they tested various title ideas, and they tested the title *Roger Corman's Frankenstein*—and it tested very well. So they called me and asked me if I would like to do the picture. And as a matter of fact I said I'm not particularly interested in doing it. But then Thom Mount, who had been head of production there, left to form his own company, and he called me. I had been thinking about it, and I said that if I could come up with something new . . . the reason I don't want to do it is that there's been so *many* Frankensteins, I didn't want to be the hundredth version of *Frankenstein*.

I remembered a little bit later the book that Brian Aldiss had written in the early 1970s called *Frankenstein Unbound*. I thought it was a good basic idea, and I had a couple of ideas of my own that I thought

I could blend with Brian's ideas and come up with something that would be quite original. And as a result, the final title is *Roger Corman's Frankenstein Unbound*, so I made the film.

WIATER: Was that why you wrote the screenplay, to ensure your ideas would reach the screen?

CORMAN: Yes. I never intended to write the final screenplay. What I did was write the first draft of the script, and then F. X. Feeney and Ed Nemayer came in and did drafts after mine, based upon on my version. What I was writing was primarily structure; I was interested most in putting into place the ideas that I wanted. F.X. and Ed then came in to polish the dialogue.

WIATER: Did the old adage "Once you learn how to ride a bicycle, you never forget" apply when you went back to being a director again?

CORMAN: Yes—it applied much more than I thought it would. I was a little concerned about what it would be like to be directing again. But we were shooting outside of Milan on the first day, and I was really wondering what was going to take place. I arrived on the set, and the set wasn't quite ready. And I said, "All right, fellows, now let's get these props over here, and these set dressings over here . . . Place the camera here, let's get those extras ready . . ." And I was working again, just as if I had been doing it the previous week and never stopped.

WIATER: Since you'd been away from directing for so long, had anything changed that really surprised you as you stepped behind the camera again?

CORMAN: A lot less had changed than I would have thought. The equipment is a lot lighter and more portable, the film stock is faster. Things like that. But these are incremental changes.

WIATER: What about stylistically then? How did you handle the horror element, when we all know that "times have changed" in terms of what audiences expect in order to be scared?

CORMAN: I handled it more akin to what I did in the Poe films, in that I handled it indirectly, but I did acknowledge—at least in recog-. nizing my own line—that the world *has* changed, and that there *is* a more graphic rendition of violence than there was. So I would say the violence is a little more graphic than I did in the Poe films, but not as graphic as it is in some other films of today. In other words, I moved a little bit with the times, but not totally.

WIATER: You're often affectionately referred to as the "King of the B Movies." Could you tell me what that title means to you, and do you feel it's an accurate one?

CORMAN: I think it means somebody doesn't understand the motion picture business. Because B pictures were a product of the 1930s and most of the 1940s. During the Depression, the major studios had an A list and a B list of productions. The B list would be a supporting feature, the idea being that if you could get people to come to the theaters, you'd give them two pictures for the price of one. So there would be a cheap second feature to go along with the top feature.

I started making films in the 1950s, and by that time this practice had died out. I never really made a B picture. Nobody's made a B picture since 1945 or 1946. As a matter of fact, *Le Mains*, the French newspaper, wrote an article on my coming back as a director, and it started off "the Pope of Pop Cinema Returns." *That* was kind of nice. [Chuckles.] So I'll ride with that title.

WIATER: Why do the horror and science fiction genres continue to be so popular, when just about every other kind of genre film—from Westerns to "youth runs wild" movies to gangster films—have all but faded away?

CORMAN: Horror films and science fiction films and fantasy films in general appeal to basic drives and wishes within the human mind. Whereas a Western or a picture about the Hell's Angels in the 1960s will appeal to a surface manifestation of a society. And when Hell's Angels are no longer in the news, and people aren't thinking anymore about cowboys, and cowboys become the latter-day equivalent of knights in shining armor—in other words, they become historical sub- jects—they're still valid subjects for motion pictures, but only if you can find something universal within them. So therefore, as a genre, they will fade. Whereas the concept of a horror film . . . the very first story ever written in the English language was *Beowolf*, which was kind of a science fiction-horror-fantasy tale. It's been with us forever, and it will *always* be with us. So it's what's universal that remains.

WIATER: Speaking of horror, why are the extremely violent, so-called splatter movies so popular? Yet you've never made one, in spite of their obvious commercial success in recent years.

CORMAN: They are just that—slashing, slapping, splatter movies, which depend to a large extent on just filling the screen with gore. I try to be a little more indirect. However, I'm not that much against them—I've never made a splatter film, though my company has made a couple of films, such as *Slumberparty Massacre*. Which in a way are that type of film, but we hope are a little bit different in that they're told from a slightly feminist point of view—the women always defeat the killer. Those have been successful for us, it's just that I personally would rather work in a more indirect or subtle manner.

WIATER: I remember seeing a television spoof of low-budget filmmakers, where the director said you needed two primary ingredients to succeed: a big chest and a big chase.

CORMAN: [Laughs.] It's not that far off the mark. It's obviously not a complete or accurate answer, but there is some truth in it. The real answer is much more complex, but certainly those two elements can't hurt.

WIATER: One of the things you're renowned for is your ability to figure out what popular trends to exploit, before anyone else is even aware there is a trend. Where does that ability come from?

CORMAN: I don't feel that I am that much different from the audience, so I would say to myself, What type of film would I like to see? (As a low-budget film, knowing that the idea has to be different from one in a more expensive film.) And if it's an idea that is interesting to me, it will probably therefore be interesting to the audience.

WIATER: So your gut instinct is to see that the movie will first and foremost appeal to the "common man?"

CORMAN: I think so.

WIATER: What keeps you going? Haven't you already done it all, seen it all, as a filmmaker? What new challenges can there be for you?

CORMAN: There is still some challenge. Some sense of fun, excitement, and creative satisfaction. However, there is a little bit less of that than there was at one time, and I probably will start to slow a little bit, very possibly this year. I will continue to make films, but I probably won't be making quite as many films as I've done in the past. If I do too many films, it's more like work and less like play. It is still fun.

WIATER: It's been said that one of the reasons you've "worn so many hats" in Hollywood is because you never seem to be satisfied with having someone else produce a movie or direct it or write it. You always seem to end up doing the project yourself just to make sure it's done the way you originally planned.

CORMAN: That's probably a fault within me. Because it would be better if I could delegate more, and as I say, I am trying to work less and making a conscious effort to delegate a little more authority.

WIATER: Do you still have the same mental list of favorite films that you've directed? Is it still the Edgar Allan Poe films? *The Intruder*?

CORMAN: It varies from time to time. One day I'll say I like this film, and the next day I'll say I don't like any other film. But in general it stays about the same.

WIATER: You mentioned *Slumberparty Massacre* as treading the fine line between a horror film and a splatter film. What do you say in response to the critics who think a movie like *Stripped to Kill* is of even less value, or who merely dismiss it as violent pornography?

CORMAN: I think any time you make a film, you're subject to controversy. One person will say, "I see this message in a film," and another will say, "I see that in a film." All I can see is that I did the best I can in a film. It reminds me of the old joke about the guy taking the Rorschach test—you know, the inkblots? So the doctor shows him one splattering of ink and says, "What does this make you think of?" And the man says, "It makes me think of sex." So the doctor shows him another and asks, "What does that make you think of?" And the man says, "It makes me think of sex." The doctor goes through the whole book, and every single inkblot—which is an abstract pattern—it makes him think of nothing but sex. And the doctor says, "Does every picture here make you think of sex?" The guy says, "You're the one showing me dirty pictures."

WIATER: A fair rebuttal. Yet some critics say that the constant deluge of violence in the movies is making some people desensitized to violence in real life. People use this as part of an argument about why there should be censorship, why we should have a MPAA ratings board for the cinema.

CORMAN: I am opposed *always* to censorship in any form. At the same time, however, and this may be a surprising answer, but I do think that violence has gotten somewhat out of hand in the motion picture industry. I don't think there should be any censorship of it, but the content of the ratings board—in terms of violence—could be a little bit stronger. If a person wants to make a film with a lot of violence, okay. But I think some of those films should get an X rating for violence. I would be in favor of modifying the ratings code slightly, and making the code a little bit tougher on violence, and a little bit more lenient on sex. I think excessive violence can have a harmful effect on young people. Whereas at the same time, seeing a woman's breast really isn't going to hurt anybody.

WIATER: Would you agree that it's the recent advent of the videocassette that has saved independent filmmakers like yourself from going the way of the disappearing drive-ins where so many of these films were originally destined to be shown?

CORMAN: The videocassette industry has arisen at the right time to help the independent filmmaker. But at the same time it's arisen to help the independents, it's hurt in a different way because it's hurting their chances to ever play in theaters. The theaters are now slanted toward major studio projects, and the independents are slanted more toward the videocassette market. So you can say, which came first, the chicken or the egg?

WIATER: Is that the thinking now with the films you produce at Concorde? In other words, it's known from the outset which films are going to get theatrical release and which are going to be sold directly to video?

CORMAN: Yes. But almost all of our films get a theatrical release. As a matter of fact, *Variety* the other day, in summing up the industry for the year, stated that Concorde is the only production-distribution company in the United States that makes low- and medium-budget films on a regular basis and then is able to distribute them in the theaters.

WIATER: If Roger Corman had never gone into the film industry, how would it be different today?

CORMAN: I don't think the film industry would be that much different. I don't really believe I've made that great of an impact. What little impact I've had would be in that I've helped the development of independent productions. I think independent film productions would have happened without me, but there might be fewer independents without me. I think I've been able to show that it is possible to exist— and even possibly prosper—away from the major studios. Following your own path.

WIATER: I would think that another major contribution you made was giving so many young directors their first big break in the industry, such as Martin Scorcese, Paul Bartel, Jonathan Demme, Joe Dante, Francis Ford Coppola, Allan Arkush, Ron Howard . . .

CORMAN: That might be. But I would think the very best of them, one way or the other, their talent would have come through. It might have taken a few years longer, but I think that the really brilliant filmmakers will eventually be recognized. Always. [Pauses.] Let me change that—almost always.

WIATER: What is Roger Corman's perspective on the *auteur* theory, where the critics give the lion's share of the creative credit to the director above anyone else?

CORMAN: On most films, the director *is* the dominant creative force. But it is not always that way. So I would say the *auteur* theory is correct most of the time. But more times than the critics think, the most important person is the producer. Sometimes the most important person is the writer, and occasionally, the most important person will be the star. But, in general, the most dominant creative force is the director.

WIATER: What does the next ten years hold for Roger Corman?

CORMAN: I haven't thought that specifically about it, because I'm so much involved with just working from day to day. But I will say that probably I will continue to make films. I will make fewer films, but I will try and put more of my personal thoughts and beliefs into them, and I will delegate other people to do the production. Hopefully they will be better films.

WIATER: And will you ever be directing again?

CORMAN: I will probably direct again, but it won't be immediately.

Wes Craven

Henri Bollinger

As the story goes, it takes all kinds to make a world. So it naturally seems odd that someone with a strict religious upbringing, and who was formerly a professor of humanities, would now be internationally recognized as a writer and director of horror films. Odder still that someone who never desired to be associated with this genre while trying to break into the film industry would eventually be the creator of one of the most successful series of all times—the *Nightmare on Elm Street* movies. (No less than four sequels, with a total box office of more than $250 million.)

But Wes Craven happens to be that kind of person.

Although clearly best known to the public as the creator of Freddy Krueger—that supernatural child killer who can come back to life through the force of a person's nightmares—Craven had already made his mark in horror right from his very first film.

Released in 1972, *Last House on the Left* still qualifies on many critics' lists as one of the most shocking and violent motion pictures ever made. Although supposedly inspired by the events in Ingmar Bergman's classic *The Virgin Spring*, this movie is more easily recognized for its unrelenting scenes of rape, murder, castration, and torture. If Craven never made another movie, this film would still prove he knew how to rivet an audience to the seat.

Over the years, Craven has also done some memorable television work, including episodes of the recent CBS-TV "Twilight Zone" series, and directed several made-for-television movies, including "Chiller" and "Invitation to Hell."

But success for Craven has been, in a sense, a double-edged sword. For though he is universally recognized as one of the most successful directors of horror films, Craven would actually like to switch gears completely and make a comedy! The reason why is what I found most fascinating during my conversation with the man, who nonetheless will always be known for directing a few of the most frightening pictures ever made.

I spoke with Wes Craven while he was in preproduction on several projects for Alive Films, of which *Shocker* was the first production in a multiproject deal.

SELECTED FILMOGRAPHY

Last House on the Left (1972)

The Hills Have Eyes (1977)

Deadly Blessing (1981)

Swamp Thing (1982)

A Nightmare on Elm Street (1984)

The Hills Have Eyes II (1984)

Deadly Friend (1986)

The Serpent and the Rainbow (1988)

Shocker (1989)

WIATER: In terms of your career overall, has it been a blessing or curse being best known as a director of horror films?

CRAVEN: It's a blessing in the sense that, from a business end of the film industry, I'm now in a structured deal that allows me a fair amount of artistic freedom to express myself. But the down side of it, for reasons that I've spent my entire career trying to puzzle out, is that I've been doing *only* horror films. Even though that was not my original intent when I entered the film industry, and not my original fascination with this area in general. So I've been tackling the whys and wherefores of that for most of my adult life.

WIATER: But some critics, myself included, believe it takes a very special talent to work in this genre, exploring the dark side of human nature.

CRAVEN: I was raised with a very strict religious background and that created a lot of inherent rage, and in a way I just stumbled onto this way of expressing myself. Another thing is when you become very good at something that is as extraordinary as horror films (and I use that word as a neutral term), it's extraordinary in the sense that this is not something most people express an affinity with. Most people shy away from dealing with emotions such as rage, extreme anger, and other bizarre and irrational behavior. Most adults are uneasy with dealing with any of that, and don't actively explore it artistically.

I went through a period in my career when anyone that I met was astonished to see that I was the person making these kind of films. I've gotten out more in recent years and met other directors working in this genre, and they all tell similar stories. People react to Clive Barker in the same way. Sam Raimi is like that—they tend to be fun-loving people. Very upbeat, very "normal" people. Yet the audience, and many of the critics, still assume we must be very strange and unhappy people.

On my set, I've often had people tell me this is the happiest set they've ever worked on, or it's the most fun set they've ever been on.

WIATER: Yet the fact that you make horror movies does show some undeniable fascination with the more unpleasant aspects of life. Any reasons why?

CRAVEN: I don't know what it is. Maybe it's some sort of exorcism of the way you really feel about the horrors of life so that you can control it. Personally I've felt, quite often in my life, helpless in the face of the overwhelming weight of the world itself. I know that by making films like these, I at least have some sort of handle on it. Almost giving myself some sort of shield . . . so people will perceive me as being capable of frightening actions, and therefore they leave me alone.

WIATER: I like to believe that for those of us who openly face the darkness, so to speak, we're more capable of enjoying the light.

CRAVEN: That's how I think it works. People who criticize horror films are not acknowledging that part of life, or that part of themselves. I firmly believe that every human being has the capacity for madness and wildness in them, and horror films express this—I think—in usually a very harmless way.

WIATER: Yet some critics will always blame horror films as inspiring violence in our society, not acting as a catharsis of these same antisocial feelings.

CRAVEN: Yes. I don't think of horror films as instigation; I think of them as reflections. In general, art is like that. It's funny, because art is always the first thing that is attacked. I think this is because the arts reflect events so truly, it's frightening. Horror films often reflect a truth that is too unpalatable for the society at large, especially for the political leaders, to be really comfortable with. Like it or not, we live in a lethal world. From what I can see of our culture and civilization, it is shot through with wars and murders and tortures—a truly great amount of terrifying horror. The threat of atomic warfare has been with us all our lives, to say nothing of germ warfare or biological warfare. People don't want to talk about this, but it's always there.

This is the amazing thing of denial that I'm continually struck by: how people never mention the actual, real horrors in our world when they criticize horror films. They'd rather blame the horror film for influencing or "damaging" their children. But these are kids who are growing up with junkies in the fourth grade, you know? People are coming into their schools carrying AK-47 assault rifles, or sniping at them from rooftops. It's on the news nightly for these kids to see. It's not like the horror film is introducing them to something that's never occurred to them!

The reason some of these kids walk around with Freddy Krueger dolls is the same reason that horror filmmakers are a little bit more relaxed about the terrors around us, because they are able to handle it, manipulate it, and call it their own for the moment. That's what a child does with a Freddy Krueger doll. That's what a teenager does with a horror film: they're somehow able to identify with it and say, "This I can handle. The person who I identify most with in this film probably will survive." Most horror films, no matter how devastating the action may become, are usually hopeful in the end, with the person you identify with most *surviving*.

WIATER: Censorship battles with the MPAA have been more rampant than ever, with the film *Henry: Portrait of a Serial Killer* receiving an X just for its "moral tone." How much of a problem is it to make a film to appease the ratings board, while still being true to your own artistic visions?

CRAVEN: I have a rather sobering answer to that, as one of the reasons I want to get out of horror is that there is very, very real censorship now. I feel very much like a racing engine with a governor on it. With the exception of *The Serpent and the Rainbow*, which I imagine was regarded as a love story or a political thriller or something, *all* of my films have been censored in a very disturbing way. Especially the last three or four films. Even though I've been scrupulous in not dwelling on violence, I have been censored for *intensity*.

That just strikes me as terrifying. Because what they are saying is that it doesn't matter whether you have a bloody scene or not, it doesn't matter if there are lopped off limbs or not, what matters is that I'm simply too intense. Therefore I've been told that this very genre must be limited in its intent, which *is* to *be* intense! It's as if we're working in some kind of emotional ghetto, where we're allowed to kill each other, but just not allowed to feel anything about it. *Shocker*, for example, was censored in twelve separate sequences. Scenes that were not necessarily bloody, but judged as too intense.

It just leaves me feeling like there is simply not the freedom there that I myself need at the level that I want to make an expression. It's extremely frustrating, because I feel that the *Shocker* now showing is *not* where Wes Craven is in the nineties, it's simply the version that they've *allowed* to be out. I am a responsible adult. I think all the time while I'm making a film, Would this damage a child emotionally? Is this violence just for prurient interests? I really try to avoid that, to be just, to be accurate, to be graphic for only as long as I need to be. But that doesn't seem to be important to these people at all.

WIATER: Clive Barker has told me that a filmmaker can never even hope to outguess the censors. You never know from one project to the next what is taboo, do you?

CRAVEN: No! There are simply no guidelines to go on, there's nothing published. Nothing! They will not tell you specifically what to cut, so even while you're doing it, you don't have any guidelines to go by. Beyond that, there is no precedent to go by.

On *Deadly Friend* we had a decapitation scene that totally freaked them out. So I had my assistant go back and make what we called a "decapitation compilation" showing films made in the last ten years that had been passed which had decapitation sequences. There were scenes that had incredible goriness to them, such as *The Fury* and *The Omen*, and they didn't even look at it! The MPAA told us, "We don't even consider past films; every film is rated on the current state of values and standards tolerated in society," or some bullshit like that.

You're simply left guessing in the dark.

WIATER: I can imagine the level of frustration you must feel, if this is the situation you've had on nearly every project. After a while, don't you find yourself consciously precensoring your vision just to get the movie completed?

CRAVEN: Of course! This lack of guidelines is a very clever device in a way, because you're always precensoring yourself. You're constantly thinking, Why shoot this—it will never pass! Or even at the script level, you find yourself saying, "I love it—but it will never pass."

WIATER: But in *Deadly Friend*, didn't you have to go back and add scenes that were purposely more "intense" because it didn't preview well to an audience expecting a "Wes Craven Film?"

CRAVEN: On *Deadly Friend* the film was slanted much more on the love story between the boy and the girl. But when they test screened the film, they got in a heavy metal, hard-core audience who had been told they were going to see a "Wes Craven Film." So this horror audience was totally pissed off that there wasn't more blood and guts in it, and the studio did a 180-degree turn at the last moment, after the film was done. We were told to go out and "shoot some gory stuff," and so we shot those dream sequences, which we edited into the film.

But that doesn't alter the censorship problem; that film was neither fish nor fowl. It was meant to be a bizarre, off-the-wall love story, and along the way it became a wild and woolly horror film. But it wasn't originally designed to be that way; nobody knew what the hell kind of film it was, including me.

WIATER: As far as the marketing department is concerned, your name is now just as much of the package as the film itself. People associate you so completely with this genre, you're probably at a point where— if you were a novelist like Stephen King—you would have to use a pseudonym to do anything else.

CRAVEN: Yes, I've realized that myself. I'd love to write children's books, but now I'd have to use a pseudonym to hide my identity. On the other hand, as "Wes Craven," I can simply approach people in this industry and get deals because I *am* Wes Craven. [Chuckles.]

WIATER: To ask my most obvious question, do you regard *A Nightmare on Elm Street* as the most influential film of your career?

CRAVEN: Absolutely. It certainly is the most broadly popular, although I've had a lot of people tell me *The Hills Have Eyes* has been a big influence. But *Nightmare* certainly reintroduced the whole concept of the "rubber reality" of the dream world in a way that hadn't been used in quite a while.

WIATER: Although you didn't personally partake of the financial gains made from the Freddy Krueger marketing phenomenon that followed, not to mention the several sequels, are you pleased overall to have originated such a popular series of movies?

CRAVEN: There are no simple choices in this world, I guess. But there were certainly benefits in my being recognized as the creator of something that is viable on the market—which is a large part of being negotiable in Hollywood as a director. So the *Nightmare* films have done an immense amount for me on that level. It was also instrumental in me getting *The Serpent and the Rainbow* simply because of the magnitude of that phenomenon. I was considered by people such as producer David Ladd, who normally wouldn't have considered me except he was aware of the money that film generated.

The other thing that helped was the seven "Twilight Zone" episodes I directed, which showed a side of me that had never been allowed to be seen in my films. Those two things combined helped my career a great deal. But as for *Nightmare on Elm Street*, it never hurts in show business to be associated with something that makes a lot of money! [Chuckles.] That *is* the name of the game for a lot of people. So what it's allowed me to do since is to have this deal with Alive and Universal, in which they say, "Well, he made *Nightmare*, so let's let him do what he does best." Obviously they're looking for another Freddy Krueger.

WIATER: It's strange to note that about the time *Shocker* was released, there were already two movies out with basically similar themes, *Prison* and *The Horrorshow*. There are also elements in other films of the rubber reality you mention even before *A Nightmare on Elm Street* became a hit. Just how do you create something totally original in this genre?

CRAVEN: [Sighs.] It's very frustrating, because *Shocker* was originally conceived as a television series called "Dreamstalker," which was essentially the first and second acts of *Shocker*. It was based on a conversation I had with my editor. "Let's do a version of *The Thing* where a person is able to get into the body of another person, and you don't know who is he or who he is inside." We had that at the Fox network, and they couldn't make a decision about it. So here it is being copied and sent to every minor executive in town, saying that this is the thing Wes Craven wants to do next at Fox. It was almost a year, and finally they passed. I went off to do *The Serpent and the Rainbow*, and by that time, the idea for this had been on various people's desks for almost a year and a half. So I'm talking to Jack Sholder, and asking him what film he's going to do next. And he says, "I'm going to do this film called *The Hidden*, about a creature that goes inside people's bodies . . ."

Nightmare on Elm Street was around in script form for a few years before it finally got launched. Right around the time it came out *Dreamscape* was around, and it was very, very similar. So? [Pauses.] These things happen. I don't want to comment on how they might happen, because sometimes you simply can't tell. Sometimes I know it is coincidental, because I didn't know about *Prison*, and yet my film has elements similar to that. These things do happen.

WIATER: It was reported that there was several occult experiences that you personally witnessed while shooting *The Serpent and the Rainbow* in Haiti. What are your beliefs on this subject of the occult or the supernatural?

CRAVEN: I suspect there are ways in which the human consciousness works that in Western culture are not clearly mapped—or even admitted to. I do believe there are capacities of the human mind that are still quite mysterious to us. I don't know about the occult per se; I do know that the human mind can be persuaded to perceive almost anything that it already completely believes in. And, at a certain point, the line between belief and reality gets very, very cloudy.

For example, in Haiti I saw people do things that we would consider physically impossible—not walking on air or anything like that—but eating broken glass, leaning against very sharp machetes without them piercing the skin. Things like that. You could call it supernatural. I prefer to think of it as "today's magic is tomorrow's technology." There may be a lot of things we simply don't understand yet, but tomorrow these occurrences may be commonplace. I don't subscribe to any particular religious explanation for all this; I'm in constant wonder of life itself.

WIATER: Another film that walks the thin line between reality and belief is *Communion*, based on author Whitley Strieber's alleged encounters with an alien intelligence. Any reaction to this sort of paranormal phenomenon?

CRAVEN: There was a period in my life when, just out of high school, I read a lot of that sort of material. I *am* fascinated by it. I read *Communion*. There was a point where I said to myself, "This would make a *tremendous* horror film." Then it reached a point where I thought it went too far and sounded like somebody who had developed a bizarre psychological mind-set.

But the idea of being invaded through one's consciousness to me is a fascinating idea. Because nature is really full of one species' insidious invasion of another. The idea of laying eggs on a host that are eventually going to hatch, and then dwell under its skin and eventually digest it from within is so common in the insect world. The idea of something that invades you—from a plane of reality that is not physical but is mental—just fascinates me. The idea that a man might have manifestations that make it seem like they can see aliens "out there" that would have to be semihuman, because that's the only way we can conceive of something like that.

But do I really think they are physically out there? No.

Do I think there's a possibility of something that is from some unknown level—not from spaceships flying around in the air—invading us? Yes, I do. I can see that as a *possibility*. I don't have hard fix—and I don't think anybody really does—on what "reality" or "consciousness" is.

WIATER: This goes back to your earlier mention of the rubber reality, the idea of one level of reality melding with another. Possibly Strieber has somehow stepped over into a level of reality that ninety-nine percent of us will never even consider, so only one percent of us can possibly grasp the concept?

CRAVEN: That's the whole point. I know when I was researching *A Nightmare on Elm Street*, I ran across some literature that listed something like 200 various states of consciousness that are recognized by Western science. From various forms of schizophrenia to paranoia, to drunkenness, to hallucinations, to euphoria—there's a *tremendous* variety of ways your mind can perceive reality, and it can be different every time.

WIATER: I'm curious to know what sort of fan mail you receive. It's not too much to assume that you are almost as well known as Freddy Krueger by now?

CRAVEN: I get my share of weird letters, but no more than anyone else working in the industry who is known to the public receives. In fact, I believe the percentage of letters that I get that are bizarre is pretty low. Maybe one a month, or something like that. And they're not from people who want to rip my eyes out or anything like that [Laughs.], so much as they are like "You are the greatest filmmaker in the world, and once you've seen me, you will know I am a great star." And its postmarked from some obscure place in Germany or Canada!

But mostly they're pretty innocent letters, including little school kids who have chosen me a class project and want to know how I got into this business. Or just want to draw me a scary picture. A lot of the letters are very sweet. One of my hobbies is graphology, and some of the kids who write in seem semidepressed; there's a sense of disturbance in their writing. Not in a deep psychological level, but still they seem what I'd call semidisturbed. But the letters they write are very hopeful and very grateful.

In the last four or five years, there's a different kind of fan letter coming from older people who have appreciated my films over the years, and who want to discuss my work directly, and tell me how much they enjoy them. By and large, I don't get letters from very many demented people—though I do have it sort of lurking in the back of my mind that sooner or later I will. Somebody will say, "You deserve to die because your last film wasn't scary enough" or tell me "I'm the appointed one." [Chuckles.]

WIATER: In one sense, you are a prisoner of your success—you can do pretty much what you want as a director, just as long as it remains squarely in the horror genre. Even so, is Wes Craven a happy man at this point in his career?

CRAVEN: Wes Craven is a very happy man. In fact, I'm not even feeling a "prisoner of the genre" as much as I did before. This is partially because I was able to get a television sitcom on the air last season. Though it was not successful in the long run, it's not perceived as my failure because it was put in the hands of other people while I was working on *Shocker*. The fact that I got that show on the air, and actually sold two comedy concepts in the space of ten days made a big breakthrough in the industry's perception of me. So now I'm getting scripts that are comedies, and it shows I'm ready to step out of the genre. I think in maybe the next three years I'll probably be doing something that's completely out of the genre.

In conclusion, I just want to say I've felt like this has been a long time coming. I'm now being perceived in the business community as a businessman, and in the artistic community I've consistently shown that there is another side to Wes Craven. So as I look forward to my fifties, I want to broaden my scope. Part of it is just a matter of confidence on my own part that I *can* do other kinds of films, though I did get my start in horror.

WIATER: But you're not thinking of abandoning the genre completely?

CRAVEN: No! My model has always been Roman Polanski, who I think has shown great mastery of the darker side of human nature, and yet has had the range that any artist should be allowed to have. So I think it's going to happen.

David Cronenberg

David Cronenberg's work is so intentionally disturbing, so unrelentingly intense, that most audiences have one of two distinct reactions to his films: they are either totally disgusted or completely enthralled.

From the release of his very first feature, *They Came from Within*, Cronenberg has presented an uncompromising series of dark visions to an ever-growing audience. This grisly tale of turdlike parasites, which once they enter a human host transform that person into a raving sexual maniac, left no doubt that a major new talent had arrived. With every movie since, Cronenberg has shown himself to be one of the important filmmakers working today, whether in or outside the parameters of what is commonly catogorized as a horror film.

Born in Toronto, on March 15, 1943, Cronenberg originally intended to make a career as a writer of science fiction stories. But an inability to sell any stories, coupled with the opportunity in college to make student films, eventually changed his career goals from writer to filmmaker. (Although he has written the screenplays for the majority of his movies.)

Even though Cronenberg first gained early critical recognition with such low-budget productions as *Rabid* and *Scanners*, it was not until he made the extremely disturbing *Videodrome* that audiences finally realized he had far more on his mind than just trying to gross them out. To be sure, this film had more than its share of revolting sequences (including actress Deborah Harry burning her nude body with a cigarette, actor James Woods pulling open a vaginalike opening in his chest and inserting a gun into it); what set *Videodrome* apart from just about every other film ever done was that it was clearly an intellectual exercise as well.

In other words, Cronenberg was able to exhibit a vision that was unmistakably his own, a dark vision that found perfect release within the horror genre. With every subsequent production, Cronenberg has examined the myriad aspects of his vision in such a way that he often presents less blood and gore on screen—while remaining incredibly disturbing by what he doesn't explicitly reveal. At least two book-length critical studies of his movies have appeared, with more undoubtedly forthcoming. His movies are not always "entertaining," but many of them are regarded by *cineteratologists* as the state-of-the-art in horror.

I spoke with David Cronenberg from his production office in Toronto, where he was in preproduction for his next feature, *Naked Lunch*, based on the controversial novel of the same name by William Burroughs.

SELECTED FILMOGRAPHY

They Came from Within (1975)

The Brood (1979)

Videodrome (1982)

The Dead Zone (1983)

The Fly (1986)

Dead Ringers (1989)

WIATER: I understand you have done some television work recently. Isn't that unusual for you?

CRONENBERG: Yes, that's true. I did a pilot for *Scales of Justice*, which is a TV adaptation of a radio show that is basically documentary in style. It's a look at how the justice system works using actual cases, and the dialogue is all transcripts from court cases. So it's quite different from any of the existing law shows; it couldn't be more different from something like "L.A. Law." You just don't know anything about the lawyers' private lives. None of that is the issue. It's quite interesting for me because it's quite different from the things that I normally do.

WIATER: If memory serves, I believe your father wrote crime stories?

CRONENBERG: That is true and there's definitely that connection. He wrote and edited for a magazine called *True Crime*. Actually, there were a few magazines that he wrote for.

WIATER: It certainly wouldn't be outside your realm of interest. I write about horror as a journalist and I write horror fiction, but my leisure reading is usually crime.

CRONENBERG: That is interesting. It *does* connect, and it is very interesting to see how completely unpredictable and strange people's reactions to things are. It's quite an education.

WIATER: What is your interest in *Naked Lunch*? I've been aware of it for years as a psychedelic antinovel.

CRONENBERG: Well, I think "psychedelic" is basically wrong because it was written mostly in the fifties. It's more experimental. It's very unstructured and doesn't really have any narrative or characters in the normal sense. That was part of the challenge. But it was also a very influential book. The writings of Burroughs have been a big influence on me. His imagery and understandings of disease, obsession, and addiction—a lot of it is from science fiction and horror. I have felt his presence in my work for a long time, and I guess it's the feeling that you need to return to some sort of literary roots and deal with it sort of at the primal level. Actually, producer Jeremy Thomas and I have been talking about doing this project for eight or nine years. We actually went back to Tangiers with Burroughs about five years ago; he hadn't been there since the sixties. He is a writer whose work has been so incredibly assimilated by the culture of North America. In rock 'n' roll—I mean Steely Dan and you name it. A lot of "Saturday Night Live" was rather watered-down Burroughs, so it was interesting to try to rediscover the original stuff and see what it felt like at this distance.

WIATER: You feel that horror isn't a separate genre, that it is really a part of our mainstream. Isn't that true?

CRONENBERG: In truth, when I am making my films I don't think at all in terms of horror, and the usual questions you get asked like "What does horror mean to you, what scares you, and what are your nightmares?" That is a level that I am not functioning on when I am writing and directing. It's really a complex process, but I'm responding to things in my own life, so on one level it's all personal stuff. And then of course people would say, "Well, does that mean that your life is horrible?" It's really not. It's observations. It really all has to do with our existence as something physical, the human body as a fact of life and somehow dealing with what *that* means. Taking that as a starting point leads you into territory that is traditionally considered to be horror. But I approach it sort of from the inside out, rather than saying, "I will now create a horror genre piece."

WIATER: When I've interviewed Stephen King, he's told me that when he writes a story or novel, it's just a Stephen King tale and it's other people's interpretation that it is "a horror piece."

CRONENBERG: The problem is that Stephen King enjoys articulating his thoughts about horror, the genre, and other people's work in the genre. He is an aficionado of the genre, which I am not, really. I don't go out and see a horror film because it is a horror film and I feel I must see every horror film. I have a feeling that Stephen does. I just see what appeals to me. It's almost like being a collector. If you're a collector of horror films then you have to stay on top of what's around, whether you particularly like what's there or not. I've never been that. I think that is the difference in terms of the way we are perceived.

WIATER: My interpretation of your work is that they are true horror films, but sometimes they are not the same as what the audience assumes is horror.

CRONENBERG: I think you are right about that. It only becomes strange when you become pigeonholed and people's expectations are of a certain kind because you have been pigeonholed. I'm sure there are fans of *The Fly* who were very disappointed in *Dead Ringers*. To me they are very connected, but to a fan who is approaching it from the genre angle, *The Fly* is a good sci-fi horror film and what is *Dead Ringers*? That's where it becomes difficult. As I've said before, on that level it becomes a marketing problem rather than a creative problem. From that point of view, I don't have much to do with it.

WIATER: Most of your films have been original screenplays, but with the case of *Dead Ringers* and *The Dead Zone* they were based on published novels.

CRONENBERG: I agree with that in the case of *The Dead Zone*. But, in the case of *Dead Ringers* it's not true. Although technically and legally it was based on the novel *Twins*. I read it once about ten years before I did the movie and that was it. It was really for legal reasons that the movie was based on it, and I think that anyone who reads that book would realize that.

WIATER: What was the interest in doing *The Dead Zone*?

CRONENBERG: It was odd. I had been approached about *The Dead Zone* some years before I actually did it by a woman named Carol Baum, whose name is on *Dead Ringers* as an executive producer. She was at Lorimar at that time and she asked me if I would be interested in the project *The Dead Zone*. I read the book and I wasn't sure. I was still thinking about it when she phoned me back and said, "I'm really embarrassed, but unbeknownst to me the project has been assigned to Stanley Donen to direct and Sidney Pollack is going to produce it. So I really didn't have the right to give it to you." That was fine, because I hadn't decided whether or not I wanted to do the book as a film. So it just sort of percolated for three years and then I was sitting in John Landis's office with producer Debra Hill. Debra said, "It just occurred to me, I'm doing *The Dead Zone* for Dino De Laurentis; do you want to direct it?" I said without thinking that I *did* want to do it, which surprised me.

In retrospect you analyze why you would do this, and I realized that there are a lot of connections between that and a lot of other things that I've done. But the tone of it is quite different. It's the combination of the two that I found very attractive. The kind of characters that are in *The Dead Zone* are not the kind of characters that I write, ever. I guess I found it interesting and attractive to combine a theme that I've done before in *Scanners* and other things with the kind of characters that Stephen likes, which are very real and normal and small town, something I don't do.

WIATER: I would like a response to this quote of yours: "Tales of horror tell certain truths that are very painful and necessarily unpleasant and not in good taste." What sort of truths *do* tales of horror tell?

CRONENBERG: For me, it's really talking about mortality. We're really talking about not being infinite. It's an existential truth, it's very raw and real. It's a very basic one, which is often lost sight of with all the layers of cultural persiflage and complexity. I think we are really just talking about a mind that doesn't see why it shouldn't be infinite and eternal, and a body that tells you right from the beginning that you are very definitely finite and time bound. I really think it is the tension between those two things that is the subject of horror.

There are many different approaches. I remember an interview with Stephen King about Stanley Kubrick and *The Shining*. Kubrick said that, in a way, *The Shining* is very optimistic because if you conjecture people somehow existing after death, spiritually, still that means there is an afterlife in which we survive in some individual way. So for someone who has never believed in an afterlife, maybe that's an optimistic element. I only have one approach to mortality and it comes from my understanding of human existence. It is that you do hit that wall, you do not exist beyond your death. There is no soul or mind that is independent of the human body. I won't do a story in which there are ghosts and spirits unless there was some reason that I felt I should explore that as a premise and see where it leads me. So that's why you get that incredible variety in horror, because given that mortality is the *real* subject of horror, there are an infinite number of approaches you can take to that subject.

WIATER: So you feel that in the horror genre there are so many stories to be told that you never have to worry about "doing it all?"

CRONENBERG: I think once again that it's a matter of how you are perceived. And it's also a matter of tone. I think it is disturbing and dark stuff. It can be dealt with lightly and even humorously, but nonetheless there is that disturbing element, always. So if you're not in the mood to do that I can see why you would move on. But in terms of a lack of subject matter or approach, no, I agree with you. It's immense, never to be plumbed by one person.

Another question that one is often asked is why have things like trucker movies and Westerns all gone away and yet horror is still there? It's because horror is very much deeper than those other things. It's right there at the primal layer of human existence and therefore it is immune to trends and cultural upheaval. It of course shifts, but it is immune to being eradicated unless by censorship.

WIATER: One quality of your movies is that you feel uncomfortable while watching your films as well as after you've seen them. Where does that unease that you are able to project into your films come from?

CRONENBERG: It's because I am trying to wrestle with myself over these questions. What you are seeing is the arena itself and the action in it. This is my struggle and I'm doing it on film to come to terms with all those things myself. My approach to film in general is not film about film. I don't do direct references to other films. It's not because I'm too arrogant to do that, it's because that's not my subject matter. I think that as soon as you do a film that celebrates the wonderfulness of horror films you are put two or three steps away from the subject matter of horror films. Suddenly you are making a film about filmmaking. When you do this I think you are several layers away from the artistic process which is that basic struggle for understanding, peace, and resolution. Which is one that never ends. Quite frankly I don't expect it to happen to me either, and when you read Melville, Hawthorne, and Whitman, they all died depressed, feeling like they had failed. I think it is one's fate to die feeling that way. All it means is that it is the struggle itself which is of value, not the outcome. I think it's because what's happening in my films is right on screen; you're that close to the primal stuff and that's what is scary.

WIATER: So no matter how happy you may be in your personal life, is it always best to keep that happiness away from your creative endeavors?

CRONENBERG: Well it's not even a philosophical approach. Most statements of artistic intent, whether it's a Realist or Cubist, come after the fact of some instinctive, intuitive action. Some artists feel uncomfortable doing interviews because they feel if they articulate things, become too conscious of them, the magic will somehow go away and won't work anymore. It just depends on the temperament of the particular person as to whether that is a problem or not. I don't worry about it because when I am making a film, I forget all that other stuff. I think there is humor in my films, but you are looking for the source of obsessive attraction. For me it means it has to be something fairly serious and heavy.

WIATER: You just made your statement of intent as an artist and then you make such a powerful film as *The Fly*. What would lead you to do that film, a remake of a film first done in the 1950s?

CRONENBERG: That was also a very specific thing. I would never have thought of doing that either, because immediate thoughts of remaking the original would lead you to think that maybe you're doing some type of campy film and maybe you'll get Vincent Price to do a cameo, which I believe the original production was going to do. That would make it something else, not something bad, but not something that I would be interested in. It was really reading the script I was given that had some elements in it that really struck me as being very powerful and very much me. My project in rewriting the script was to make the rest of the script like that as well. Those basic elements had nothing to do with what I just said. I knew I could make a movie that would satisfy me. And then kind of peripherally it had a built-in audience. *The Fly* is certainly the most popular film I've ever done because it had a built-in expectation and a built-in audience, which I normally don't have. So it was just a fortunate combination of things and all I had to do was to make sure that the other people involved in the film knew what I wanted to do and agreed that that was the right thing to do.

WIATER: As the creative leader working with so many other people and all the compromises you have to make, at what point do you precensor your work or limit your imagination?

CRONENBERG: I don't censor myself at all when I write. I think as soon as you do that, you're finished. I think that one of the hallmarks of being a good director is not putting yourself into a context where you can't function properly. In other words, you have to make sure that the people you are working with are the right people, that the budget you have for what you are going to do is the right budget, and that people's expectations are the right expectations. Otherwise you are doomed from the start, and then you are playing some bizarre games that have nothing to do with the creative process. I kind of sidestep problem productions and situations if I can, so I'm not in a position where I have to self-censor. When I write a script I don't think about the budget, I don't think about how hard it may be to do something, or impossible. If things happen right, then you don't end up self-censoring or even compromising.

WIATER: So for you there is excitement as a writer and then there's a different excitement to make the motion picture?

CRONENBERG: Yes, they are quite different.

WIATER: What are the critics' biggest misconceptions of your work?

CRONENBERG: I think it is coming around. Let's talk about reviewers. Pauline Kael was talking about the difference between a critic and a reviewer. A reviewer experts that their readers will not have seen the movie, and a critic expects that the readers *have* seen the movie. I've gotten different responses from both. Of course the reviewer is always going to give you a more superficial look because of the pressure of the hype of the industry. Their reactions to films are rather tainted, I think. It is very easy to click into well-established channels of thought, especially if they don't have a particular empathy for your filmmaking, and I've had to deal with that a lot, just in terms of let's say acting. It was understood and anticipated that your low-budget horror film would have bad acting in it. It was almost a given. For years after my films didn't have bad acting in them they were just saying that the acting was bad and the effects were good given the fact of the low budget. Gradually, people began to see that it was actually a good performance despite the genre. You get to an overload point where you can't read what people write about you anymore.

The basic misconception is that they have a preconceived impression of the genre, and then they assume that your film is within the genre. As soon as they assume those two things you click into whatever the trend of the time is. You are asking a reviewer or critic to see your work for what it really is, which might seem like a simple thing, but it's something that you rarely get.

WIATER: Regarding Clive Barker's *Nightbreed*, could you tell me a little about your experience of working as an actor in this film?

CRONENBERG: I loved working as an actor. It's almost like seeing your life from the point of view of one of the other characters in your life. It's suddenly like you are your wife or child instead of you. You get a chance to see yourself from a totally different perspective. Clive's set was as relaxed as my own. It was like one of those sixties drug experiences where suddenly you are outside yourself and seeing yourself as though you are a different person. Filmmaking is very complex and the more you know about it, the better you are. It was a very positive and exciting thing to do. You don't have all the other complexities and politics to deal with. You are there to be the kid who gets to be someone else.

It was Clive's idea to be the serial killer. He called me up out of the blue and said he thought I should play this character. I think it was because of an interview he had seen me doing. He thought I was so rational and so reasonable, and yet I made those movies. His character was supposed to be a psychiatrist who was supposed to be the same. It was a rather theoretical reason for doing it, and I pointed out that he probably wanted a real actor to do it, but if he insisted, I certainly wasn't going to argue. It was great fun!

Robert Englund

Abrams Artists & Associates, Ltd.

Once upon a time, when you planned on going to a horror movie, the next thing you thought of was the name of the actor appearing in the film. Of course, we're going back a few years—say thirty or forty years ago. This was the heyday of the star system—the Clark Gables, the Humphrey Bogarts, the John Waynes—each genre had its own superstars. In horror, you had such actors as Boris Karloff, Bela Lugosi, and Peter Lorre, to name only the brightest of the dark stars. Even up until the sixties, there were horror actors such as Christopher Lee and Peter Cushing capable of directly attracting an audience, no matter what the name of the film.

Needless to say, the star system—at least in the horror genre—is for all intents and purposes dead and buried. With the exception of the semiretired Vincent Price, the great horror stars of old have all left us. And with the exception of

Caroline Munro, there are also no recognizable actresses—once fondly known as "scream queens"—who have made their names known to the moviegoing public via this genre.

Yet in terms of current actors becoming famous for portraying monsters, there has been one noticeable exception to this rule where the special effects are now the star.

That actor's name is Robert Englund.

In the tradition of Karloff, who became a Hollywood legend by having his face transformed by makeup in the classic *Frankenstein* (1931), Englund has made his mark in the history of horror cinema with his portrayal of the razor-fingered, hideously disfigured, and unkillable child killer, Freddy Krueger.

The rest, as the time-honored cliché goes, is history. Ever since the first *Nightmare on Elm Street* film appeared in 1984, no one would have dreamed (so to speak) of the tens of millions that the eventual series would gross over the course of four sequels (to date).

Beyond the movies themselves, the "Freddy Krueger phenomenon" has also become one of the most lucrative merchandising tie-ins in the history of horror. There are Freddy Krueger games, Halloween costumes, masks, toys, plastic models—even a talking Krueger doll with the voice of Freddy being none other than (of course) Robert Englund. Not since the Universal Studios monsters of the 1930s and 1940s has a supernatural creature taken the public's fancy. And as the other time-honored cliché goes, Englund is laughing all the way to the bank with his definitive interpretation of "the boogeyman of the 1980s."

When I interviewed Robert Englund, he was working on a number of television and motion picture projects, including the syndicated *Horror Hall of Fame*. And waiting for the next *Nightmare* to begin.

SELECTED FILMOGRAPHY

Eaten Alive (1976)

The Fifth Floor (1979)

Dead and Buried (1981)

A Nightmare on Elm Street (1984)

976-EVIL (director only) (1989)

Phantom of the Opera (1990)

WIATER: Looking back on that fortuitous decision, what made you decide to audition for the role of Freddy Krueger?

ENGLUND: At the time I had just been playing the benign, nerdy alien "Willie" on *V*, which was the number one, highest rated television miniseries ever created. My contract said that the miniseries could serve as a pilot for a series. So I had to do the series whether I wanted to or not. So I made a certain peace with myself at that point. Because *V* had been the number one, top rated miniseries for ten hours, I thought, "Well, here's the next five years of my life" doing the series. I could live with that—here's where I finally get my big bucks to put my kids through college or whatever.

At the same time my personal life was coming apart. I had heard about Wes Craven, and this movie—*A Nightmare on Elm Street*—fit perfectly during my hiatus from *V*. So between the miniseries, and the time the television series was to begin, the movie fit in like a piece in a puzzle.

They originally wanted a giant stunt man that didn't talk to play the part. I'm not sure whether I convinced Wes I was right for the part, or the casting director convinced him. I know that when I went to audition, I greased my hair back, and I penciled in, with a regular pencil, a little bit of a baggy line under my eyes. I hadn't been drinking the night before, but I looked that way in that I had five o'clock shadow, and I wore all black—I was in my punked-out phase. I had an oversize black sportcoat, black T-shirt, black slacks, and I had black boots on.

I also kind of played staring games with Wes. But I was never really sure I had gotten the part. Then, when I knew I got the part, Wes was totally open to me, so maybe he did always want me. Maybe he didn't . . . ! But he knew I was a hard worker. I had worked with Tobe Hooper, and maybe he had called Tobe by then.

WIATER: As we both know, Tobe Hooper has had a number of bad breaks in his career as a director. Would you ever work with him again?

ENGLUND: Oh, yeah! I love Tobe—I just wish people would leave Tobe's films alone. You hire Tobe Hooper, you want to get Tobe Hooper. You don't want to shit on his creativity. I remember when

I was working with him on *Eaten Alive*, people were trying to tell Tobe to put more sex and violence in the movie, as if you have to tell the director of *Texas Chainsaw Massacre* that!

WIATER: You're now known worldwide as Freddy Krueger. Do you feel that because of that recognition, you may eventually be stereotyped and offered only roles in horror films from now on?

ENGLUND: No, because I had done more than twenty motion pictures before doing *Nightmare on Elm Street*. Some of which I'm not too proud of, but some are now classics, such as *Stay Hungry*. So I was already known in the industry and had a full body of work out there. I had done some major plays, and had done half a dozen movies-of-the-week at around that same time. So I was known around town as "Robert Englund, the dependable character actor." Had Freddy Krueger been my first big break out of the gate, I'd be on the shrink's couch right now! [Laughs.] You know? I'd be stuck with this. Or I'd be happy just to slay a guy *out* of makeup. So no, I don't carry that horror stigma—I just starred in *Ford Fairlane* with Andrew Dice Clay, and I'm out of special makeup in that, doing my Billy Idol impression.

WIATER: But there's no denying you are being marketed as a horror movie star. It's where your marquee value obviously lies.

ENGLUND: I have to say that my big bucks still lie in horror. I'm hosting the "Horror Hall of Fame," which is kind of like the Oscars for horror films past and present, and that's where I get my annuity for the dues I paid in horror out of projects like that. It's hoped the show will be on every Halloween as a special. I'm also doing "Shadow Theatre" for cable television, where I'm going on as Robert Englund, and I'll tease myself a bit and parody the horror host, kind of like Joe Flaherty did on "SCTV." So those things are lucrative for me, and they free me up to do other projects.

WIATER: Now that you're a bankable horror star, what sort of roles have you turned down since working on the *Nightmare* movies?

ENGLUND: It's very hard to top Freddy! I've turned down countless roles that have been offered me. I've just said no to them because I'm *proud* of Freddy. He is a definite footnote in the history of horror films.

WIATER: Yet, in terms of playing monsters in makeup, you have done yet another interpretation of the classic *Phantom of the Opera*.

ENGLUND: When that came along, it was almost impossible to say no to, because of the Broadway musical, because of the rediscovery of the original source material, and because of the opportunity to do something *so* different from Freddy—

WIATER: Perhaps, but he's still a scarred and deformed monster—

ENGLUND: But I had promised my agent I would do one more film in makeup, because I have a lot of cachet—I can't begin to tell you the money and the projects I've turned down! But I knew I would be in good company with this film, and I'm pleased with my work in it. It was my first chance to work in Europe, in Budapest. And yes, it was very lucrative, which is why these projects come to me originally.

But by playing the Phantom, it was a chance to show that side of a very articulate, very passionate, almost swashbuckling man—there's a different kind of sexuality in torment there. It was also a chance to show people that I could play a period role. There're a lot of actors who look like fools in a historical costume. In our production, we were not trying to do anything but show the dark side of that source material. About the only major liberty we took was transposing the location from Paris to London. And it's melodramatic, it's operatic, and over the top—intentionally over the top because of the nature of the work.

I did it so I wouldn't have to keep saying no to all the other offers for horror movies. I think in ten or twenty years it will be part of a marathon with all the other ''Phantom'' movies: when you can sit down and watch the Lon Chaney one or the Claude Rains one or the Jack Palance one. Or Herbert Lom or the Michael Crawford musical version—and somewhere in there will be the Robert Englund one. And I'll be in very good company.

WIATER: But you have no regrets with being forever identified with playing the hideous Freddy Krueger?

ENGLUND: I'm *proud* of what the *Nightmare on Elm Street* films stand for, as a sort of dark, twisted comment on a certain moment in our culture—with Freddy Krueger as a sort of logo for all the sins being passed on to the present generation. It was also not only the first horror movie to dwell entirely in the Hollywood dream sequence, but also had a monster with a sardonic sense of humor. That's also a first. You only have to look at our list of imitators to see how many people have borrowed from that in the last five years.

WIATER: Who created the wisecracking persona of Freddy Krueger? Most critics give you the credit.

ENGLUND: Now, this is a weird point. I want to go on record to say that Wes Craven deserves *all* the credit. Wes Craven brought all of that out of me. Wes sometimes gets upset at what he considers the silliness in some of the films, but I think it would have been a mistake if we had just stayed with the violence. And I'm not saying that as any defender of the PTA mentality. I'm saying it because there is a logic to the *Nightmare on Elm Street* movies. The logic is, the real reason these movies are a hit has nothing to do with Freddy Krueger.

It's because they take place in a nightmare. It's the common denominator that everyone of every age and nationality can relate to. Everybody's had a bad dream! *That's* the real reason.

If I've done anything to contribute to the character, it's that I can improvise that kind of sardonic personality, and some of the better lines have come from me. The posture of Freddy is all mine, that pelvic walk, the way he favors that clawed hand—that's all me. And my incredible sense of energy, working on these movies. I realize now that not everybody can do it. I'm in that makeup fifteen, sixteen, seventeen hours a day. I think that's part of why I make the big bucks because there is an athletic nature to it, as well as psyching one's self up every morning. I'm in my forties now, and that stuff takes a lot out of me.

WIATER: It's not too difficult to imagine that there will be *Nightmare Part 6* by the time this book is published. What are your thoughts on continuing the series? Or is the series over?

ENGLUND: There's a desire to make another one. I'm proud of the series, real proud of the series, even though there's elements in each of them I don't think work. I'm real proud of the last three especially. I think a prequel would be nice because it would give the whole series a sort of horror mythology of the times. Maybe in ten years the whole series could be rediscovered by another generation with Freddy as the boogeyman of the 1980s, who became a sort of symbol of the horror of the times. So a prequel would make a nice bookend. Which is not to say I wouldn't put the makeup on, but I'd like to see who Freddy was *before* he got torched.

WIATER: Haven't you ever gotten any negative comments from the media for playing such a hugely popular figure of evil?

ENGLUND: Oh, I understand that; there's a certain validity to their reaction. One of the problems is that the media itself gets a little lazy. One of the first mistakes the media made—because the movies began as cult movies—they assumed Freddy was a "cult hero." As opposed to a cult *figure*. There's a *big* difference. Nobody wants to grow up and be Freddy, but a whole lot of people wanted to pay their six bucks and be scared by Freddy! I think the horror renaissance proves there's some kind of need for horror in our culture.

But when Freddy was misinterpreted as a cult hero, parents were naturally worried that their adolescents were taking this idea seriously and in the wrong way. Consequently, adults—who at that time had not found the fun in these movies—lumped all horror movies together. And you and I know there are some horror movies that are just gratuitously violent. Some perhaps to a level of pornography. But these people want to criticize *all* the horror movies equally. So when I run into those people, I try to stress to them that the main difference with the *Nightmare on Elm Street* movies is their wit, and the fact that they are taking place in a *fantasy*. They are not taking place in reality. They are not movies of reality-bound violence; they are imaginative fantasy scares. And there's a big, big difference there. The viewer always knows, *this is just a happening in a dream*.

WIATER: I know there has been some backlash against the toys made in the likeness of Freddy, including a talking Freddy Krueger doll that was taken off the market because of pressure groups.

ENGLUND: That was a protest group in Canada, led by a Canadian Jerry Falwell, against Matchbox Toys in Canada. But haven't those guys proved themselves already as being some of the most misguided, corrupt, and pathetic people around? As far as I'm concerned, they've set religion back a hundred years.

But I've been on several talk shows with psychiatrists, and they all say that the horror movie is very, very necessary. My own experience has been with terminally ill patients, terminal adolescents, and they have a huge fascination for the horror movie. Being in the hospital wards, these movies take their minds off the very real horror in their own lives that they face. I think there's some kind of substitution that goes on, that watching these movies fulfills some kind of need for our society.

I once would go on a talk show apprehensively whenever there was a psychiatrist on, because I thought they were going to be against horror movies or against me. But in all instances, the shrinks were on our side. In fact, they made very eloquent cases for the necessity of catharsis, being in the dark on a group level, that comes from the horror film.

WIATER: To a certain degree, I imagine some of the criticism is directed at you personally—that you must be "warped" to be playing this sort of character. That sort of standard charge.

ENGLUND: Yeah—by the "politically correct" people. I mean, I'm out there shopping for antiques on the weekends at old barn sales, my friends all have babies, and I go broke every Christmas buying presents. I just get so appalled when these people lose all sense of what is fun and give horror films this blanket condemnation, because they imagine these films have something to do with contributing to the violence in our society. [Angrily.] *The violence in our society?* My pat line is "What the hell was Jack the Ripper watching when he was doing his thing? What was Hitler watching?" It offends me that the people working in the horror business don't get the respect that they deserve.

WIATER: A few years back you directed your first feature film, entitled

976-EVIL. Was horror a natural first choice to make your debut as a director?

ENGLUND: No. You have to understand that I'm from live theater, and I've directed a lot in the theater. I've been around the block, too, as an actor—some twenty feature films and another dozen made-for-television movies. But since I've been directing theater since the early 1970s, I was ready to direct a feature. I had been told since I was twenty that I should be directing. I always thought I would start by working on some small television project such as an "Afternoon Special" or a "Wonderworks." But when it fell into my lap to do a feature film as my first project, I couldn't say no. Outside of pornography, I probably would have done *any* feature film offered me.

I don't know exactly how it all began. My name came up, and people jumped on the idea. For one thing, my agent had gone to the Cannes Film Festival that year, and he realized that there is much more respect for the horror genre in Europe. And they were able to quite literally raise money for the film just on my name alone. I went in to the producers and made my pitch, they were taken with my energy and my knowledge, and we went and made the movie.

WIATER: As someone who has made all sorts of movies, from comedies to dramas to action films, what do you really think of horror as a genre? You just mentioned there is more respect for it in Europe than here in America.

ENGLUND: I have learned to rediscover the horror film. Now I don't want to be a spokesman for horror, and I don't want to defend it, even though I am called upon to do so on many occasions. But being a reasonably bright man, there are a couple of things that I have realized in focusing my attention on the genre over the last couple of years, which is how many great directors have come out of horror. How it's a place to really show what style you've got. And how many incredibly great actors have come from horror, and there are others still working in the genre who haven't made the transition yet, such as Jeffrey Coombs in *The Re-Animator*. Brilliant actor!

I'm thinking of Brian DePalma's work—I think the uncut version of *Sisters* is just a brilliant movie for all time. It's just a remarkable film. More recently, *White of the Eye*. I think that's an extraordinary film. And *Paperhouse*. And a couple of years ago, John Carpenter's remake of *The Thing*. Every single actor in that movie is a major star now. Those effects by Rob Bottin were exquisite! Exquisite effects! It's a brilliant movie, superior to the original. The musical scoring, everything! . . . Carpenter is one of the few people who's ever been able to top something like that.

WIATER: When the *Nightmare* series finally concludes, how do you think your role in it will be remembered? You seem to be very pleased to have been a part of it from the very beginning.

ENGLUND: It was spectacularly lucrative for me, and it made it easier to turn down other projects I don't really want to do. I can pick and choose a little more, perhaps option and produce a little bit. But what I'm probably going to have to do, given the nature of the phenomenon, I'll probably have to go back and do one of my comedy nerds on television. You know? Hopefully the show will be a hit, because I love doing comedy. That's what I'll probably have to do as an antidote to Freddy—that might be necessary over the long run. But in terms of hindrance to the career, it hasn't been.

I hope the generation who originally saw the *Nightmare on Elm Street* films will fondly remember them from when they saw them the first time with an audience in the summer of their adolescence. Seeing them in the dark, with their friends. I hope another generation discovers them. I think they might hold up for another generation, too.

WIATER: In general terms, what is your advice to actors just starting out in the business? As you say, you've been around the block a few times.

ENGLUND: Well, my advice is that you have to love it enough to do it wherever they want you. This concept of living in New York or Hollywood to find work is wrong. You work, you know? Actors *act*. They don't wait on tables and all that stuff—they *act*. And if you're good at all, you'll find a theater somewhere in America where you sweep the stage or understudy, or do small parts and then work your way up through seniority and paying dues. And if you love it, you'll know you have to do this for the rest of your life. And there's great, great theater going on all across this country!

I just encourage people to act. If you get a job in a movie, in your hometown or near your hometown, and then you make some connections, and they ask you to come to Hollywood to do some postproduction work, that's fine. If you're near New York or Southern California and you have access to these places, that's fine. But you should always be working, whether it's in a class or a university or regional theater or summer stock. There's so much good paraprofessional and regional theater now that you can make a living in. I'm not saying you're going to get rich, but then you have that sort of a test you have to pass for yourself. I once thought I was never going to do movies or television—I was too good for it! [Chuckles.]

WIATER: From all appearances, I take it then you are happy with the way your career has turned out?

ENGLUND: Oh, yeah! I have nothing to be *unhappy* about. I'm recently married, I have a beautiful wife who's in the business, I've got a dog, and I've got a house down here on the seashore. . . . I'm in pig heaven. [Laughs.]

Stuart Gordon

From time to time, a new talent appears on the horror scene and is responsible for a motion picture that quickly earns a reputation as a landmark in the genre. In 1985, the film destined to become a classic was *The Re-Animator*.

Its first-time director was Stuart Gordon.

Like his colleague Clive Barker, Gordon entered the world of movie-making from the theater stage. As founder and artistic director of Chicago's Organic Theatre, Gordon already had twenty years experience of what it took to get an audience's attention. Working with producer Brian Yuzna and screenwriter Dennis Paoli, he blasted his way into the field with a movie based on some obscure stories by an otherwise famous horror writer, H. P. Lovecraft. To say the least, it was an impressive debut for all concerned.

In his cinematic version of these Lovecraft tales, Gordon takes the idea of a young scientist bringing the dead back to life to the ultimate in shock. *The Re-Animator* contains such bizarre images, and gory scenes so outrageously grotesque, that audiences either had to laugh out loud or left the theater in utter disgust. Ultimately, the movie would gain a cult reputation, partially because of the infamous scene where the head of an undead doctor attempts to perform an unnatural sex act with the strapped-down, nude heroine. Regardless of how mainstream audiences may have reacted to *The Re-Animator*, the fact remains that *cineteratologists* now regard it as one of the most important films of the 1980s, just as George A. Romero's *Night of the Living Dead* was a taboo-breaker for the 1960s.

Stuart Gordon's career has continued to climb, though perhaps not as quickly as fans of his premiere film would have liked. His second film was also inspired by the writings of H. P. Lovecraft, and in many ways is just as shocking as *The Re-Animator*. However, Gordon's third film, *Dolls*, was basically a Grimm's fairytale for adults, while such long-delayed projects as *Robot Jox* have so far been unreleased in this country. Another Lovecraft film, *The Shadow Over Innsmouth*, literally never made it off the drawing board, even though such veterans as artist Bernie Wrightson and Dick Smith were involved in the preproduction stages.

I had my conversation with Stuart Gordon as he was preparing to get production underway with a new version of Edgar Allan Poe's classic tale, *The Pit and the Pendulum*.

SELECTED FILMOGRAPHY

The Re-Animator (1985)

From Beyond (1986)

Dolls (1987)

WIATER: Oliver Stone once said that to be a successful director of horror films, you have to be a "visual sadist." Do you have any response to that interpretation?

GORDON: I think you have to be a masochist as well because you have to know what scares you and be able to return the favor.

WIATER: Oliver Stone directed two horror films early in his career, and he felt that he didn't have the right stuff it took to be a horror director. I was wondering if there is any particular talent that separates horror directors from mainstream directors?

GORDON: In my own case I was affected very much by horror films when I was a kid. I was scared to death, I had nightmares that would last for weeks after seeing a film. My parents, because of that, told me that I wasn't allowed to go see them, which of course only made me want to see them more. In reading other interviews, it seems to be true of a lot of people who make horror films, that as kids they were terrified of the films. So I think that is a good preparation, you know what scares you and it's a sort of therapy of turning it around and scaring someone else.

WIATER: Was it the idea that you didn't enjoy being scared or that you *did* enjoy being scared? Sam Raimi told me that he didn't enjoy being scared, and this was his way of getting back at his own fears, to confront them.

GORDON: I think that's true. I think that you *have* to have an overactive imagination. One thing that I've found about horror movies is that whatever you can imagine is far worse than what you can portray. The thing that really scares you in a movie is when suggestions are made to your mind, and then your mind does most of the work. It's an unpleasant feeling; you feel like you're going to throw up or pass out. But when it's over you feel a kind of relief, and it's a positive feeling. It's like a roller coaster ride after it's over, you always say, "well let's do that again!" I think the ideas are similar, the idea of facing your own death and surviving.

WIATER: When you were a youngster, was it a particular group of films? I can date myself by saying that I was watching "Thriller" and "Twilight Zone" as a very young lad, as well as the Roger Corman films with Vincent Price in the early sixties that made an indelible impression on me.

GORDON: One of the films that really scared me was *The Tingler* directed by William Castle. I was out of there, I didn't stick around for the end of that movie, I was gone. I think the earliest one I can remember is *Abbott and Costello Meet Dr. Jekyll and Mr. Hyde*. I saw the movie again recently and realized that the movie ends with Abbott and Costello turning into monsters, so it didn't have a very comforting ending. This movie didn't end, it just kept on going. I think that's what scared me.

WIATER: Continuing with childhood influences, in literature you were obviously well associated with H. P. Lovecraft.

GORDON: No, actually it was in college, which would put it in the late sixties. But I was a fan of horror and ghost stories since I was a kid. I remember reading *Dracula* in Chicago in the summer when it was really hot and muggy. I would sleep with all my windows shut and locked. That book was so scary that I would just sweat it out. I kind of agree with Oliver Stone, I think it takes a certain type of person. I would even go further to say that all people who direct horror films look the same, too.

WIATER: Describe that please?

GORDON: Sort of large, heavy-set sometimes, usually with beards. I keep running into various versions of myself all the time. [Laughs.] There was one article I read about Stephen King that he was sort of using his writing to get back. He wasn't one of the kids that fit in. He wasn't the most popular. He gets his revenge by taking people apart in stories. I think that could be part of it too, that your imagination triumphs over your problems.

WIATER: Why horror? I know you were a founder of the Organic Theatre in Chicago and obviously it wasn't Grand Guignol or a horror theater.

GORDON: Well, we did some plays that were definitely horror plays. We did a play based on the life and writings of Edgar Allan Poe. We did a ghost story, *The Beckoning Star*, and we did use some blood affects in our show. I like to do other things besides horror movies as well. I think it's almost Freudian in a way: My father died when I was young and I think horror movies deal with death in some form or another and sometimes it's the ability to triumph over or conquer death. I think there is a definite connection between my father's death and my having done the movie *The Re-Animator*.

WIATER: Sometimes writers and filmmakers go to extremes, of course. I'm talking about people in the horror genre trying to belabor the point that they had "normal" childhoods and normal parents.

GORDON: You could say the same things about ax murderers. They seem so "normal." Your next-door neighbor seems so normal, always keeps to himself, and then chops up his whole family. I think that "normal" exterior is a good camouflage. Then, instead of going out and chopping up your family, you do it on film.

WIATER: So many people like to think that horror movies and horror fiction are a bad influence. Why are some people so obsessed with protecting our "precious youth" from horror?

GORDON: It's funny, because I think the way they go about protecting them does a lot of damage. Particularly the MPAA. If you are going to murder someone in a movie, they want it done with no fuss and no mess, no blood. The lesson they are teaching is that violence is painless and fun. My feeling is that if you are going to show violence in a film, you should show how it *really* is. It should be ugly and upsetting, and there is a lot of blood. Anyone who's seen a newsreel knows how much blood there is when someone is shot or stabbed. When you portray violence without the reality, I think you are encouraging it. The argument is 180 degrees opposite of what they intended. I think that children should be protected in that they and their parents should know the content before they go see it. But I think as long as you give them fair warning, it is up to the individual to make the choice.

WIATER: Do you think that in today's moral climate, things are getting worse instead of better?

GORDON: Yes, I definitely do. I think the standards of the MPAA are getting much more strict, and they're not allowing certain things to be shown anymore under an R rating. I've gotten into arguments with them over this scene or that scene. I would compare it to another film, and they would say that if that film were being rated today it would be rated differently. One of the ones that they are the most upset about is *Friday the 13th*, that they gave the initial film an R rating back whenever that was, and now it has sequels that they have to deal with.

WIATER: How is that affecting your current film projects? Do you have to precensor your imagination because you are dealing with a lot of money and the producers will say, "Why even try because it's going to get cut out by the MPAA?"

GORDON: You do run into that. Oftentimes, though, I think you can find alternate ways of shooting something so the audience will still get the idea without showing everything, and sometimes it's more effective.

WIATER: When you did *The Re-Animator*, which was shot in 1984 and released in 1985, did you say at that point, "The hell with it, we're just going to do it?" It's really hard for me to fathom how in today's climate *The Re-Animator* could be made, and I'm wondering how it could have been made even six years ago.

GORDON: I think we were incredibly naïve. We were concerned, but when we were making the film, we thought we could get an R rating, believe it or not. One of the worries that we had was the male nudity because we were told that if you have any full frontals of men, then it is automatically an X rating. So we went to great trouble to make sure that you didn't see anyone's genitals. They even created these things for the actors to wear called a merkin, which is sort of a codpiece. We never used these things but when we got to the last day of shooting we were doing a sequence and someone said the actor was exposed. So we said, "Let's put a merkin on him." It turned out that the prop guy had thrown them out because we never used them. What we ended up doing was painting it black. That was how naïve we were. [Laughs.] It turned out when we showed it to the MPAA that they said no way they would give it an R rating. I think if we had tried to cut that film, we would have ended up with a twenty-minute film.

WIATER: Correct me if I'm wrong but when the movie came out on cable wasn't it the unrated version, or was it the R version? If memory serves, Cinemax or Showtime was actually showing the unrated version, but with their own R rating over it.

GORDON: No, that's right, they did show the unrated version on cable TV. I think that it should have been an R-rated film, anyway.

WIATER: When Orson Welles made *Citizen Kane*, and whenever he made a film after that, people would say, "Okay, Orson, tell us more about *Citizen Kane*!" Are people saying that to you, "Stuart, we know you've made other films, but tell us more about *The Re-Animator*," as if that is your *Citizen Kane* already?

GORDON: It was a very strong introduction of my work and it does stick with people. That doesn't bother me. I also think it has to do with the fact that it's been around the longest and it's taken all these years for an audience to be developed.

WIATER: You're probably aware that the *gonzo* critic Joe Bob Briggs has called *The Re-Animator* the "drive-in film of the decade."

GORDON: That's terrific, I didn't know that.

WIATER: Tell me about your made-for-television movie called "Daughter of Darkness"? I was wondering how that experience was, in the sense that you had to go by the standards and practices of network television right from the outset?

GORDON: I was curious to see what was allowable on TV. The most intriguing thing that I found out was that most made-for-TV movies are trying to appeal to a female audience because in all their research they found that it is the women who turn on the TV and prefer made-for-TV movies. Horror films are notoriously a guy's thing so there was an interesting challenge to see if I could interest a female audience. In a sense "Daughter of Darkness" is sort of a cross between one of those Barbara Cartland romance-type books and Bram Stoker.

WIATER: That was shot overseas, I believe.

GORDON: Yes, it was shot in Budapest, although it's set in Bucharest, Romania. One of the other things that happened was that about less than a month before "Daughter of Darkness" aired the revolution took place. So the film, which we had done a great deal of research on to try to get it as accurate as possible, suddenly became a period piece. It became sort of a historical epitaph.

WIATER: It starred Anthony Perkins, and I know you're a big fan of *Psycho*. Did you swap anecdotes or did he tell you any anecdotes about *Psycho* and working with Hitchcock?

GORDON: Yes, he did, he was full of wonderful stories. He worked with some of the greatest directors, and he is a fascinating fellow. He is also a great fan of the horror genre and has great knowledge of it. He told me a funny story about Hitchcock when they were doing *Psycho*. He and Martin Balsam had been rehearsing the scene in which the detective is questioning Norman Bates about the woman who had been staying at his guest hotel. Balsam kept interrupting Perkins, not letting him finish his lines, asking the next question before he could answer the one before. They liked that and later in the day Perkins was looking through the storyboard that Hitchcock had done on that scene and discovered that the entire scene was shot in close-up, which meant that there could be no overlapping of the dialogue. He said to Hitchcock that he would like to show him the scene that they had been rehearsing. Hitchcock said that he didn't really have time right now, and Perkins said, "No, I really think you need to see this." Finally, Hitchcock realized that something was going on and he said, "What's the problem?" Perkins told him that he thought it would be better if he shot it with a two-shot instead of close-up. He realized at that moment that here he is telling Hitchcock how to shoot a piece. In a long, ominous moment, Hitchcock takes the storyboard and tears it up.

He said that the stories about Hitchcock being so immovable and such are just not true. Hitchcock was much more flexible and he did listen to the actors.

WIATER: Let me continue with that thought on directors, Hitchcock being an obvious one to name about influences.

GORDON: Well Hitchcock, definitely, I think *Psycho* was a curious movie because it broke all the rules. I'm a big fan of Roman Polanski. *Rosemary's Baby* was a great film and I watched it a lot before I directed *The Re-Animator*. His work in that movie is so subjective that it makes the audience become Rosemary. I also love Stanley Kubrick's work. His work in *The Shining* I think is great, the way he moves the audience through the story. The cameras are constantly in motion.

WIATER: Are there some other directors outside the horror genre, or was it always just horror directors?

GORDON: There are other areas I enjoy. I am a big fan of the Marx

Brothers and Fellini. I think both their movies are full of surprises. The worst thing for me in a movie is when you know everything that is going to happen in the first five minutes of the film. It's like it was written by a computer. So I like it when they mix it up, pull the rug out from under you. When the directors surprise and startle you.

WIATER: This gets to the humor in your films. I think George Romero's films are very humorous, as are Polanski's and Kubrick's, with a lot of black humor that I think only the sophisticated viewer appreciates.

GORDON: When Hitchcock referred to *Psycho*, he always referred to it as a comedy. It took seeing it three or four times before I started picking up on the comedy. He said that there was a very fine line between getting someone to laugh and getting someone to scream. One thing that I've learned is that laughter is the antidote. When you think you don't have to laugh, then you are basically blowing away the intensity. You have to be careful when you do that, you don't want to be laughing at the expense of the fright. It's best if you can alternate the two, build up the tension and then release it with a laugh. It is a double degree of challenge. You're walking a tightrope, and if something becomes inadvertently funny, the whole thing is over.

The thing I have found is that you'll never find an audience that wants to laugh more than a horror audience. I did a lot of comedies in Chicago, and a lot of these audiences are just going to sit there with their arms folded like make me laugh. Whereas in a horror movie you welcome any chance to laugh. Something to take you away from the oppressive scariness of the piece. So it's always a good idea to give the audience that moment.

WIATER: One unfortunate situation for you is that *Robot Jox* has been held up for so long. Is there still a possibility of that film being released?

GORDON: That's true, it has been finished for over a year now. If it had been released when it was supposed to have been, it probably would have done well. The premise of the movie is one that comes out of the Cold War, two superpowers, and the world is a whole new ball game. It's been released on video in Great Britain and done extremely well. In fact it did better than *Lethal Weapon II*. But I'm still keeping my fingers crossed, I haven't written it off yet. It's too bad, I think movies have life spans.

WIATER: I would like to know a little bit about your relationship with Dennis Paoli. I understand that you have known him for many years, and it's unusual for a director and screenwriter to work on more than one or two films. What is that special chemistry you have, beyond your obvious friendship, that you work together?

GORDON: Dennis and I go all the way back to high school together. We wrote comedies together as part of a comedy group called The Human Race. We were able to work our way through school doing this. I think the fact that we are such good friends allows us to be honest with each other. We kind of complement each other. Dennis's strong suit is dialogue and mine is stories, so we are a good team. The bottom line is that we enjoy working together.

WIATER: What is the fascination that keeps you interested in the horror, fantasy, science fiction field?

GORDON: I like stories that take you somewhere that you've never been. They take you somewhere and show you something new and exciting. Science fiction, fantasy, and horror are the bread and butter, that's what they thrive on and they explore. I like stories where anything's possible. I think movies are like dreams, and they don't need to be ruled by reality.

WIATER: What about the sense of telling the philosophical truth? Both Romero and Cronenberg have stated in interviews that it is only in horror films that you can speak about the unspeakable in terms of death and decay. *The Fly* was a good example.

GORDON: I think that is one of the great strengths of horror and fantasy films. But when they do talk about these things they have to talk about them in parables, in a way. They couldn't talk about AIDS in *The Fly*, but everyone could feel what it was really about. The parable is like the Bible, where the exact details of the story are exaggerated or invented. But I think with any form of great art you have to tell the truth. I agree with the idea that there are certain topics that people would not be able to talk about unless done as a parable.

WIATER: It's the same thing with humor, which brings me back to your work. As you mentioned Hitchcock with *Psycho*, the idea that these are comedies. I have always found that comedians understand death and horror better than anybody else.

GORDON: That's true. When I was doing the research for *The Re-Animator* I talked to a lot of pathologists and discovered that they have very funny, very black outlooks. It's the same thing that if you're going to do a job like that day in and day out, you *have* to be able to laugh. I think that's one of the reasons why *The Re-Animator* ended up the way it did, trying to incorporate that approach, that view of humanity that comes from hanging out in the morgue.

WIATER: In terms of *The Re-Animator*, are there things that you yourself determined were too off the wall or over the edge?

GORDON: We pretty much threw everything in there that we could think of. There was very little self-censorship, although we did cut back a particular scene. Earlier on in the movie there is autopsy and they are removing the brain from a corpse. During that sequence I talked to a pathologist who explained move for move exactly how things were done, which we shot in great detail, cracking open the skull and using a corkscrew-type device. This scene went on much longer than it probably should have. The reaction from the audience was kind of weak, and they had a hard time recovering from this. So that scene was cut way back.

WIATER: Let me switch over to *Dolls*, which I enjoyed a lot, but with the running time, and maybe I'm just falling into a black hole by saying this, was that film cut? Is there a longer version of *Dolls* or was it meant to be a relatively short running time?

GORDON: It *is* a short film. Part of that was that this was the first film I did in Italy, and they work at a quite different pace. It's not that they're not, they're wonderful craftsman and artists, but they have their own way of working. We found that we had to cut things or never shoot them in order to make our schedule. So that film is short due to the reality of the situation. But the things that were cut I wouldn't say were necessary for telling the story. I don't think this film could have been much longer and worked as well. It's interesting that you mentioned that because I've talked to a lot of people who have seen the film, and I've never met anyone who complained about it being too short. The original script was longer, but I think that the film is as long as it needs to be. It's a satisfying film.

WIATER: Would you go back to H. P. Lovecraft if that opportunity presented itself?

GORDON: There're so many wonderful stories! I think a lot of people are finally picking up on that. It's too bad that he's not around to appreciate the fact that he *is* appreciated.

WIATER: Films have been based on H. P. Lovecraft stories before. What do you think he would have thought of your interpretations if he were alive today?

GORDON: I think he would be a little shocked by some of the films because he approached things with sort of a Victorian view. He was much less explicit when writing a story. But I think he would have been pleased overall.

WIATER: Is it true that today's audience has forced you to always be explicit? You can no longer go for just the hand on the back or the shadow on the wall to make an audience be scared?

GORDON: I think you ultimately have to show them something if there is something to be seen. You can't just go with the Lovecraft "cop-out." He would talk about this *thing*, but he would never say exactly what it *was*. Film is images. I think it is still possible to scare an audience with suggestion. Like I said, imagination is the greatest weapon that you've got. I think it's a combination of both those things. You should show the audience just enough to get the idea of what they are seeing, but not too much. I used to think with horror movies that the movie was over as soon as you saw the monster. No matter how horrible something is, once you've seen it you feel better. So it's the anticipation of the horrible thing that really scares you. When that moment comes you really have to deliver it and knock someone's socks off.

WIATER: But is there a point where there won't be anything left to scare an audience with? Are we going to reach the point where they say, "We've seen everything in the horror film and even Stuart Gordon can't give us a new chill?"

GORDON: No, I don't think we will. The horror movie has been around forever. Before the horror movie was the horror story. The new filmmakers will come up with more scares. When Romero did *Night of the Living Dead* people were running out of the theater, and now it's being shown on network TV uncut. I think the same thing will be true of *The Re-Animator*, that it will eventually be looked at as a period piece. So I have faith in my future generation. And that's part of what you do, you always try to top what has been done before. You see what the level is and top it, that's what filmmakers are doing all the time.

WIATER: Sam Raimi told me when they did *Evil Dead* they went to every horror movie they could find and said, "Now we have to top everything that is the best about these movies."

GORDON: Exactly! And the only way you can go is further. The imagination is always working.

Gale Ann Hurd

I t's an obvious question, and certainly one worth pondering: Why aren't there more women involved in the cinematic world of dark visions? Certainly filmmakers since
the beginning of the industry have exploited womens' fears
and fantasies. Certainly a horror film doesn't hesitate to show
women as victims, or, at the very least, as "damsels in dis-
tress." Yet it's undeniably odd that, with the obvious exception of a few actresses, women are not traditionally identified
with the horror or science fiction genres. Not as writers, directors, and certainly not as producers.

Then you have someone like Gale Ann Hurd.

A 1977 graduate of Stanford University, Hurd began her
career in the film industry as an executive assistant for Roger
Corman. She quickly moved on to become head of advertising
and publicity and had her first chance to cut her teeth as a
producer with the Roger Corman space opus *Battle Beyond*

the Stars. Working with her (now ex-) husband James Cameron, Hurd has continued to make a name for herself as "a class act" in genre films, including *The Terminator*, *Aliens*, and *The Abyss*.

In person, Hurd has the typical attributes of someone who has made it to the top of her chosen profession: a cool grace, a relentless intelligence, and an ability to answer any question as if she had been pondering it for hours, not seconds, before. She never hesitated to speak her mind, although she was diplomatic in never naming her detractors. ("I'm outspoken, not stupid," she would tell me with a smile.) For in spite of her impressive string of box office successes, not every film—including *Bad Dreams* and *The Abyss*—has been well received, either by the public or the critics.

Regardless, it's obvious that Gale Ann Hurd will continue to be associated with some of the finest horror and science fiction—and here she indicates nongenre—films that Hollywood has ever produced. I spoke with Hurd at a horror convention in New York, shortly before her latest production, *Tremors* was released.

SELECTED FILMOGRAPHY

Battle Beyond the Stars (1980)

The Terminator (1984) (producer, co-writer)

Aliens (1986)

Bad Dreams (1988)

Alien Nation (1988)

The Abyss (1989)

Tremors (1990)

WIATER: Let me first say that Roger Corman is also profiled in this collection, and I'd like to know to what extent should he be given credit—or blame—for your career decision to specialize in horror and science fiction films?

HURD: I wouldn't even be in the film industry had I not had the pleasure of working with Roger. So anything you can say about my career, at least indirectly, is attributable to Roger Corman. He recruited me right out of college. Not only was Roger my mentor, but he was actually my recruiter.

WIATER: So did your interest in this genre come about because of working for Corman?

HURD: I was an aficionado of speculative fiction from the time that I was a teenager. I used to review science fiction genre books for the local paper in Palm Springs.

WIATER: So you've always had an interest in science fiction and the fantastic?

HURD: Absolutely.

WIATER: Then, growing up, you must have already known who Roger Corman was as a filmmaker?

HURD: Let's put it this way—I had heard of him. But since he hadn't published any novels, my exposure up until the time I went to work for him had been limited somewhat to science fiction writings as opposed to the literature of film.

WIATER: In other words, you weren't a B-movie buff or a drive-in movie fan, where many of his films regularly played?

HURD: I don't think I'd ever been to a drive-in.

WIATER: [Pauses.] I find that a little shocking—a fan of Roger Corman who'd never been to a drive-in! Where did you get exposed to genre movies then?

HURD: I had seen the weekly syndicated television shows like "Thriller," and watched movies on late-night TV. I'm a bit of an insomniac, so I caught a lot of those core films on TV rather than the big screen. Of Roger Corman's films, I saw *X: Man with the X-Ray Eyes, Masque of the Red Death,* and *Pit and the Pendulum.*

WIATER: With your track record of box office hits, why are you staying with the fantastic? Certainly you could do a drama or a romantic comedy if you wished?

HURD: I *am* doing other genres. I have a feeling that I will always return to science fiction because I think that it finds its perfect medium on celluloid. The wonderful thing about science fiction and fantasy is that you can create worlds that we've never seen before. It's perfectly suited for cinema.

At the moment, I have a number of projects in the starting gate, but the gun hasn't gone off yet. I can tell you that one of them is science fiction, one fantasy, and for the other two, one is a drama and one is a thriller.

WIATER: Science fiction may be perfectly suited for cinema in principle, but in terms of getting a project into production, wouldn't it be much easier to do two dramas a year than to spend two or three years of your life producing a massive special effects–laden movie?

HURD: I think it's all a matter of quality, not quantity, and what challenges the particular individual. I enjoy the collaborative process, and when you are doing a large special-effects film, you get an opportunity to push the outer edge of the envelope, which to me is very exciting as a producer. Also, I think you can incorporate other genres within science fiction and not just come up with a hardware movie.

The characters in the films that I've done are very important and there is a tendency by some to give them short shrift. Oftentimes the critics look at films and the minute there is a special effect, they dismiss it from any other possibility of critical acclaim. Although I think we've seen that begin to shift, with the Academy Award nominations for Sigourney Weaver for *Aliens* and Jeff Goldblum in *The Fly*, and many more accolades than the genre has received previously.

WIATER: To what extent does fan input affect your own judgments on which projects you choose or pass on?

HURD: I have to vote on a project with my own sensibilities and not try to second guess what other people will like. It's really just too great a commitment on my time and my life to determine in advance what's going to appeal commercially to an audience. So I don't use that criteria. However, I think what helps me get through some of these projects is the knowledge that there *is* an audience clamoring for great science fiction and horror films. I don't think there is any other genre that has attracted that kind of attention. In a sense, hero worship.

WIATER: Worship in a sense that there are people who enjoy going to the movies, and then there are people who will see *every* decent science fiction and horror film they possibly can?

HURD: Right. And they scrutinize my films in that genre a lot more than perhaps audiences would be doing in other genres. I think that science fiction and horror fans *are* very critical. They just don't embrace every film that comes out.

WIATER: It is difficult for most of us to understand what a producer does, precisely. Is there anything unique about your position as a producer, in the sense that you do such films as *The Abyss* and *Tremors*, which are certainly more of a technical challenge than, say, a contemporary love story?

HURD: The wonderful thing about producing in the true sense (as opposed to people who simply acquire the title contractually—I'm talking about the people who earn it) is that producing films that are truly challenging across the spectrum allows the producer to continue to learn about techniques and technology. At the same time, to try to keep the delicate balance between showcasing just the effects and perhaps ignoring the emotional core of the picture. I love challenges like that! To me, the ultimate compliment is for someone not to be aware that what they saw was an effect.

WIATER: So as producer, you are there pretty much from the inception to the release. You don't just put your name on it and walk away to yet another project.

HURD: Well, obviously every case is going to be different. I take responsibility—you have to—to earn the credit of producer. It's not something that you simply negotiate.

WIATER: To what extent do you read critical reception into your films, or doesn't that really affect your perceptions at all? For example, the critics, by and large, seemed to strongly dislike *Bad Dreams* and on the other hand seemed to strongly favor *Tremors*.

HURD: I don't think that critical response affects the kind of film I'll do next. In some cases filmmakers are so influenced by the response to their last picture that it determines the kind of project they'll do next. That doesn't influence me. After I read a bad review, I wish I could call the reviewer up and explain some things that they missed. It is very difficult as a filmmaker since you're not able to have a dialogue with a critic. Which I understand—I think that critics couldn't then be as objective as they are. But at the same time, I've found that certain facts are invented in some reviews.

With respect to *Bad Dreams*, one of the problems that we had was that *Nightmare on Elm Street III* had come out prior to *Bad Dreams*. Both films had similar elements. We didn't know about them, they didn't know about us. In the Monday-morning quarterbacking, many critics said this film is trying to come in on the coattails of *Nightmare On Elm Street III*, not even realizing that in the filmmaking process, we were both shooting at the same time. I'd never read their script, the *Elm Street* people never read mine. It was an unfortunate coincidence that one *Nightmare* preceded us, because I think it would have had the reverse effect had we come out before them. I think that Andy Flemmings, the director of *Bad Dreams*, is extremely talented.

WIATER: Yet at the time you read the screenplay, there didn't seem to be anything you could have foreseen as being derivative of the *Nightmare on Elm Street* series? Concidentally, Wes Craven had a similar problem with ideas crossing over with his movie *Shocker*.

HURD: The idea of the dream warriors, where they had the dream counseling—when I saw *Elm Street III* I just went, "Oh, no!" I knew then exactly what was going to be said about our movie, but at that point you have to say to yourself, We came up with this idea independently, we're treating it differently anyway, and hope that the audience saw that difference. I don't think many critics are sufficiently familiar with the horror genre to be fair critics.

WIATER: Some critics automatically equate horror films with trash—period. So it doesn't matter how hard you try to say something, they're just not going to listen.

HURD: You know what I really like though? This is why it is very difficult for me to take a bad review seriously.

There have been—no names mentioned—two extremely well-known critics, and both panned *Aliens*. I mean we're talking slam-dunk, gave it maybe a two on a scale of one to ten. When they reviewed *The Abyss*, they reviewed it in negative terms while being complimentary to a film they had previously panned. They remembered reviewing *Aliens* positively when they hadn't! I thought it was so funny, because as a filmmaker, believe me, *you remember*. If they had bothered to drag out their actual original review, they would have realized that they had simply torpedoed it.

WIATER: It would almost be funny if it wasn't true. John Carpenter's *Halloween* is a similar case in point. It was totally dismissed when first released, and the critics have since reversed themselves, saying: "Why isn't Carpenter as good a filmmaker as when he did the classic *Halloween*, a masterpiece of horror and suspense?"

HURD: That's why to me it's very amusing and I think the audience are the people who really cast their votes: because they are paying and the critics do not.

WIATER: Another unfortunate coincidence for *The Abyss* was the fact that it was "the summer of underwater science fiction movies," and two other films—*Deep Star Six* and *Leviathan*—in a sense stole most of your intended audience. Did you get any sense of that—that others were making these films to perhaps cash in on your massive production?

HURD: Oh, absolutely. I am fairly certain that the reason these two films were green-lighted was because they knew that our preproduction was going to be so long that they could start shooting and be out before we were even into postproduction. You run the risk of that everytime you gear up on a difficult film that you hope to be precedent setting.

But there's nothing you can do about it. We tried to be as security conscious as possible about the screenplay. In fact, we had a lot of misinformation, people thinking it was a movie about gill-breathing people, which I thought was very funny, and who insisted that they had excellent sources. But at the same time there was no way to hide the fact that it was definitely an underwater film that had an alien presence in it.

So you do the best you can, and I don't think you can be put off by the competition. Everyone starts off even in a sense. In a similar situation, of all those "body-switching" movies, *Big* was the most successful. So I think that *The Abyss* had other problems, and it wasn't just the audience being set up with that kind of underwater science fiction film again. I don't think there was ever a clear marketing campaign as to exactly what the audience was going to see. I don't think it was ever clear in anyone's mind—it was a ill-defined movie from the marketing sense. And I don't think we ever got the ending right.

WIATER: Was the ending tinkered with after the studio previews, or was it while you were making the film, you really didn't know how to end the story satisfactorily?

HURD: There were two problems. One was that the film was very long, and Jim and I consciously decided without pressure to reduce the running time. But every screenplay that Jim writes is a very carefully woven tapestry, and when you start to remove certain threads the whole cloth suffers. We simply didn't have the time in postproduction—because there was some pressure to get the movie out—to rethink anything. So *The Abyss*, in my mind, was a victim of the release date. It *had* to be a summer movie.

WIATER: Do you have a "wish list" of directors you'd like to be working with, or doesn't that enter into your creative menu when you first agree to take on a project?

HURD: There are so *many* directors I would like to work with; I don't think I could list them in one sitting. Just to see someone's work on the screen is not the same as going through the collaborative process, so to me the marriage of producer and director is extremely important. It is an experience that is so collaborative that personalities are just as important as the vision.

WIATER: Then are you satisfied, creatively, to be "just" a producer? Most movie fans have been lead to believe that the director is the true creative star of the show.

HURD: I enjoy most aspects of being a producer, as when I'm working with someone like James Cameron, who is very much a visionary. With him I have a great deal of creative input, but in the creative realm he has ultimate authority. I've worked with other directors with which my input has been far more overreaching, as it were. It's really a question of talent as well as experience. The more films I do, the more experience I have and the greater assistance I can be to a director. But at the same time I am not a stand-in for the director. I don't believe in using the director as my mouthpiece. If that were the case, I might as well be directing myself.

WIATER: But in terms of being a producer as a career position, you never feel that perhaps you are missing out in making that collaborative effort succeed to its full extent?

HURD: Absolutely not. The only area that producers lose out on is financially. The directors' salaries at this point are ranging up to $6 million per film. Oftentimes directors are dropped in at the last minute after a producer has lived with the film starting with the very germ of the idea. Yet the maximum salary for any producer, no matter how successful, is $1 million. That's quite a disparity. In addition, producers are the only ones in the creative team who do not receive residuals. Every time a film is sold to videocassette, television, et cetera, that triggers residuals for the director, the writers, and the actors.

Producers are the only ones who have to wait until the film actually breaks even, and that never happens. [Laughs.] After a while, it was impossible to hide the profits on *The Terminator*, because that only cost $6 million. *Aliens* is still in the red! . . . It really makes me wonder why they continue to do sequels to unsuccessful movies.

WIATER: Are you seriously considering further sequels to *Alien*? I must confess that that film and its sequel are among my all-time favorites.

HURD: I have no ownership on the *Alien* franchise. Jim Cameron and I were both for hire, as it were, on *Aliens*. David Giler, Walter Hill, and Gordon Caroll are the people who continue with that property.

WIATER: What about *The Terminator*, your first big hit?

HURD: With respect to *The Terminator*, I do have control of the rights, and there will be a *Terminator 2*, and Jim will commence directing that this fall [1990].

WIATER: But you haven't said if you're for or against sequels in general.

HURD: My feeling about sequels is that I can't look at the original as a cash cow to continue to exploit an idea and remake the same movie. I've already done a sequel to someone else's movie, and it makes even more sense to do a sequel to my own. If there is a new direction that a sequel can take you, then I think it's worth making. It's also easier to get them financed.

WIATER: I spoke with John Carpenter as well for this book, and he informed me he was offered *Total Recall*, being released this summer, more than eleven years ago. It is really that simple—that studios would rather make a sequel to an established "cash cow," rather than take a risk on making an original film that can just as easily fail as succeed?

HURD: I believe the studios have as their motive maximizing profits. When you have to spend $10 to $14 million to open a film and generate awareness simply to get people who are potential audience members familiar with the title and the idea and the cast, it obviously makes sense if you've got something that is presold. That's one of the reasons that there are so many sequels. You don't have to spend all that money up front to create audience awareness. Consequently, you can use that money to build an enormous opening weekend. Hopefully, if you've done your job right, you can have a $100-million-grossing film. The audience continues to vote for sequels, and as long as they're successful, studios and filmmakers will continue to make them.

WIATER: A few years ago there were a spate of remakes, including *The Thing*, *Invaders from Mars*, and *The Blob*, which really didn't catch fire at the box office. What are your feelings on remaking classic motion pictures?

HURD: Any film that is well made has won its place in the annals of film history, whether or not it is a completely original idea, a remake, or a sequel. To me, that's immaterial. I think that the mistakes that the studios have made is that the original films are more familiar to the audience than the studios believe they are.

WIATER: When given the opportunity, you would prefer to work with original material, correct?

HURD: I really prefer to start with a clean slate. I think that all of us carry around as part of our knowledge that we've gained a lot of bits and pieces of the films we've seen and the books we've read. So I think that subconsciously the films we grew up loving are influencing us every day.

But I don't think there is one particular film I would like to recreate. I think it's difficult when you remake a film in that the more we know about the film, the more shortcuts we take in terms of storytelling because we *are* so familiar with it, and the audience is never up to speed. They can't read things into it that are ironies from the original or tributes to certain filmmakers or certain sequences.

WIATER: To date, all the films you've produced have been original screenplays. I was wondering, with your background in reading speculative fiction, why there hasn't been a particular short story or novel that you'd want to make into a great movie?

HURD: There have been a lot of projects that I have wanted to option. But most of the classics have been purchased and are sitting gathering dust. Right now I'm in discussions with some tremendous science fiction authors about adapting some of their work. It is primarily short stories.

I find that short stories and novellas are the ideal length to expand into a feature film. When you try to adapt a novel it seems to me that you lose some of the texture that is the greatness of the novel. You simply don't have enough time in one and a half to two hours to tell a very complicated story, whereas you have 400 to 500 pages to develop ideas in a novel.

WIATER: What's your opinion of the television series version of your movie *Alien Nation*, which appeared recently on the Fox network?

HURD: I'm hoping that the viewers who have come out and protested to get it back on the air are successful, because it was canceled. I do think it is in very good form to help people to see science fiction in a more socially conscious way. It's a show with a message that has done well. I noticed it's the only Fox Television series that the Viewers for Quality Television approved of.

WIATER: With your background as a screenplay writer, what effect does that have on your creative input to a project? When you are reading screenplays how much of that experience comes into play before you even put on your producer's hat?

HURD: I am very sympathetic to writers. If I pick up a screenplay, I read it all the way through. I don't think that I have ever started a screenplay and not finished it because I know what it's like to look at a computer screen or a typewriter with a blank page in it. It's absolutely unnerving. It is the most terrifying thing to know that ultimately you have to create a work of entertainment or art out of whole cloth. So I'm very sympathetic to writers! At the same time, I'm also very critical. I tend to get involved in the editorial process when it comes to developing a screenplay, which I think is a direct result of having been there myself.

WIATER: You're here to promote your most recent production, *Tremors*. Can you tell me what it was about that particular screenplay that you fell in love with?

HURD: I loved the characters. I thought they were two people that we wanted to see time and time again, the way that when you read a great novel and reach the last page, you wish you could pick up the next volume and keep going. I felt that way about Val and Earl. I liked some of the choices that were made in the script, which were conscious decisions not to say where the worms came from. Unfortunately, I have discovered that the audience won't buy this! To me, I thought that was quite bold and people would applaud it. Instead, every marketing research poll showed that the audience wanted to know where the damn things came from! [Laughs.]

If you really go back and look at it, there is no way that anyone *would* know. We wouldn't know as individuals. I always like to take the logic test when I make decisions about scripts, and to me the logic held. I've also realized now that sometimes you have to suspend that logic to make the audience happy. I thought *Tremors* was terrific and wasn't a movie I had seen before. It was certainly an *homage* to a lot of movies—but it was fresh and original in and of itself.

WIATER: Considering the amount of negative press you eventually received for *Bad Dreams*, what sparked you to choose this project, which admittedly made for a pretty grim horror film?

HURD: I really liked the psychological aspects of the picture, because to me it was a psychological horror film as opposed to simply a slasher movie or a film that created scenarios that couldn't exist. I think the idea of an individual psychology, and the horror that we create in our own minds, is extremely interesting. I liked the idea of a character that no one believes, sort of a Cassandra. And it turns out of course that they were right all along. That's very interesting. Also the fact that it was a picture starring a young woman in the horror genre, which I know has been in the true in the past, but traditionally they've been very male orientated. I like the idea that this character was the main focus of the story and not the villain.

WIATER: Excluding the problems that arise that are beyond your control, as occurred with *Bad Dreams* and *The Abyss*, do you have any major regrets? That is, are there films you wished you had tackled differently, or wished you perhaps hadn't tackled at all?

HURD: I honestly don't second guess. I think that you can't look back, you can only look forward. You learn from the choices that you make as you go along. I don't want to second guess myself and create a whole "What if?" scenario. You can only respond and react within the moment. It is not a one-man band. There are a lot of people who are collaborating and have influence, and I don't think that on my productions there has been a unilateral voice that has said, "You have to do it this way." It was only after listening to a lot of people's opinions, and then trying to make the right choice.

WIATER: All through our talk you've mentioned the collaborative process in filmmaking. What do you think is the most misunderstood part of your role in that process?

HURD: There is a fiction that is perpetuated that what I do as a producer is very glamorous. I would say that the filmmaking process, with respect to the films I've been involved with, is extremely *unglamorous*. It involves getting up every morning at four A.M., being on call twenty-four hours a day, not having any time off for up to two years, and not having the wonderful feast with celebrated movie stars and driving around in limos and having private screening rooms. . . .

I have discovered that when I go into a new city that hasn't hosted a shooting crew before, they are quite surprised at how hard we work and how diligent we are. There aren't the wild and crazy parties, because no one has the energy after work to get into any trouble. But that's why believing in yourself and believing in your own abilities is *so* important. It also helps if you can get by on only two hours sleep! [Laughs.]

Michael McDowell

Michael McDowell

Michael McDowell is the only talent I know who gave up a successful career as a horror novelist to strive for an even more successful career as a horror screenwriter. Before he became known as the creator of the fabulously successful horror-comedy *Beetlejuice*, McDowell had already carved an enviable niche for himself as a popular horror author. His novels include *The Elementals*, *Katie*, *Gilded Needles*, *Toplin*, and the epic six-part *Blackwater* series. When his career as a novelist was just getting underway, no less an authority than Stephen King called him "the finest writer of paperback originals" in the country.

Born in Alabama in 1950, McDowell has lived most of his adult life in Massachusetts since moving there to attend college. He eventually received a doctorate in English ("which I did absolutely nothing with") and decided while in graduate school to try for a career as a writer. Since 1978, he has been a full-time writer, and now divides his time between Boston and Los Angeles. I had every intention of including him in my previous volume of interviews, *Dark Dreamers: Conversations with the Masters of Horror.* However, at McDowell's request, he has perhaps found a more suitable home here in *Dark Visions*, as his last novel in the genre was published in 1985.

Obviously, Michael McDowell did not abandon the horror genre—he only shifted gears from one medium to another. Through a curious case of mistaken identity, McDowell had the opportunity to submit a teleplay to the syndicated horror anthology series, "Tales from the Darkside." (He eventually wound up being involved in no less than sixteen episodes.) However, as a screenwriter, McDowell became an "overnight success" with *Beetlejuice*—a movie so successful it spawned an animated cartoon series, as well as a phenomenal amount of toy merchandise. No one was more shocked and pleased at its success than McDowell himself.

Meeting with McDowell, I am always left with the impression that here is a person who, if he ever unleashed his imagination full force, would knock the industry on its ear. His wide range of talents has yet to be used, either as novelist or screenwriter.

I spoke with McDowell at a time when he was working on several projects simultaneously: one simply titled *Pet People*, and another an adaptation of Stephen King's last Richard Bachman novel, *Thinner*.

SELECTED FILMOGRAPHY

Beetlejuice (1988)

High Spirits (1988) (uncredited)

Tales from the Darkside: The Movie (1990)

WIATER: *Beetlejuice* was a wonderful movie for many reasons, not the least of it being the extremely dark sense of humor. Knowing your past history as a horror novelist, I have to ask if the earlier versions of your script were much darker in tone than what audiences saw on the screen?

MCDOWELL: That's interesting—my tone *was* much harsher. For example, the people from New York were not as endearingly clumsy as they are made to be in the movie. But Tim Burton, the director, made them warmer characters—made both sides warm—and that made them much more interesting, and much more accessible.

WIATER: Did you have any contributions to the film while it was in production, or was your job finished in the sense that the producers bought the script and politely told you to go away?

MCDOWELL: I sold the finished script. Tim became very interested in it from the first draft, though he was not attached to the film until later. I did two more drafts, and then my partner, Michael Bender, and the Geffen Company fired me. [Chuckles.] And they "fired" me because the script was going in a way it shouldn't go. They hired another screenwriter, who did a very good job of it. But I had become friends with Tim, and was working with him on other projects, so I was around, talking about the script and everything else while they were making *Beetlejuice*. It couldn't have been nicer.

WIATER: Your general opinion was that you were pleased the way it turned out?

MCDOWELL: [Laughs.] My general opinion was that I was extraordinarily lucky! Lucky in the fact that it was my first screenplay. That it sold at all. That having sold, it was made. And that having been made, it was made by someone as good as Tim Burton. So to say I was pleased . . . is quite mild!

WIATER: What's your view of this "Beetlejuice industry" that has appeared, years after the initial film was made? The toys, the games, the costumes?

MCDOWELL: I find it odd that I should write this script called *Beetlejuice* and have this character . . . and that it should be so *popular* . . . that is fairly astonishing to me. To hear complete strangers saying, "Beetlejuice, Beetlejuice, Beetlejuice . . ." I find it quite wonderful and surprising.

WIATER: You chuckled when stating that you had been fired from *Beetlejuice*. I don't quite see the humor in that situation.

MCDOWELL: Being fired out here in Hollywood is not the same thing at all as being fired from a regular job. It is *not* the same thing. There are often good reasons for firing someone from a job out here, and they have nothing to do with competency. Or whether you want to go work with that person again. So I don't harbor ill feelings at all. People often have to do things that have nothing to do with how much they like you—or how good you've been. People don't forget. And if you're good, they will work with you again—and they will tell other people that you are good. Of course, you can be kept on a production, and if you're bad, people will pass that word on as well.

WIATER: Before moving on, I know that you had some involvement in the horror-comedy *High Spirits*. Can you tell me what that entailed?

MCDOWELL: I worked with Neil Jordan, the director, on the first draft. I like Neil very much, and I had a good time with him. We had a mutual parting of the ways because Columbia put the film into turnaround, and it became a different project. Neil needed different things out of the script, and I was not the person who could bring to the script those elements that he needed. And that's all.

Neil and I took a trip through Ireland with his two daughters and a producer, in what we were told was the only limousine in Ireland. [Laughs.] And we went from derelict castle to derelict castle picking up ideas for atmosphere and locations. We just had a wonderful time! I enjoyed working on the project, but after that, I really didn't have anything else to do with it.

WIATER: You've always approached writing in a very logical and methodical way. How do you describe the process of screenwriting versus your method of writing a novel?

MCDOWELL: It's a question of having 2,000 elements to get into a screenplay, and only having 124 boxes in which to put these elements. And so, every box has to have a peg that is 8-sided, and every peg has to do double, triple, and quadruple duty. Do you understand what I mean?

WIATER: I believe so. Years ago, you told me that you were the sort of writer who, if a publisher asked for a 200-page novel, with 16 characters, about underwater Nazi zombies, that is precisely what you'd deliver. It's writing just what is necessary to make it work.

MCDOWELL: I actually still agree with that. These screenplays *are* exercises, and they have to be treated as exercises. It's wonderful when you can do the exercise, and then sneak in something on top of that. Putting something of yourself in it. Because when you're actually writing, working it out, so much of it can feel like choreography. And blocking. Getting your characters on, getting them to move about, getting them resolved.

So it's not like writing a novel.

It's as if I had 600 pages of a novel, and all the things I brought to that novel, all the aspects that I developed and tied onto it, that I suddenly had to do that in 115 pages. And not lose any of it in the translation. You also have to have a Hollywood audience in mind—not necessarily a film audience—but a Hollywood audience that ultimately judges you. This is not a negative comment because I work out here, but it is part of the system, and it's very interesting.

WIATER: You've written screenplays for *Tales from the Darkside: The Movie*, and teleplays for the same show in its television form as "Tales from the Darkside." Precisely what is the difference between writing horror for television versus horror for the screen?

MCDOWELL: I don't know how this answer will sound, but it's actually true. One form has commercials, and the other form is much longer. Now, what that means is you have a different rhythm for each. And what's particularly hard is that not only do you have to think of telling a story, but you've got to have an "electrified story." That is, it's got to produce jolts now and then. A normal screenplay works like one of those little wooden trains that children have that go around a track. But with a horror screenplay, you've got to electrify that track so it produces jolts at certain points along the way.

So, here's what we have. In working for television, for a show such as "Tales from the Darkside" or "Monsters"—which are thirty-minute shows—you have a very specific time frame. These are five-eight-eight: five minutes, eight minutes, and eight minutes. And you have a progression of jolts in those frames. It's a very tricky business to get everything in there for budgetary considerations, and tell a good story, too. But those are great fun, and they take all of your concentration.

WIATER: You once told me in working for "Tales from the Darkside," that the best chance a writer had of selling a script was if it only contained two characters and two sets.

MCDOWELL: Well, sometimes that's all you get. [Chuckles.] Now, I cannot sound as if I'm making fun of them, because I loved working for Laurel, the production company. They have never failed me. They have taught me a lot, and I love those kind of constraints.

WIATER: One show you wrote—"In the Closet"—nevertheless works precisely on the constraints of two characters and two sets. It's a perfectly constructed teleplay.

MCDOWELL: But I had a good pattern for that. When I was given the opportunity to write for the series—which came about in a very strange way—I asked to see a sample script. I was given George Romero's script for the pilot episode. I looked at that and I took it apart and I imitated it. I put my story in its format, with the peaks in the same places, and figured out how long scenes were and so forth. And it worked.

I also got another script accepted because in this case it had one set and one actress. [Laughs.] It was called "Answer Me" with Jean Marsh. But I enjoy the constraints. It's like working in a hothouse and forcing bulbs. Sometimes they bloom bigger and grander if you decrease the size of the pot.

WIATER: But doesn't writing for television prepare for you writing for the motion picture screen?

McDOWELL: The fact is, they have totally different rhythms. You can't simply take a half-hour show and make it into an hour-and-a-half movie. It just doesn't work. To me, it's almost as different as a novel and a short story.

WIATER: Yes, but for adapting a short story to the screen, isn't the half-hour television anthology the perfect medium?

McDOWELL: Yes and no. You're thinking of it as "How do I preserve the short story?" and I'm thinking of it as "How do I fill out a segment?" I've adapted several short stories—usually with a fair amount of success. But I feel a duty to keep all that I can of any original—except when it's my own work.

WIATER: Not many people are aware that your first novel, *The Amulet*, was first created as a screenplay.

McDOWELL: You have to understand that I had written six unpublished novels before that! I was looking for a way to get some money for my efforts. This is embarrassing, but I had no idea what the screenplay format was. My original draft was ninety-eight pages, and was totally in the wrong format. So I doubled its length in novelized format and that sold to a publisher. Then my editor had me double that in length. But it's embarrassing how little I once knew about the screenplay format.

WIATER: Yet I've heard there are actually two kinds of basic format for a screenwriter: a script that will sell the concept, and then another script, the actual shooting script. But initially you have to be successful with writing the concept screenplay, don't you?

McDOWELL: First let me say it's better to learn from a bad script than a good one. Because with a good screenplay, you're not going to know what makes it good when you're starting out. But with a bad script that gets produced, then you may have a chance to figure out what makes it work. I'm sure people could tell *Beetlejuice* hadn't been written by someone working in Hollywood, but there was something about the script that they liked, and they bought it.

If your script is good, there is somebody somewhere who will read it. The appetite for scripts out here is voracious.

And every three months there's a script that everybody is talking about. You'd think with all the thousands and thousands that are registered with the Writer's Guild, there'd be more. But there's always only one. Once it was *The Lost Boys*. Once it was *Heathers*. And once, I'm happy to say, it was *Beetlejuice*. It's usually the script that gets passed around and everybody says, "Wow! This is great! It'll never get made." [Laughs.]

WIATER: You've written a number of successful novels, both in and out of the horror genre. Why haven't you done the obvious—adapt your own novels into screenplays?

MCDOWELL: I'm too close to them. My sister, who is also a very good writer, is working on *The Elementals*, with my partner. Once they take it out of the book, and I can look at the screenplay *as* a screenplay, that's different. But I can't look at one of my books and try and make it into a screenplay. Why? Because I'll look at something and I know why it was there in the novel, and I'll think it also has to be there in the screenplay. Adapting a novel to the screen is not the shortcut many people like to think it is. In many cases it can be a longer and more torturous process, because you keep thinking of what you have to put in.

WIATER: You have the distinction of being both a successful novelist and a successful screenwriter. Which do you now prefer?

MCDOWELL: I wrote over thirty novels. [Long pause.] I wrote over thirty and that was enough for right then. You can choose to be a writer out here, working in the movie industry, but it is definitely a business. Yet because of the Writer's Guild, the scale minimum for a screenplay for even a low-budget film is over $25,000.

WIATER: In other words, most novelists are struggling to get $10,000 for a book, while a single screenplay could net them two or three times as much?

MCDOWELL: That's right. Absolutely—I make more money at this. But it's not because I don't make as much money at it that I no longer write novels. It's really because I enjoy being out here with my partner, Michael Bender, and my sister, who works as our assistant. And you're talking about writers who "only" get $10,000. Now, $10,000 can be a lot of money; it really can, as I remember *very* well.

WIATER: Do you miss writing novels? People must be disappointed not to see new books forthcoming with your name on them.

MCDOWELL: I'm always surprised that anybody knows my name! [Laughs.] That's nice to hear. I miss writing novels, because I don't have the absolute control over writing that I used to have, or have the larger patterns of rhythm that I love. I have started a book—I have maybe 200 pages—it's a big book. I didn't think I could write much horror after *Blackwater*. I felt that I'd "shot my load" as they say. [Chuckles.]

WIATER: A fascinating little quirk about your career as a professional writer is that there are apparently several other writers also named "Michael McDowell."

McDowell: I keep a list on my computer of the other Michael McDowells. Before I get it, would you like to hear how I first became connected with "Tales from the Darkside" and Laurel?

Wiater: Please go right ahead.

McDowell: Well, I was sick in bed one day with the flu. And a man called on the telephone and said, "Hello, my name is David Vogel, I'm the producer of 'Tales from the Darkside,' a television show. Are you Michael McDowell?" And I said, "I am." He said, "I would like to buy your story 'Slippage' for the show. You *are* Michael McDowell, the horror writer?" He waited for a response, and finally I said, "You have the wrong Michael McDowell, horror writer." [Laughs.] I told him, "You want Michael Kube-McDowell." And he was so embarrassed, he said, "Well, uh, do *you* have anything?" So I said, "Yes, I do." And I didn't. So I went upstairs and I wrote something, real quick. And that was "Inside the Closet." I sent it to him, he bought it, and I ended up doing four episodes that same season.

But here are the other Michael McDowells: there's me, there's a Florida highway patrolman who's my first cousin, there's a reporter for the Boston *Real Paper*, there's a gay writer from Baltimore who had a byline in *Christopher Street*, there's Michael Kube-McDowell, there's an environmental consultant that I saw on CBN, there's a University of Oregon graduate who owes money on his student loan bill, there's an editorial production consultant for *Bay Windows*, a gay periodical in Boston, and I just came up with another one the other day: Michael McDowell is the editor of a hard rock fan magazine. Of these, five are writers. But I feel I got there first, so I get to use Michael McDowell without the initial. [Laughs.]

Wiater: Any other literary projects you're involved with at present?

McDowell: One of the few things that I'm doing now—though I haven't worked on it in a while—is a project with Harry O. Morris, who illustrated my last novel, *Toplin*. My agent said to me one day, "Well, what do you write for pleasure? You always have contracts for everything—don't you do anything for yourself?" And I thought, Well, I don't, do I? What do I really want to do for myself? And I thought I'd better have *something* for the good of myself. So I wrote something that I thought was close to myself. It's called *Revolt of the Bondage Models*. And the way I'm writing it, it's coming out in script form.

It's not about graphic sex, the way you'd think it might be from the title, but it's something that definitely is *not* going to be produced quickly. But I showed it to Harry Morris, and he liked it very much, and he's going to do photographs for it. So we're going to have *Revolt of the Bondage Models* the script, as well as stills from a movie that doesn't yet exist! He sent me one photograph to show me what he's thinking of, and it's really quite wonderful. So it is something that is close to me—fetishism. [Laughs.] Mostly women's fetishism. I never thought anybody ever did fetishism right, except Michael Blumlein, the author of *The Brains of Rats.*

WIATER: Curiously enough, Anne Rice told me this was part of her reason for writing erotica—she couldn't find anyone handling S-and-M themes in the way she thought they should be properly done.

MCDOWELL: That's right! So it's a very strange story, but it works on its own terms, and I'm very pleased with it so far.

WIATER: Although you've gone outside the horror genre on some projects, it seems apparent you still have a great respect for this genre. Why are you still fascinated by it?

MCDOWELL: [Long pause.] I am always a little . . . surprised . . . that these things can work. Still. Not only for an audience, but horror can still work for *me*. That's one reason why I'm with horror. Another reason is it's part of the way I make my living.

Also, for the sake of the art, I should stand up for horror. I get real mad when people try to put it behind them. And I have been fortunate in that I have not been stereotyped out here in Hollywood, coming from my books, and coming from *Beetlejuice*. I have gotten jobs to do all sorts of genres: I've done male action-adventure, swords and sorcery, women behind bars, heart-warming fantasies, women buddy capers. . . . So I consider myself lucky that I wasn't pigeon-holed—I don't know why. I guess it's partially because I've always been willing to do other things. So I don't like to exploit horror in that way, but I will always come back to it. I love genre, and I think horror is very important. I'm proud of my association with it.

WIATER: So you've never looked at horror simply as a genre to be a stepping-stone to something more "relevant?"

MCDOWELL: [Angrily.] There is something wrong with that way of thinking. Things don't work that way—on *any* level. I don't think you should be petulant about what you do. If you take on a project, you should find some way of doing it with a good heart. I find it contemptible when people slough something off, or when people think a project isn't worth their best effort on it. It makes me furious: "Oh, what are people going to think of me if I throw myself into this project, body and soul?" You know? "People should think I'm saving myself for something better."

I'm appalled by that attitude. I love working in horror—because I find it very difficult to do. I think it's very difficult to find new jolts—

to find new ways of twisting the knife. And new places to stick the knife.

WIATER: Fellow horror writers such as Clive Barker and Stephen King have tried their hand at directing a motion picture. Any interest in this area?

McDOWELL: I've actually turned down offers. There are people who want to direct and do nothing else. I'm not like that. I like to write. I love the business side of the industry. But I will direct someday because I should—because I'll be more competent in other areas. I mean, I'll be competent in directing—I don't think anybody will lose money on a movie I direct. Now that sounds like hubris, and I don't mean it to be. What I mean by that statement is that hiring me will pull the budget down low enough so nobody will lose money on something I direct! [Laughs.] Another aspect is that I'm so easily bored, and to be a director, and to do it right, takes so much concentration on *one* project for *so* long a time, that I'm very reluctant to get into this.

WIATER: Directing possibilities aside, what's down the road for this Michael McDowell without the middle initial?

McDOWELL: Now that's an interesting question. In a weird way, I've stopped thinking about the future. Because this is the future I've always wanted to get to. A future in which I'm doing what I want to do, day by day. It's very interesting right now, and I don't have a five-year plan. Except, if a five-year plan means that I hope I'm as happy working then as I am now. And being able to say what I really think, even if it's sometimes to my detriment.

Caroline Munro

Steve Swires

A las, the great days of Hollywood's "Scream Queens" are all but over. As most readers of this book who are over forty will recall, there was a time when "Hollywood Horror" also meant horror stars: Karloff, Lugosi, Chaney, Lorre. The same held true for the ladies: there were actresses, such as Evelyn Ankers in the 1940s, Beverly Garland in 1950s, and Barbara Steele in 1960s who were best known for their work in horror and science fiction films.

Of course, special effects are the "horror stars" of today's dark cinema. No one goes to see a horror movie because of the actors—if anyone is a "star," it's usually now the monster itself! (Especially when one considers the number of films starring Michael Myers in the *Halloween* series, Freddy Krueger in the *Nightmare on Elm Street* series, and Jason Voorhees in the *Friday the 13th* series.) One of the few legitimate actresses to enter the genre when audiences were still paying to see human flesh rather than torn flesh is British-born Caroline Munro.

Although Munro has of course appeared in other films outside the horror and science fiction genres, she remains today one of the few viable contenders for the position of a movie "scream queen." She made her first genre appearances with Vincent Price in the *Abominable Dr. Phibes* and its equally campy sequel, *Dr. Phibes Rises Again.* She also has the distinction of being a "Hammer girl," that is to say, she appeared in several of the British studio's productions, including *Dracula A.D. 1972* with Christopher Lee and Peter Cushing, and *Captain Kronos: Vampire Hunter.* She is the first to admit that a number of early roles simply called upon her to wear as little as possible while screaming as much as possible.

Most recently, she has appeared in a number of European productions not yet theatrically released in the United States, including *The Black Cat, The Howl of the Devil,* and *Faceless.*

One of the most delightful aspects of speaking with Munro is that she doesn't take herself too seriously—she is more content with enjoying life than worrying about immortality on the silver screen. An obvious example of her priorities is that I spoke with her while she was baking a cake for her husband's birthday.

SELECTED FILMOGRAPHY

Abominable Dr. Phibes (1971)

Dr. Phibes Rises Again (1972)

Captain Kronos: Vampire Hunter (1974)

The Golden Voyage of Sinbad (1974)

At the Earth's Core (1976)

Starcrash (1979)

Maniac (1980)

WIATER: The first thing I would like to know is what your current projects are. Your work hasn't appeared in America lately.

MUNRO: Last year I did a film in Italy called *The Black Cat*. The experience was very enjoyable. I worked with a director that I had worked for before, Luigi Cozzi, who did *Starcrash*. I played a very interesting part; she is *very* evil. I played the villainess rather than the heroine. The heroine was played by a French actress, Florence Guerin, and she is very good, I was very impressed. The rest of the cast was mostly Europeans. There was one American, one was an Italian prince called Urbano Barbarini, who is doing very well over here doing television. He is a real-life prince, so that was interesting.

I did a television show in England at the end of last year. It was a detective spoof called *The Armchair Detective*. I played a Spanish maid in that and it was "whodunit." There were just five of us in the cast, and they were wonderful. It took a couple of weeks to do and it is an hour long. It will be shown sometime this year. But this year has been quite quiet. I had been offered a film in Spain, again by director Jess Franco, who I had worked with two years ago on the film *Faceless*. But I couldn't take the job because I had been decorating our apartment so I had my hands full.

WIATER: Can you tell me what the status is with the *Doctor Who* film?

MUNRO: I thought you might ask about that! [Laughs.] Everyone wants to know about this. It's all going ahead as planned, but it probably won't be until early next year. That's as much as I know.

WIATER: Has your role been selected? Do you know what character you'll be playing in the movie yet?

MUNRO: Yes I do. It isn't the assistant at all as many people think. Again it is the bad person. Actually there are two bad people, one being a man and the other his lady love. Her name is Zilla. I have not read the entire script as yet, I prefer to wait until I know everything is set. I always do that with projects, because anything can happen and you might not get to do it. Until I am actually doing it, I don't believe it.

WIATER: What keeps drawing you back to horror, fantasy, science fiction films? One reason that you are a known quantity is that fans of this type of film can see you in these movies time and again.

MUNRO: That is an interesting question. I find the genre interesting, but also it seems to be the type of work that I have been offered. I don't seem to be mainstream and I'm not sure why. I have done a few mainstream movies, *The Spy Who Loved Me*, *Golden Voyage of Sinbad*, and *At the Earth's Core*. These were fantasy, but they were more family oriented. I started in the early seventies doing this sort of thing. I did a couple of the Hammer horrors and from there, that was the sort of work I was offered. I would love to do something mainstream, but it *is* sort of tricky. People in England are very blink-ered. They tend to think that what you've done is what you can do, rather than giving you a chance to try other things. With the television and various roles I've been doing abroad, at least I've been given the chance to experiment with myself and try to do other things. But, it is very hard to convey this to producers and directors. I am not a pushy person I'm afraid. I don't go out and sell myself or have managers. So it's sort of the work I've been offered. As much as I like it, I'm also getting a lot of experience and working with some interesting directors and some very good actors. I'm grateful for all this, but I'd like to do other things, obviously.

WIATER: So you don't really mind being typecast?

MUNRO: You can't knock the fact that you will always have work because you are associated with a certain type of film. Look at Chris-topher Lee and Peter Cushing, although he really started in light com-edy. I came into it in a very funny way. I started out doing some modeling, so really all my experience and learning has been done on the film set, which at times is very hard but can be very good. At the time you are plunged into the deep end and you have to really have your wits about you.

I have to look at typecasting in a very positive sense. At least if I am working, that's great because people want me for what I can do. But the last few years and roles I've been doing abroad, and I don't think they've been seen, have been slightly different from just running around in leopard skins screaming. They've had a lot more substance, and I suppose that's because I'm getting older so you mature and you hopefully get a chance to play different characters and people see you in a different light. But there of course have still been a lot of genre films. And *Dr. Who* is the same sort of culty thing. I would like to do something "normal" for a change. [Laughs.]

WIATER: Has the fact that you were a model been a blessing or a curse in your career?

MUNRO: Beauty is in the eyes of the beholder and beauty fades, I do believe that. In England actors are meant to be theater trained, and it makes it hard if you haven't had experience that way. They all tend to go to drama school and a lot of them come out very much the same: same package, voice, and look, which is very good for stage. But for film you don't need that. I think that as long as *you* believe it on screen then the audience will believe. It's not very simple to do, but it is a simple thing when it works.

WIATER: Isn't it just as challenging to play against a supernatural monster as it is to play against a handsome leading man?

MUNRO: Well it is because the supernatural monster isn't there! In

The Golden Voyage—and a lot of my films—*nothing* has been there! They gave you a little drawing of how tall the monster is and what it looks like. So it's all in your imagination. You just have to imagine it and it's up to you to make it believable. If you believe it then the audience will believe it. But it *is* tricky, but I think I prefer working with monsters than handsome leading men. [Laughs.]

WIATER: Could you tell me a little more about working with Christopher Lee and Peter Cushing?

MUNRO: That goes back a few years. What lovely men! About two months ago I attended a "This Is Your Life" for Peter Cushing. It was a surprise and it was great to see him again because he is the ultimate gentleman. He is so charming, so unspoiled, such a professional, and such a funny man. I did *At the Earth's Core* with him in 1976. He had a quirky little character in that as the doctor. He was just so funny and charming, and so helpful too. I was relatively a newcomer in those days and I went in sort of apprehensive because here I am working with the great Peter Cushing and I'm just a little person. But he was so sweet, welcoming me in and showing me the ropes.

I did *Dracula A.D. 1972*, which was one of my first films, with Christopher Lee and I found him terrific to work with. He is so believable as Dracula. I didn't have to do much acting in that, I just looked at him and that was it. [Laughs.] I was there, I believed it. I believed that he was going to bite my neck and I was going to turn into a vampire. He had wonderful tales to tell about all his travels to research Dracula. I saw him recently when I was with my father. He plays a lot of charity golf. I couldn't speak highly enough about the two of them.

WIATER: Tell me about your workings with Vincent Price, if you would, on the two *Dr. Phibes* movies.

MUNRO: He again is in the same league as the others. Again he was charming, very witty, and a wonderful cook. He used to bring his pâté early in the morning onto the set. Then I would just go and lie in a coffin. *That* was a very hard day's work! It's kind of strange to have that on my genre résumé that my first genre role was as a corpse. Because I was with Hammer at the time, they wouldn't allow my name to be shown on the credits. I suppose they had to have me in the second one for the continuity. That was the easiest thing I've ever had to do. You just have to hold your breath, which sometimes is a bit tricky, but other than that it was lovely.

WIATER: Have you found that horror films have changed in the last twenty years?

MUNRO: Terrifically! The Hammer films were more like a Grimm's fairy tale. They had a gentleness and a sort of romantic style to them. The first time I became aware of it was when I went to New York and I saw the director of what was to be *Maniac* and he took me to see *Halloween*. That's not generally the type of film that I tend to see. I prefer lighthearted films or films with more substance. But I saw *Halloween* and it took my breath away when I saw that. And, of course, working on *Maniac*, that certainly enlightened me. I had *no* idea that films had gone that far. To tell you the truth, when I flew back to New York to see the opening of it, it really shocked me because I didn't think it was going to be as graphically violent as it was. It was brilliantly done by Tom Savini; the special makeup effects were wonderful. A lot of critics really liked it and it did well in New York, but a lot of women's groups really attacked it. That film really made me think, but then again, I didn't stop doing them.

WIATER: What films have you refused to do?

MUNRO: Certain films I've said no to thinking that they've gone too far, or it just looked awful and tacky. But then of course you're totally in the hands of the director and the editor really, as to how they put it together in the end. The script can look fine and then all these extra scenes have been added and you think, My goodness, when you actually see the film. I tend not to go to see the films if I can help it.

WIATER: What two or three films would you recommend to someone who is not familiar with your work?

MUNRO: I suppose *Captain Kronos* would be a great favorite of mine because I had such a lovely time doing it. And, I suppose the character of Carla would be the closest to me, not that I was awfully good in it. I was still learning. I think if I was given the chance to try again now, I would do it differently.

The Spy Who Loved Me is another one; I had a very short part in it. The effects were wonderful, and it is such a big, spectacular film, and Lewis Gilbert, the director, and of course Roger Moore.

I would definitely recommend *Starcrash* for children. I think that is great fun with all the costumes and effects.

As far as recent ones go, having not seen them, it is very difficult for me to say, but it's the parts that I really enjoyed. I was getting close to what I want to do as an actress in, say like *Faceless* or the little one I did in Spain called *Howl of the Devil*, which has not seen the light of day. I think they ran into financial problems. And of course *The Black Cat*. All totally different parts but I know that I got close to what I wanted to do, but whether they will ever get seen is another matter. Although I believe *Faceless* has been shown in France and did very well there. Whether it will come out in video in America or England, I don't know.

WIATER: As far as your fans and fan mail go, have you ever perceived that it's different than if you were a mainstream actress, or do you think that fans are more dedicated because you are known for doing horror and fantasy films?

MUNRO: I honestly don't know because not receiving mail from being a mainstream actress and the fact that I haven't talked to other people about fan mail makes it very difficult. But I do find that fans are very loyal.

WIATER: Is that part of the reason that you enjoy the work, in the sense that the fans are so loyal to you?

MUNRO: I think so, because you are hopefully giving them something that they want and the response is so good. When I go to conventions in the States the reception is so warm that I think, How can I not do what I am doing? If these people are enjoying what I do, then it makes me enjoy it. Also, I think that I am not that ambitious because if I was I would have stayed in the States after I did *The Spy Who Loved Me*. Cubby Broccoli, the producer, said, "Well, now's the time, you must stay over here and I can help you." But I thought, Well, I've got my family over here, and even if I keep doing little European productions, at least I can stay close to my home. So that's the choice that I made. [Pause.] Maybe things wouldn't have been different. Maybe I wouldn't have gotten any more work, or maybe got a different sort of work, and professionally I don't think I was ready. But now I feel I could tackle any role, and do it justice.

WIATER: Bluntly put, you haven't done nude scenes in your films. This is something that would seem obvious for some actresses to further their careers.

MUNRO: I don't think it would have gotten me more film work. Everybody's done nude scenes—it's nothing special. If I were going to do one, I would want it to be a bit special and it certainly wouldn't be now because everybody does them. I don't think it is necessary and I would feel uncomfortable. I've got fairly explicit clothing in *Captain Kronos* and *The Black Cat*, but I didn't feel it was necessary for me to be wandering around nude. For me the obvious doesn't work; I prefer a little mystique in things. If I were going to do it, I certainly wouldn't do it now. I would have done it twenty years ago when I was a lot younger and a lot fitter.

But at the same time, there's nothing wrong with nude scenes and they can be done beautifully. I'm certainly not a prude, what other people want to do is fine. But, I don't think you get more work because of it. Having said that, I have lost several parts for not doing it. So yes, I *have* lost work, but whether I would have gained work, I'm not sure.

I have no regrets, though.

WIATER: Do you ever get a sense about why people seem to be attracted to horror and fantasy films?

MUNRO: I think that with the horror, people *like* to be frightened. That's a basic, sort of primal instinct. People enjoy being frightened. As a young child I used to watch *Dr. Who* from behind the sofa with my hands over my face, but with my fingers open. It gets rid of the tension to have the jumps and screams of horror movies.

I think we all enjoy the fantasy film because it takes you away from the mundane things of life. You can escape with people, and then you can come back if it's a bit scary and get back to normal. Those are the basic instincts that we have, and that comes from childhood. Children are always playing games and fantasizing. They can do it without material things, as adults seem to need; children use their imagination. When you lose that sort of thing it's sad. I was about twelve and you suddenly realize that you have lost the power of play. You think you should try to be a little bit grown up. You suddenly lose that wonderment, and I think that's a sad thing because it's almost like losing your innocence. I think it is important to hold on to the child in you if you can.

WIATER: Do you think you are able to when you're acting?

MUNRO: Yes, I actually do. It may be not as good as when you are a child, because as a child you are much freer, but you can still do it. I think most actors feel that way. For me, I had such a wonderful childhood, I never wanted to grow up. I always wanted to be Peter Pan. But unfortunately you have to grow up and pay the bills and such. That is why acting is so good. I think everyone needs a bit of fantasy. It's like when we see "Dallas" or "Dynasty" over here. Very few privileged people live like that. It makes me smile, but it *is* fantasy.

WIATER: Out of all your films, was there one that was the most memorable?

MUNRO: Well, all the films I have done have had some very good times and obviously some very hard times. Whether it's conditions that you're working under, being on set and it's meant to be bright sunshine and it's pouring with rain or snowing and you're wearing something very skimpy. Or it may be that you have learned the script line for line and the director says, "We've changed the dialogue and we're going to shoot it in five minutes." When I was younger things like that scared me to death, but now I think that it is a challenge and try to do the best I can.

William F. Nolan

William F. Nolan

William F. Nolan is one of those people for whom the cliché *multitalented* is, for once, a very accurate description. Although he may ultimately be best known as the author of the *Logan* novels (*Logan's Run*, with George Clayton Johnson, *Logan's World*, *Logan's Search*), he has in fact written over 50 books and been published professionally more than 800 times. He is a novelist, short story writer, editor, biographer, poet, literary critic—you name it in the endeavor of writing, and Nolan has probably done it. Actually, to describe more fairly all of his accomplishments, one would need a book to do so—and it's entitled *The Work of William F. Nolan: An Annotated Bibliography and Guide* by Boden Clarke and James Hopkins (Borgo Press, 1988).

Born in Kansas City, Missouri, on March 6, 1928, Nolan has spent his professional career exploring just about every possible genre, from science fiction to mystery to horror and suspense. After a lifetime of purposely excluding himself from being "typecast" within any one genre, Nolan recently made a major career decision to concentrate in what he prefers to call "dark fantasy." So far, this has resulted in the publication of his first horror novel, *Helltracks* (Avon Books, 1990), and second collection of horror stories, *Nightshapes* (Avon Books, 1991), following his *Things Beyond Midnight* (Scream/Press, 1984). With Martin Greenberg, Nolan has edited his first genre anthology, *Urban Horrors* (Dark Harvest, 1990), and has had his shorter fiction selected for more than sixty horror anthologies. To further illustrate his renewed devotion to this genre, he has written an instructional volume for Writer's Digest's Books entitled, sensibly enough, *How to Write Horror Fiction*.

However, for the purposes of *Dark Visions*, I met with Nolan specifically to learn more about his adventures in the screen trade—for both television and feature motion pictures. (He has also done teleplays for American anthology series such as "One Step Beyond" and "Darkroom.") Often working with producer-director Dan Curtis, Nolan has been over the years a screenwriter on such movies as *Burnt Offerings* (1976), adapted from the novel by Robert Marasco, and his original *Terror at London Bridge* (1987). However, he is best known for his motion pictures made for television, often working with producer-director Dan Curtis.

I spoke with Nolan as he was completing a teleplay for a sequel to *Trilogy of Terror*, again for Dan Curtis.

SELECTED FILMOGRAPHY

The Norliss Tapes (1973)

Burnt Offerings (1976)

The Turn of the Screw (1974)

Trilogy of Terror (1975)

WIATER: You've collaborated with some famous fantasy authors in the past, including Richard Matheson and the late Charles Beaumont.

What's it like to work with someone else on a script? Is it just the two of you sharing ideas, or is it more involved than that?

NOLAN: Let's face it, film and television writing is a collaborative medium all down the line. There are usually more than a hundred people involved in each production. You end up "collaborating" with the set designer, the art director, the wardrobe and makeup people, the special effects experts, the unit production manager—and each actor, as well. Not to mention the considerable input a writer usually receives from network or studio executives. So you can go into it with that sort of mind-set. Every person has his or her own particular vision of what the finished product should be, so you can see that collaboration is the very basis of television and film production.

In the initial stage of collaborative writing you try to work with people who operate on your creative wavelength; you look for a creative rapport. And that's exactly what I shared with Dick Matheson and Chuck Beaumont. We had a lot of fun writing together, tossing ideas back and forth. It's like having two heads! However, if you end up collaborating with a writer who's *not* on your wavelength it can be hellish. That's why I have refused to work with certain people— who shall be nameless. We'd be butting heads over every scene and character and line of dialogue.

With prose work, it's just you and the page—and the only collaborator you've got is your editor. With scripting, it's like working on a circus. All kinds of people have input into the final product. I always say that if a writer can't tolerate collaboration, he or she should stay away from scripting. Prose writing helps keep me sane. I'd go wacko of I just did scripts without the novels and the stories and articles in between to balance things out.

WIATER: Tell me about your most recent television project, which is a sequel to the justly famous "Trilogy of Terror." That film was adapted from three of Richard Matheson's stories, and the sequel is an adaptation of three other stories, correct?

NOLAN: That's right. I adapted Henry Kuttner's "The Graveyard Rats," Philip K. Dick's "The Father Thing," along with an original story by Dan Curtis based on Matheson's devil doll, "He Who Kills." These three will form a "Movie of the Week" for ABC called "Trilogy of Terror II."

Actually, the Kuttner segment is practically an original. All I started with—in the published story—was a character who gets trapped underground in a graveyard and has to battle a horde of killer rats. That's all I had to work with. I had no conflict, no developing dramatic situation, no buildup, no interesting characters. I had to create ninety percent of that story. The last three pages—the last three minutes on the television screen—will be Henry Kuttner's "The Graveyard Rats." So, again, we have a collaboration—in terms of adapting another writer's short story. The Phil Dick teleplay was much easier. Everything basic was there in the story; it just had to be expanded and dramatized.

WIATER: The most memorable of the three stories from the original "Trilogy of Terror" has to be the one with the devil doll going after Karen Black. That was based on Matheson's story, "Prey." How is it that Matheson wrote the script on that one and you ended up adapting the two other Matheson stories?

NOLAN: Well, Dick and I have often chuckled about this, since everyone vividly recalls the devil doll segment he scripted, yet no one remembers the two that I wrote!

What happened was Dan Curtis asked us to adapt these three printed Matheson stories—and Dick naturally picked the strongest of the trio. I really don't think the *quality* of our scripts differed, but Dick knew he had the gem of the lot. That sharp-fanged little devil doll made a deep psychic imprint on everyone. Happily enough, all these years later, I'm finally getting my shot at the devil doll. Curtis (who will produce) worked out a terrific sequel idea—and I think this new segment will have the same jolting effect on viewers as the original did. It'll give 'em nightmares.

WIATER: From the screenwriter's perspective, is it easier to compress a novel to "fit it" onto the screen, or is it simpler to "expand" a short story?

NOLAN: Each has its individual problems. A short story is far less complex than a novel and is usually simpler to adapt—providing it's written to fit a short visual format, such as the segments in "Trilogy" or in an anthology show such as "Twilight Zone." (Incidentally, I wrote a segment of "Twilight Zone" for Rod Serling way back when—my first script sale. Sadly, it was never produced.) But if a short story must be expanded into a full-length film, it can be murder to pull off. I was asked the adapt the classic Henry James ghost story, "The Turn of the Screw," for a two-part miniseries. Which meant solid extension of the basic novelette. My main concern was to maintain the spirit and intent of the original—and I believe I managed to do that. At least, the critics thought so.

With a novel, you have this great mass of material, with subplots and multiple characters, that must be compressed for the screen. A book can bend in all kinds of directions, like a pretzel. But a script has to have a direct dramatic arc that must build, crest, and then pay off in the end.

When I adapted Robert Marasco's novel, *Burnt Offerings*, with Dan

Curtis, we had to throw out the first third of the book entirely. We built our arc from that point forward. On the other hand, adapting *Logan's Run* for the screen was fairly simple, since the book was written with a script in mind.

WIATER: But even though you did an adaptation of your own novel, your screenplay was never ultimately used. Why?

NOLAN: This sort of thing happens all the time in Hollywood. MGM *did* purchase the screenplay I wrote with George Clayton Johnson—which was faithful to the novel—but they had this idea of turning the book into a futuristic James Bond–type of film. Our script didn't "fit." During several changes of management, over the eight years MGM owned *Logan's Run*, various executives had various ideas about how to do it. The final shooting script was written by a man who knew nothing whatever about science fiction. Or about the logic of fantasy. Which is why the film was a dramatic failure. But MGM was happy; they made a pot of money from it. Actually, the whole look and thrust and treatment of *Blade Runner* was what should have been done with *Logan's Run*. That was the kind of hard-edged world our novel projected.

WIATER: In terms of other new projects, aren't you currently attempting to adapt a Peter Straub novel to the screen?

NOLAN: Yes, I've been working on *Floating Dragon* to make it a two-hour television movie. And it's a real toughie. I had to eliminate a great deal of material from the book, including a major subplot. In a 2-hour television film, you don't really have 2 hours; because of commercials, you have 97 minutes of actual screen time. And since one script page equals a minute of screen time, we're talking about a 97-page script for *Floating Dragon* from a 515-page novel that has all kinds of characters, viewpoints, and subplots. It becomes a matter of selection and compression.

Sometimes you'll take three or four characters from the novel and combine their characteristics into one person. Let's say for example you have a newspaper editor, a reporter, and a photographer who are working together on a story. You might combine all those into the editor of the newspaper, and make it a small newspaper so that he has to do his own photography and his own research. But you'll use parts of the characters' dialogues and their actions in the novel for your screenplay. So it *is* a compression situation. When I had finished my first long outline I had created new material and compressed old material.

I sent the treatment to Peter in New York and he told me how much he liked it—then presented me with forty-seven pages of notes! [Laughs.] But actually they were "detail" notes, not "basic approach" notes; he was indeed happy with the way I'd handled his book. I kept his notes in mind in doing the final draft of the treatment.

WIATER: No script on it yet?

NOLAN: Not yet. The production company I'm working with has to get a network okay before I can go into script. It may happen, or it may not.

WIATER: Unfortunately, previous films such as *Full Circle* or *Ghost Story* didn't really capture the spirit of Straub's writing. Any other novels of his that interest you?

NOLAN: I tried like hell to adapt *Shadowland*. But I could not lick that book! It's an illusionary novel, and much of it is in the mind of the narrator. I couldn't find a way to translate it visually. The first job of every screenwriter is to say, Can this be visually transformed into script format? Some books can't be done—by me or anyone else. Books are sometimes bought by producers simply because of the name of the author or because they're best-sellers and the producers want to brag, "We have the movie rights to so-and-so."

WIATER: Could you tell your wonderful anecdote about the modern remake of *The Mummy*, which you were hired to undertake in 1977?

NOLAN: This is an absolutely true story—I will not add to or dramatize it in any way—I'll simply tell it exactly as it happened. Producer Stan Sheptner calls me up one day and says, "Look, I've got ABC interested in a new version of *The Mummy*. I'd like you to take a crack at scripting it. Do you know anything about the original movie?"

And I say, "Are you kidding? The Karloff classic? I love that movie! It's *horror noir*." So he says, "Okay, come on over we'll talk about it." So we talk. He says the network executives wanted to bring it back to life via scientific means, and do I think that bombarding the tomb with gamma rays would do it? And I say, "Sure, why the hell not!"

So we have our meeting with ABC, and the network people tell us that pyramid power is "very big right now." (This was during the time that pyramid power was a big fad in this country, like the Hoola Hoop once was.) Can we get pyramid power into this story? And I say, "Absolutely, I can give you pyramid power!" So they say, "Fine, fine! Get to work!"

For weeks Stan and I plot the story. One plotting session after another. Which is incredible, because usually I can wrap these things up in outline form in about a week. But Stan was always coming up with new ideas, and, in addition, the network is saying, "Give us more pyramid power!" And I tell them, "I gave our hero a pyramid-shaped refrigerator, and in his backyard he reads under a pyramid-shaped umbrella. But if you want more, I'll give you more."

Then the network executives say, "We want a really mean, fast mummy. We don't want him drag-footing along like Karloff."

So I say, "Fine. You got it. This guy will move like Mick Jagger."

"And he's gotta be *strong*," they tell us. So I devise a scene where the mummy tears a parking meter right out of the concrete and smashes it across the windshield of this cop car and the car goes across the street and smashes into a dry-goods store. And the mummy skitters off down the street, slowly unraveling as he goes, still wrapped up in his mummy shroud after being brought back to life with the gamma rays.

So the whole concept is getting worse and worse, and I'm starting to think, How did I get ever get into this mess? But I want to get paid for my efforts—I'm only getting $7,500 for this outline, and the real money is on the other end when I get a go-ahead for the actual teleplay. So I persuade myself to stick with it, because at that time, it would have been $25,000 for the script. (This happened thirteen years ago. My rate is now considerably higher.)

Finally, Stan and I go back to the network for the final meeting. The ABC executives tell us, "We love it! You've got pyramid power, the gamma rays, you've got a damn strong mummy, and you've got him moving fast. We love the scene where he kills the blonde in the swimming pool and the cops find this little unwrapped piece of mummy shroud floating in the water. So . . . we have some good news and bad news for you."

Stan and I are sitting there, and we say, "Fine. Give us the good news first." And the executives says, "You have a green light. It's a *go* for scripting." And I say, "That's great!" (I could see the $25,000 worth of sugar plums dancing in the air.) "What's the bad news?"

"The bad news is that we want *one* more change."

And I say, "Hey, no problem. I'm Mr. Change. You name it, I can handle it. What do you want me to do?"

"Drop the mummy."

There was this long silence in the office. Stan and I looked at each other, and I remember saying, "You want to do *King Kong* without the ape?" And this executive says, "We don't *need* the mummy! All we need is the mummy's curse. After they enter the tomb in the first act, all of our characters die, one by one. At the end, there's this big question mark on the screen. Did the curse of the mummy destroy these people, or was it life itself that destroyed them?" The executive turns to me. "What do you think, Nolan?"

And I say, "I think I'll leave." And I did. I walked out and that was that.

Now you see how easy it is to go crazy out here in Hollywood. It's Alice down the rabbit hole. Madness personified.

WIATER: You've been involved in a bit of controversy regarding the so-called splatterpunk school of explicit horror, right?

NOLAN: [Grins.] A bit . . . yeah.

WIATER: Considering how graphic most horror films have become in the past twenty years, where should a screenwriter working in this genre take a moral stance? Would you censor another writer's choice to be so graphic?

NOLAN: Never. I don't believe in censorship in any form. I think there's room for the "splatterpunks" as well as the so-called quiet horror in the genre. Personally, I don't happen to like splattering gore, on a printed page or on the screen. I don't approve of it, but that doesn't mean I'm trying to stop it. I just don't want to have anything to do with it. I've never written a *Friday the 13th*–type film. And I never will.

WIATER: Would you elaborate further on your reasons why?

NOLAN: Well, to me, that kind of horror desensitizes people, instead of frightening them. It's not true horror, it's revulsion. I call it the "vomit bag school." The ax in the brain, and squashed guts in your dinner plate. I think it works against the very principles that I love about horror on the screen and in print.

WIATER: In what way?

NOLAN: I like to be frightened—I don't like to be revolted. I don't enjoy reading a splatterpunk story about a woman being nailed to a cross, about exactly how the nails are being pounded through her breasts. [Grimaces.] In the fright genre you can do a great deal with indirection rather than by desensitizing the audience with overtly graphic, violent acts of horror.

In "Trilogy of Terror II" I only describe the legs of the victim sticking out of the bathtub. We don't have to see the cut throat. It's enough for the coroner to say, "Her throat was cut straight across." We don't have to see it—and we especially don't have to see the throat actually being cut.

The imagination can create greater horrors than we can ever show on the screen or in a book. As a writer, I don't give my readers or viewers any more information than they need. What is primary in creating true horror is the mood and the buildup. And the suspense. It *isn't* the ax in the brain with the blood running down into the guy's mouth and his eyeballs popping out. I prefer to let the reader and the viewer create the ultimate horrors within their minds. The human mind can conjure up far greater terrors than any set designer. Charles Beaumont called it "the fiend in you."

WIATER: So what about the ideals of the splatterpunk school—which says in part that you must go over the edge, that you must shock and revolt the audience to make a truly lasting impression?

NOLAN: I don't think it will prevail. Of course, there will always be violence in some form in horror, because horror and violence go together. Indirectly, at least. But I don't think you're going to have this overt, graphic violence for too much longer. The last *Friday the 13th* and *Nightmare on Elm Street* films didn't do well at all at the box office. Viewers are tired of people being chopped up. Even though you have more freedom on the screen than you do on television, that freedom can be abused and misused. And the same thing is true with the printed word.

WIATER: It does seem odd that a popular writer of horror is saying that contemporary horror has "gone too far."

NOLAN: I want to make one important point. I'm not rigid in my tastes. I can appreciate violence—even overt violence—if it's coupled with really good characterizations, fine stylistic writing, and it's by someone who knows what he or she is doing. A good example would be Joe R. Lansdale's *The Nightrunners*. But most writers just don't know how to handle violence. They think if they nail a woman to a cross, that will do it. With crude, graphic gore you very quickly reach a point of saturation; you're soon looking for something with more depth to it, and I believe that's where the better writers are going to be coming in and staying with us, whether in books or on the screen.

I like to think I'm one of them.

Vincent Price

As discussed in the Introduction to this volume, one of the seminal film experiences in my life was seeing Vincent Price in the 1960 production, *House of Usher*. (Not coincidentally, it was directed by Roger Corman, another boyhood idol of mine.)

In the history of the movies, there have been only a handful of horror superstars: Lon Chaney, Boris Karloff, Bela Lugosi, Peter Lorre, John Carradine, and Vincent Price. Sadly, all are gone except for Price. (And I haven't forgotten British stars Christopher Lee or Peter Cushing. Alas, Lee no longer wishes to discuss his great career in horror films, and Cushing is all but retired from the industry.)

For all intents and purposes, Vincent Price is the last of the great horror stars.

Although he's made a number of films in practically every genre from Westerns to historical romances to mysteries, he will always be most admired for his work in the horror genre. He has done his best work when frightening several generations of moviegoers, from the 1940s right through the early 1980s.

What probably endeared Price to many youngsters (myself included) in the early 1960s was that he always seemed to be having so much *fun* in his movies, no matter how grim his role or how diabolical the circumstances. Born May 27, 1911, Price has made very few films in recent years, seemingly content to do guest appearances on various game shows and in television commercials. Even so, his legacy in the horror genre is undeniably impressive, with Price always adding a touch of class—and sardonic humor—to whatever production he chose to participate in.

On a personal note, I have to add that it was a great honor to have the chance to meet Price when he brought his one-man show to the University of Massachusetts a few years ago. For in his spare time, Price has been lecturing at various colleges and universities for more than thirty-five years. His presentation was equally memorable: "The Villains Still Pursue Me," a history of villainy interwoven with personal anecdotes from his own long career of playing so many great villainous roles.

In person, I found Price to be unfailingly pleasant, good-humored, and more than willing to answer any question asked of him. It was partially because of seeing his Edgar Allan Poe films as a youngster that I eventually decided to pursue a career that would allow me to interview my favorite personalities in the arts. Especially those involved in the arts as dark dreamers, or who possessed dark visions in their souls.

(In preparing this volume, I contacted Price for a new interview. Ironically, his reply was this interview was so complete, he didn't honestly feel he could add anything new to it.)

SELECTED FILMOGRAPHY

The Invisible Man Returns (1940)

House of Wax (1953)

The Tingler (1959)

House On Haunted Hill (1959)

House of Usher (1960)

The Pit and the Pendulum (1961)

Masque of the Red Death (1964)

Tomb of Legia (1965)

Theater of Blood (1972)

The Abominable Dr. Phibes (1971)

Madhouse (1974)

House of Long Shadows (1983)

WIATER: Why so few films in the past decade? The ones you made in the early 1970s, such as *Theater of Blood*, and the two Dr. Phibes movies are considered among your best.

PRICE: I *was* sent some scripts. But the last ones I did make, the ones I really enjoyed like *Theater of Blood*—which I think is a marvelous movie—or the Dr. Phibes films, were send-ups. So everything that was sent to me after that were exactly the same story. Done in a different way or with a different plot, maybe, but significantly the *same* story. Or they were overly violent. Since I'm active in other areas, I didn't really need them—so I didn't do them.

WIATER: You said earlier that today's films are simply no longer suspenseful.

PRICE: I think they've lost a sense of *humor*. And I really think that humor—and I don't mean "funny" or "send-ups"—I just mean they have to have a basic sense of humor. But some of these films are really terrible. They are violent, they have no writing in them at all! They're just a series of technical acts of violence. And I know how they're done, so they don't take me in. [Chuckles.] But one I saw the other night on television with Charles Durning—"The Night of the Scarecrow" I think it was called—and it was mar-vel-ous! I was terrified. I was on the edge of my seat. Yet it was simple; there was very little violence in it at all. It was just this wonderful suspense film, with a kind of sly humor.

WIATER: What are your thoughts on the belief that some critics have where horror films can carry over to inspire acts of horror in real life?

PRICE: I think there is some of that. I don't think there can be any question about it—but it depends on what you mean by seeing a horror picture. My definition of a "horror picture" is *Taxi Driver*. Which I think is one of the most terrifying pictures I ever saw. Or *Marathon Man*—they were really frightening pictures to me. Well, *Taxi Driver* was the inspiration for that little fellow who took a pot-shot at President Reagan. And sometimes I do think they *do* have an influence, but no more influence than the front page of the newspaper. These were valid films, but I think there was too much of it; we got down to a point where we had no humor at all. Everything was so serious, you know? And so boring! There *is* fun in life.

WIATER: You must get a lot of offers for projects still, especially from young people just starting out. Do you ever take on any of these offers?

PRICE: Oh, yeah! I do a lot of them, too. A bunch of kids came up from San Diego one time, with a young Japanese-American boy who was a brilliant photographer. And he showed me some stills he had done of a film called *Annabelle Lee*. It was very simple—but it was so beautiful! He asked me if I would do the narration for it, because they then thought that with a "name" attached to it, the film would get some attention. And they did—they got right up to the Academy Awards with it! [Laughs.] But it was fun to do . . . just fun to do! I think that a person who has been in the business so long is there to be used. I love doing it.

WIATER: But it has to be something very special to pique your interest?

PRICE: Well, I've been in the business nearly fifty years now, and I try not to accept things that aren't a challenge. I mean, I won't do another mystery show or another horror show unless it really is witty. And fun. And scary. And everything is *right*—or I don't want to do it. I don't want any part of it. I just did this summer Gilbert and Sullivan's *Rudigore*. And it was mar-vel-ous! My God, the challenge of doing it with an all-English cast, doing Gilbert and Sullivan in England! It was really wonderful—I've never worked so hard in my life. I was a basket case at the end of it, but it was worth it.

WIATER: So was this the reasoning behind your most recent feature film, *House of the Long Shadows*; the project contained all the desired elements?

PRICE: Yes, I thought it was a reversion, going back to the old-fashioned kind of show. I don't know how it turned out; I hear it's not being too well cut, but I don't know. I haven't seen it.

WIATER: Your co-stars were Peter Cushing, Christopher Lee, and John Carradine. Was it the first time the four of you had all worked together on a project?

PRICE: It was the first time we'd been in a picture together, and we've all done pictures together—except not the four of us at once. It was very much fun, because I enjoy those men, and they enjoy me, and we're great friends. So that's jolly.

WIATER: Of all the legendary horror stars you've worked with over the years, who was your favorite?

PRICE: I think Boris Karloff. He had a marvelous sense of humor, and he always struck me as very funny, because there was that funny sort of lisp he had. And that strange complexion—which was green—he was a funny man. He was always very sinister, but at the same time he struck me as being hysterically funny, so I adored working with him. I loved him as a person, too.

WIATER: Do you see the Price family becoming another acting family like John Carradine and his sons, who are all actors?

PRICE: Oh my God, I haven't got that many kids! [Laughs.] No, John is really extraordinary—all of his kids have done so well. Very talented. My daughter is a college student and loves theater, but I don't know if she's going to do it or not professionally. My son is a writer. And he's a very good poet—he's been published all over the world. The money you make from poetry, let me tell you, you'd starve in the first three weeks. I asked him one time, "Doesn't it bother you?" And he said, "I'm the richest man I know." And he is—he lives his life the way he wants to live it. He edits a magazine now that's a very successful little magazine. But it's just constant work. He works harder than anyone I know, for less pay. But he's *happy*.

WIATER: You co-authored a book with your son called, appropriately enough, *Monsters*. It seemed like a work long overdue, since your previous books have been about cooking or art, and not about this aspect of your career that you're best identified with.

PRICE: Yes, but it was a very serious book that my son and I did about the things in life and in mythology and religion—in all history of things that are larger than life—"the monster." Chaos. The Leviathan. These things that were there right from the beginning of folklore and mythology and that had to be overcome by man. The kind of subliminal fears that people have of things larger than life. The dinosaur, King Kong—they're very obvious ones, but it was really a much deeper book than that. I think the publishers—who finally went out of business—were very sloppy in their handling of it. They wanted it to be a kind of facetious book, to be about movie monsters and everything else. Well, there have been dozens of those, and we didn't want to write another one. It got very good notices, but it wasn't the kind of book the publishers wanted, so they didn't push it.

WIATER: Then do you see yourself as representing the end of an era in terms of horror stars? There doesn't seem to be any "son of Kar-

loff'' or ''son of Price'' around to carry on the tradition of great
screen villains.

PRICE: Oh, I think there are! Bruce Dern, for instance, is a marvelous
heavy; he's wonderful at being mean. Oh God, can he be mean and
nasty! He could be wonderful in this kind of picture if he ever wanted
to make one.

WIATER: Your villains, especially in the Edgar Allan Poe adaptations,
were always both terribly cruel, yet terribly tragic figures.

PRICE: That's what I tried to explain in my show: ''that there but for
the grace of God go I.'' The most interesting of the villains are the
ones who have been *made* villains through circumstance.

WIATER: Like my personal favorite, Roderick Usher in *House of
Usher*?

PRICE: Yes, like Roderick Usher. If you lived in that, *you'd* be very
strange!

WIATER: What do you think of the recent radio series, the ''CBS
Mystery Theater'' with host E. G. Marshall?

PRICE: The only thing I have against the E. G. Marshall ones was
that they were a little old-fashioned. They were sort of consciously
old-fashioned, as if, here we are: we're listening to an old medium.
Radio is *not* an old medium. It's a very present medium. I do a series
in London called ''The Price of Fear'' for World Service on BBC,
and the listening audience is a hundred million people, which ain't
bad! [Laughs.] These stories are written by the very best writers in
England, and they're all written especially for this series. I was sent
two tapes before I left London, and they are incredible. All the top
actors of England do these stories. And I've been the host, the connection between them.

WIATER: I've heard more than once that you feel *Theater of Blood* is
one of the best films of your entire career?

PRICE: When I did *Theater of Blood*, we had Michael Hordern, who
had just been made a knight, we had Harry Andrews, who's considered the greatest supporting Shakespearean actor in the business, we
had Jack Hawkins . . . every single person in that company was a
huge star. They came out from plays they were doing in the West
End, only about an hour's drive to the movie studio. They did their
day's work, and the movie was shot around them. I was the star of
the picture, and I would have to stay late to do all the fill-in scenes
so that so-and-so could go back and do his play in the National
Theatre! Which is bloody well right, you know? [Chuckles.] It's more
important that I should have them working with me, than to do a little
extra work for the privilege of having them. Diana Rigg. My wife,

Coral Browne . . . incredible people! Twelve of the greatest actors in England.

WIATER: What was Diana Rigg like to work with? She's become a cult figure because of the 1960s television series *The Avengers*.

PRICE: I loved her. She's marvelous.

WIATER: Yet why have you occasionally chosen to work in projects so obviously beneath your talents, such as the 1965 fiasco, *Dr. Goldfoot and the Bikini Machine*?

PRICE: *Dr. Goldfoot and the Bikini Machine* was one of the funniest scripts I ever read in my life. It was a musical. They cut out *all* the music. They shot the musical numbers, because it was Frankie Avalon and myself, you know, and it was a very funny picture. Then the producers got so terrified of it that they destroyed it. You have no control over that, at all.

I did a film one time called *Up in Central Park* with Deanna Durbin, who was the greatest star in the business at that time. And they cut out all the music—and it's a musical comedy! They cut out one of the biggest hit songs of all time. Now, *I* didn't say, "Cut it out."

Sometimes you do dogs. [Pauses.] I did one in Italy once—mainly because I wanted to go to Italy—and also it was not a bad script. But—they *lost the soundtrack*. They had never kept a complete script. There were seven people in the cast: two of them spoke Tiawanese, two of them spoke German. I spoke English, and the rest of them spoke Italian. So they had to get lip-readers to look at the scenes to find out what the hell we were supposed to be saying! Because they lost the soundtrack *and* the script. Now, what do you do about *that*?

WIATER: It must also be frustrating to have a film you've worked on barely released, or released in a different form than you'd imagined. For example, it doesn't seem as if the British film you did with Peter Cushing called *Madhouse* ever played widely, if at all, in the United States.

PRICE: I know it . . . it's now just coming out in England, almost ten years later. Don't ask. It's sometimes terribly disappointing. You can never tell—it's a business. It should be an art form, but it's a business. You just never know.

WIATER: There've been several 3-D movies in the past few years. Do you see the form ever becoming as popular again as it was when you made *House of Wax* in the 1950s?

PRICE: I don't really think so. The one that's made the most money of them all was *House of Wax*, which made millions of dollars, and still does every time they rerelease it. And people take their kiddies to see something they're never going to see again because you might already wear glasses, and then you've got to wear 3-D glasses on your glasses. The funniest thing about making *House of Wax* was the director was a man with one eye—so he never saw the 3-D effect. You have to have two eyes going very well to be able to see 3-D, and he had one glass eye. He never saw a thing!

WIATER: Any chance of an autobiography? *Vincent Price* by Vincent Price?

PRICE: No! [Laughs.] Everybody's written one. You know, anybody can write anything they want to about you. Somebody did a thing called *Vincent Price Unmasked*. I don't know what it's about; nobody asked me about it. They can write anything they want about you. I wrote an autobiography—*I Like What I Know* in 1959—but it was not what I've *done*, but what I've *seen*, and that to me was a much more interesting way of doing it. I might like to write one, but not just about my life in the movies.

WIATER: Any great villains you feel you've missed out on playing onstage or in the movies?

PRICE: Not necessarily, no. Oh—I suppose so. King Lear. As I've said, we've always got Shakespeare.

WIATER: Is there anything besides acting that you're most proud of in your career?

PRICE: That I've done everything. I've done musical work, I do a lot of symphony work, I do a lot of poetry reading and records of poetry. I do college lecturing, which is very much a part of my life. A lot of different things. I know it makes people highly suspicious because we're a nation of specializers. But I couldn't care less; that's the way I wanted to live my life, and the way I have. I think my life and career have all

been a whole to me.

I found that the cookbook that I wrote really has been a marvelous introduction to another world, an introduction that I wouldn't ever have had, had I not written that book. A book I wrote on American art has given me an entre to places I would never have had, had I not written *that* book. I'm a very lucky fellow. But I worked for it— very hard.

WIATER: Have you ever heard this quote from Roger Corman about your work? "The keynote of his art lies, I believe, in his uncanny ability to embody and project the effects of mental aberration. He is rightly noted for his speaking voice, and suave, polished presence through which he can convey eerie graduations of a sinister motivating force."

PRICE: My God, did he say that? [Laughs.] I couldn't agree with him more!

Sam Raimi

Melinda Sue Gordon/Universal Pictures

O ne of the personality traits most likable about a young turk director like Sam Raimi is that he is so affable. Unlike most directors in the film industry, who are insulated from their fans, Raimi makes no hesitation that he sincerely appreciates his fans and that they have been instrumental in making his only two horror films cult favorites. Raimi is included here because he is definitely one of the directors to watch in the 1990s, especially since his first two horror films—*The Evil Dead* and *Evil Dead 2: Dead by Dawn* are so highly regarded by fans and *cineteratologists* alike. (Even though *Evil Dead 2* is not so much a sequel as it is a bigger-budgeted remake of the first motion picture.)

A native of Detroit, Raimi is now all of thirty years old. He has only three independent features to his credit so far, the first two never seeing release as major features, with the third film, *Crime Wave*—a bizarre comedy-thriller—virtually having no theatrical release whatsoever.

Like his colleagues John Carpenter and George Romero, Raimi has made a name for himself by mounting his first features totally outside the traditional Hollywood studio structure. Although the *Evil Dead* films are clearly hindered by their very low budgets, the degree of energy and sheer creative output is nothing short of stupendous. Raimi is a burgeoning talent who appears clearly to be destined to be a director of highly stylized, highly charged motion pictures.

For the moment, his future looks bright. In spite of what may appear to be a poor track record as a filmmaker, Raimi has since broken into the big time in Hollywood: co-writing and directing a major studio production for Universal Pictures entitled *Darkman*.

I met with Sam Raimi while he was in postproduction for *Darkman*. Incidentally, next on his list is another independent production, the eagerly awaited *Evil Dead 3*.

SELECTED FILMOGRAPHY

The Evil Dead (1983)
Crime Wave (1985)
Evil Dead 2: Dead by Dawn (1987)
Darkman (1990)

WIATER: It appears you've graduated to the big time with your current project, *Darkman*. What can you tell me about it?

RIAMI: It was produced by my partner, Robert Tappert, who also produced *Evil Dead*, *Evil Dead 2*, and *Crime Wave*. We're currently in the editing stage. We've just received a rough cut and showed it to Universal. They were pleased, and now we are taking it to a finer cut, with a few more weeks of cutting. I've been lucky enough to acquire the services of Danny Elfman, whom I'm a big fan of, to do the music. He can really add a lot of soul and character to scenes that might just have a trace of it. He really brings it out, makes it very full, and realizes the dream that you're trying to convey.

WIATER: I understand you had a ninety-day shooting schedule, which is fairly lengthy for any motion picture being made nowadays.

RAIMI: You've got it right. It was about ninety days, which is a very long shoot. But this picture has so many locations that burned a lot of time, traveling to and from different locations, set dressing it, lighting it, and a lot of moves, packing and unpacking equipment. . . . But it went very well; we shot it on budget and on schedule. It was shot primarily in Los Angeles, although some of the miniatures were shot in San Francisco. In this picture I had a chance to experiment with miniatures in ways that I haven't before, composing them with live action photography. I had a chance to do some multiple element, blue screen composite shots using more elements than I ever had in the past—that was interesting!

I also had a chance to work with Intervision. That's a matting process using mirrors and holdout painted mattes. The goal of it is to put your characters into situations that either would be too dangerous to actually shoot them in or maybe a situation that couldn't really exist. Or you couldn't build it because it might be too big and too expensive. In *Darkman* there's a final confrontation between Darkman and the villain on top of high steel, eighty stories above the city on a partially completed skyscraper, where they duke it out. Because it was too dangerous, I had to resort to a technique of faking it, and Intervision had the most opportunities to fake things a lot of different ways. So we went with it and it worked out really well.

WIATER: Now that you're playing with the big boys, so to speak, by working for Universal, how did that change your cinematic vision? Or was it just a case that you had bigger and better toys to play with, but essentially little changed with your filmmaking techniques?

RAIMI: A lot of things *did* change. First of all, there's a lot more input from a studio than there is from independent sources of finance, as far as the script itself. So this script went through twelve different drafts before it was actually made, and a lot of writers were brought on. So it probably wouldn't have been the same movie even from the script had I made it independently. Certainly not that number of writers would have worked on it, nor would there have been as many drafts.

So you really have to please the people who are financing and distributing the picture as much as yourself, it appears, when working with a studio. At least that's the way it is in my case, where I don't have that much power. I'm a small-fry filmmaker so I can't tell the studio what to do, I just have to play by their rules. But I knew that going in, so it wasn't bad at all.

WIATER: But to go from low-budget, independent features to being carried by a major studio does have its benefits in the trade-off, no?
RAIMI: The additional monies that come with making a studio picture helped. So I was able to work with a higher quality actor than I'm used to working with because I could afford them. The same for all technicians—usually I work with people that I can afford and like. This time I could work with supposedly the best in the business. That was wonderful.

I don't mean to put down anyone that I've worked with in the past. I just mean that it's nice to be able to afford supposedly Hollywood's finest craftsmen to surround yourself with. A director's job is just to direct the different departments and the actors, and it really boils down to the quality of the person you have working on the picture.
WIATER: But it says something for your talents that Universal is willing to risk a major theatrical release with you at the helm.
RAIMI: It's a good break, it's different. Most important, I've only made pictures that have been unsuccessful stateside, theatrically. I had made two pictures that were unrated and they could only get very limited releases. So working with Universal I was I hoping to tap into their giant machine of distribution and marketing to really get my picture off for the first time. This is picture number four for me as a director, and I've never had a real release yet. So this time I hope they will give me a full-blown release, and I'll play cards with the big boys. [Laughs.] Then I'm very happy to return to my quiet life.
WIATER: I understand your next project will be *Evil Dead 3*, and that it'll be an independent production, as were the first two films. Then you'll be back to having almost total control once again, won't you?
RAIMI: Yes, and that's very satisfying, creatively. When you do exactly what you think the audience wants to see or exactly what pleases you. See, that's a tough enough equation for me as it is. What *do* they want to see? Well, I have no idea—I'll just take the best guess I have.

The toughest part of the equation come when you work with a studio, and you're dealing with not just what you think the audience wants to see—which is already an impossible guess—but then you have to deal with what another group of people—the executives—think the audience wants to see. And even though they can be very intelligent people, I'm already dealing with so many guesses in the equation that it just adds another unknown factor. It's difficult to argue your point so far, because you can only be sure that the audience wants to see what you had in mind versus what the studio executives think the audience would like to see. You're always talking hypotheticals, like "They think they want this" versus "What I think they want, which is this."

WIATER: Given the fact that your previous features weren't box office successes, why do you think Universal hired you then?

RAIMI: Well, I believe that they enjoyed the craftsmanship of *Evil Dead* and *Evil Dead 2*, and made the conclusion that, had those movies not been basically X-rated pictures and had the subject matter been more "mainstream," as they call it, they would have been huge financial successes. I think they felt that I could make a reasonably okay picture for them if the story matter was acceptable to the mainstream audience that they go for. So I pitched a story to them, about a man who could be anyone, who could change his faces, and they liked it.

They said, "Great, write it as a treatment," and I wrote it. They said, "Great, write it as a script." They said, "Great, write it again as a script." I wrote it again as a script and again and again and again until after twelve times they said, "Great." Then I said, "Okay, I have to make it or leave now."

At that point they let me direct the picture.

WIATER: So you purposely were trying to make a "maintream picture," rather than stretch the boundaries of the horror genre? Make a larger audience aware of what you can offer?

RAIMI: Exactly. It was difficult for me to attempt because I usually go for more what I like, and this time I am sort of second guessing the audience a little bit. I'm trying to please them specifically, which is strange. It's probably where you go wrong. But who knows, I'm out on a limb. [Chuckles.]

I've never made a love story before, and this is a love story. I've never made a movie that has real characters in it, and that's what I'm trying to do here. So it's very different for me. Also, the movies I've made in the past are very low on plot, and very high on thrill and chill. So this one is just the opposite, it's low on style, thrill, and chill, and it's high on plot, story, and characters. See, I wanted to make a movie where the audience could feel something for the main character, which I've never been able to do. So it's kind of a big, bold experiment for me, although it probably seems very common for the average filmmaker, what I'm going to be doing with *Darkman*.

WIATER: Do you think you've finally "made it" in Hollywood? That you've reached the point where, career-wise, you're living out your wildest dream?

RAIMI: [Pauses.] God, I don't know anyone who has ever reached that point in any profession, in any position in their life. But I do feel satisfied creatively. I've got my bills paid for the first time this year. [Laughs.] I'm not in debt, so I can create—and that is my wildest dream, I guess.

WIATER: For a lot of people, that *is* living out one's wildest dream— in the sense that the traditional American success story is to be out of debt and doing just what you want for a living.

RAIMI: Yes, it's true. I've at least bought myself a little breathing space, and I now have time to write and create films, which has always been a great dream of mine to do that. But I have a lot of dreams. I want to travel in outer space. I want to create a solar energy company. I've got a lot of things I want to do.

WIATER: But you're happy, overall, with your first experience working with a major studio? Not everyone is.

RAIMI: This was a very satisfying experience for me. I felt that the entire cast and crew were there pushing for this film. It's great to be at the helm of this big machine. It's so big in fact that sometimes, even when I no longer want it to go forward, it's terrible weight moves nonetheless.

WIATER: Even though you've yet to have a big commercial success, you know that your films have attracted a fairly substantial cult following. There are people who will go to any picture that has your name on it, just as they would with a George Romero or a Tobe Hooper. How does that affect you?

RAIMI: I don't know if I'm in the same class as Tobe Hooper or George Romero, actually. They've got great bodies of work behind them in the horror field. I've just made two pictures. These guys are the masters of horror. I like to refer to myself as "the apprentice of suspense" because I feel it's not too bold a title yet. [Chuckles.] But I'm on my way. If I keep making horror pictures, then I'll be "the journeyman of fear" and "the next master of terror."

WIATER: Do you recall the first horror movie you ever saw as a kid?

RAIMI: I always had an interest in what they were all about. My sister brought me to the first one that just *terrified* me. She snuck me into *Night of the Living Dead*. It was playing on a double bill with *Freaks*. I was so terrified, so utterly freaked out at this show, that it definitely left a lasting impression. In fact, George Romero's work has greatly influenced the first—and therefore all—the *Evil Dead* movies. It's in a small cabin, isolated. A few people are battling against the undead. . . . So his *Living Dead* left a very big impression on me.

I really didn't fall in love with horror until after I made *Evil Dead*. At the time, I had been making comedies in college with my brother Ivan and my partners Robert Tappert and Bruce Campbell. I made a lot of comedies; I loved comedies, loved Jerry Lewis, and we wanted to make our first feature. So Robert determined that the best way to get a return on our investors' money—if we were really going to go out and get investors—was to make a horror picture.

Back then they were always playing at the drive-ins. So we tried to learn how to make a horror picture. I sat through about two months of horror movies at the drive-in: cheap Italian ones, really bad ones . . . I saw all these movies and then tried to make one myself. I made a little one in Super-8 called *Clockwork*, which was a five-minute movie. That worked okay: it had a scare in it and some suspense. Then I wrote the *Evil Dead* screenplay and a thirty-minute version of that called *Within the Woods* in Super-8. Then I made *Evil Dead*, the feature.

But I still didn't like horror films until after I started to watch more of them. I really like *Halloween*. And then I started to appreciate the art and craft of making a horror picture, and started to like them more and more since making *Evil Dead*.

WIATER: So I take it you weren't like John Carpenter, who has been hooked on horror and science fiction movies ever since he can remember? Who read *Famous Monsters of Filmland* as a youngster?

RAIMI: I didn't, but had I been exposed to the right movies, I probably would have. But now I'm into them. I was just a latecomer.

WIATER: Your two *Evil Dead* movies are pretty rough in spots, and you're not afraid to "push the envelope" in terms of gory special effects and bloodletting. What is your statement to those who say that these movies are bad for young people to see, that explicit horror films like these can only have a negative influence?

RAIMI: Horror films themselves make such a strong statement that I don't really have a problem with people saying that young people shouldn't see them, that they do "bad things." But I don't agree with that. I think that a story is a story, and a film can certainly be made to make violence seem like something that people would want to emulate. Or it can be made in such a way so that it creates a feeling of horror, fear from the act of violence.

Well, most horror films I know have violence in them, but it's used to create fear for the audience. So it's not something you want to emulate. I don't really agree with most of the criticism against horror films. But I think they certainly have a right to criticize them, and certainly horror films make such a strong statement that they deserve criticism and examination. It's always good to examine what's happening.

My only problem is when a country will determine that a picture has to be banned. I've had *Evil Dead* banned in the United Kingdom. It was a very big video seller in 1984, and the constables came in and raided all the video stores that had it and found it obscene. Well,

I had to go to Leeds to testify—they were going to throw the distributor in jail. [Angrily.] Well, *Evil Dead* is just a fantasy ghost story, and to put someone in jail would be a real crime. It would be absurd!

So I went to England to testify, to try to explain that the real crime is a small group of government officials determining for their citizens what they can—and cannot—watch. I mean, this is the old book burning. This is terrible censorship! It is mind control and I tried to explain to the journalists in England that the real danger was not horror films, but a group of people determining what the rest of the nation was capable of seeing and incapable of seeing. *Who are these people to determine that?* And if it has such a strong and terrible effect on the viewer, maybe once these censors saw *Evil Dead* they were no longer capable of making a rational decision, if their logic holds.

For myself, I like the experience of horror films. They give me a chance to laugh at my fears and investigate them and survive them, even if it's somewhat removed from the actual experience as I'm watching a film and I'm safe in a theater. But I always feel invigorated after watching a horror film.

WIATER: Isn't that odd? [Laughs.] I always feel so much better about things after watching one, too.

RAIMI: Yes—my life isn't so bad, and thank God I survived! [Laughs.]

WIATER: Unfortunately for us, the people who attack horror movies are the ones who have never tried to appreciate or understand them. To me, it's like the argument censors used to try on *Playboy* magazine: it doesn't matter how many fine articles or stories are in it—it also contains photographs of nude women and therefore must be pornographic or at the very least sexist. The sad fact is, the people who most loudly denounce it are the ones who have never picked up an issue.

RAIMI: Actually, my policy is that if it has nude women in it, it must be good.

WIATER: But it's frustrating to try and comprehend the minds of people who seem to loathe the horror genre so intensely. The idea being, if it's horror, then it has to be bad. Or at least antisocial.

RAIMI: It's tough to say what man needs. [Pauses.] I know that in early times, man was chased by saber-toothed tigers and other beasts, and he was hunted himself by other men. Adrenaline and fear were a part of his everyday life, thunderstorms, wild animals, what have you. Now in this modern, antiseptic world there's very little fear. And that's fine, I'm glad we understand things more. But who's to say that fear shouldn't be a part of our lives? That adrenaline pumping shouldn't be a weekly experience? Maybe it's an important physiological function of the human body?

Horror films are *great*. Maybe they provide a release that is lacking in our modern-day society, in our antiseptic world. Maybe they allow us to experience what we really need to experience—a little primal fear. Maybe they allow us to stay in touch with ourselves a little more.

WIATER: You're not a scientist, you're not a sociologist, you're a filmmaker; can't you consider that perhaps horror films are causing some subconscious damage to the mass consciousness of the moving-going public?

RAIMI: I think that as long as people are aware of the difference between a fantasy film and reality, then I don't believe that's true. I mean, I could hear a hundred ghost stories personally and I still don't kill a spider in the house. I still catch it in a Kleenex and let it out the front door. I don't feel a vicious desire to crush the spider, nor do I feel that it is a meaningless creature once I've seen a few horror films. I still feel that this spider has a right to live and I let it out of the house. Unless he's in my food container. Any insect caught within a food container, its penalty is death! [Laughs.]

I can only go by my own personal experience, but I don't think that I've been numbed to everyday situations of pain or violence because I've seen a lot of horror films. In fact, how long has the horror film been around, nearly a century? And there's probably more peace on earth than ever before—more communication than ever before. I'm not trying to draw a line between horror movies and peace in the world—but if times were worse right now, if it was a dark time for humanity, I'm sure that people who are against horror films would point to them as another instigator for the troubled times in which we live. They go for any argument they can!

But in fact I think that humanity is on the upswing, becoming more sensitive than ever. If anything, maybe we are living out our dangerous and terrible desires through films, so that in reality we can function as peaceful, more balanced individuals.

WIATER: What do you feel about some of the statements made against your *Evil Dead* films where—even though your male characters are killed and mutilated—you clearly had no hesitation in killing and mutilating your female characters. In other words, do you feel that there is some sort of unwritten rule that almost all horror films have to show women, preferably attractive nude women, being killed?

RAIMI: No, I don't think it's required. In fact, there was a trend toward killing beautiful women in the movies— "It's a horror movie, so we have to kill them." But for me, I was aware of the trend, and when writing the script for *Evil Dead*, I very specifically tried to make the women not the victims but rather the monsters. Where women are possessed by these evil spirits, and they are in fact the tormenters of mankind. So I tried to flip it around—make the man the one who is running around like a crazed banshee, screaming.

So I tried to do something in the opposite vein, which actually George Romero had done years before anyway. And I'm sure it had been done before him. But I don't like watching women get killed on film. Something about that isn't entertaining to me.

WIATER: Any last comments about your chosen career as a creator of dark visions?

RAIMI: I like horror films. Not only because they are scary and fun, but the world of horror offers to a filmmaker a great world in which to experiment with cinematic techniques and lighting and sound effects, because you're dealing with a world, not that we know, but the world that lies between the spaces. So it's a great canvas to paint an imaginary picture. You can move the camera as a demon might move across the room, and you can let it seem like Hell itself has erupted. You can really go crazy, artistically, with a horror film. That's really why filmically I'm attracted to them. Horror films offer so many opportunities for the aspiring craftsman who is trying to craft a picture; they offer so many artistic opportunities, too.

George A. Romero

Eric Caidin

Although George A. Romero is undoubtedly one of the most effective horror directors working today, he also happens to be one of the nicest to meet with in person. In spite of a number of successful movies in the genre, he will probably forever be known for his first feature, the 1968 classic, *Night of the Living Dead*. Independently made on a shoestring and produced in his hometown of Pittsburgh, the film has gone on to influence an entire generation of horror filmmakers.

Just as important, the fifty-year-old Romero is also known as a fiercely independent filmmaker—in more ways than one. Although he has been tempted to "go Hollywood," he has in fact made only two films that were directly distributed by major studios: *Creepshow* and *Monkeyshines*. For the most part he has worked outside of the Hollywood "system," preferring to make his own movies in his own way, most often still in Pittsburgh.

Even if he is best known for his *Dead* trilogy (which includes *Dawn of the Dead* and *Day of the Dead*), Romero has directed several other influential films, such as his modern-day interpretation of vampirism, *Martin*, and the little-seen *The Crazies*. As a screenwriter, Romero has also been involved with several popular movies, including *Creepshow 2* and *Tales from the Darkside: The Movie*. He always seems to be working.

In spite of his continuing success as a consummate film-maker (he also has worked as cinematographer and editor on several of his films), Romero takes his enviable position in the field with an easygoing grace. Like his friend and colleague Stephen King, Romero is very much aware of his good fortune and, if anything, is too modest about his considerable accomplishments. A fine book on his career is Paul R. Gagne's *The Zombies That Ate Pittsburgh: The Films of George A. Romero*.

I spoke with Romero while he was working as executive producer (with friend Tom Savini directing) on the color remake to *Night of the Living Dead*.

SELECTED FILMOGRAPHY

Night of the Living Dead (1968)

The Crazies (1973)

Martin (1978)

Dawn of the Dead (1979)

Creepshow (1982)

Day of the Dead (1985)

Monkeyshines (1988)

Two Evil Eyes (1990)

WIATER: Considering the original film is now regarded as a bona fide classic, why remake *Night of the Living Dead* now?

ROMERO: I never wanted to do it; I just sort of went along with the people who own the property. John Russo and I own the literary rights, and there's a group of shareholders who comprise Image Ten, the company that produced the original picture. Most of these people are still alive, and they've been ripped off a million different ways on the original film. And they decided they wanted to do a remake before someone else did it. So basically I just went along with it— the way I went along with the colorized version. Then I decided to be more involved rather than not, and wrote the screenplay.

But it certainly is not something that I wanted to do, or wanted to direct; it's something that I've done already. That's pretty much it. Hopefully everybody can make a buck on it.

WIATER: At the same time you're working as executive producer on *Night of the Living Dead*, you're completing the screenplay for your next assignment, as writer and director of Stephen King's *The Dark Half*. How much time did you have to script the adaptation?

ROMERO: Well, I actually wrote it in finished form—that is, in the word processor in script format—in about three weeks. I kept notebooks on it. The standard screenplay commission is three months; you can get more or you can get less. Nobody breaks your knees! [Laughs.] So it's usually whatever it takes to do right, especially if it's a fairly important project. I find that when adapting something, three months is enough. It's a lot more difficult to write something from scratch; it takes a lot longer. With an adaptation, it's pretty easy: somehow all those little switches inside your head that say, Well, it's not me, I won't blame me for this change, click in, and you breeze through it a little easier.

WIATER: We first met over a decade ago, and at that time, I had to ask the question, "When are you going to make Stephen King's *The Stand*?" Forgive me if I repeat that question, but people are still hoping to see that happen. Will it?

ROMERO: Beats me. The problem is, I don't own it anymore. My ex-partner, Richard Rubenstein, owns all the properties that we had owned together. He owns them as Laurel Entertainment, Inc. Theoretically, I was scheduled to do *The Stand*. I was also scheduled to do *Pet Sematary*, but that didn't work out because there was a scheduling conflict with *Monkeyshines*. I still would have liked to have done *Pet*

Sematary, but it wasn't meant to be. And as far as *The Stand*, I don't know.

I know that Richard has been having screenplays done, but I haven't seen any of them. The screenplay that I saw last was one that Steve had done, and I did a little bit of cut and paste on it. I didn't write anything, but I did a little editing work just to give Steve my thoughts on what we could take out and how we could move things around a little bit. I forget what we came out with, but it was long. I think we came out with around 150 pages, maybe 160 pages. At that time of course that was what was preventing it from being made. No one wants to make a long movie that's going to cost $40 million.

WIATER: Yet that's not really a ridiculous amount, considering the epic scope of the novel.

ROMERO: Steve and I always maintained that it wouldn't necessarily cost $40 million; that if we could do it efficiently with a generous schedule, and with a cast that wasn't costing us $800,000 a week, that we could probably do it for a lot less. But unfortunately what happens with movies is that there's going to be a certain amount of money invested. And the producers feel they have to protect that investment by investing even more in things like stars . . . and so you know it just mushrooms. Maybe somehow Richard will be able to get it made. If he gets a deal on it, maybe he'll even talk to me about doing it, but's he not obligated to, legally. So I don't know. It could well go off without my being attached to it at all, and probably will.

WIATER: Then I'm curious to know how you became involved with *Tales from the Darkside: The Movie*, which was a Laurel production. For that film you adapted King's short story, "The Cat from Hell."

ROMERO: I had nothing to do with that film whatsoever. Right after the original *Creepshow*, Steve agreed to do *Creepshow II*. Not to do the screenplay, but he contributed five stories. A couple of them were published stories, "The Cat from Hell" and "The Raft," and a couple of them were just idea sketches that he had. From that material I wrote a screenplay for *Creepshow II*, which was composed of five stories and a wraparound, just like the original *Creepshow*.

And of course I was working for the company, Laurel, so they owned it. I imagine they had the same deal with Steve where they just owned the material. So when Richard finally made *Creepshow II*, he only used three of the stories, so now he has two stories, just sitting in the drawer, that he owns. So he put one in *Tales from the Darkside: the Movie*, and as I understand it, he has the other one in a screenplay for *Creepshow III*. So he gets his mileage from this stuff.

WIATER: You've written the screenplays for practically all your motion pictures. Have you developed a standard method for writing scripts over the past twenty years that always just works for you?

ROMERO: I find that what happens to me—particularly as I get older—is that I just don't have the energy to devote the whole block of time, the whole three or four months scheduled, completely to it. I often thought about writing a novel, but then I realize what a commitment that is. Screenplays are in fact about one-third the size. On the other hand, they do need more careful outlining, because they are much more concise. They're not as forgiving in terms of letting you roam.

So I find that it's a process that's sort of like doing a jigsaw puzzle. It requires a certain period of really concentrated thought, which has more to do with organizing and trying to figure out what's really important. Every writer goes through that. Then the actual physical writing—particularly dialogue—what I do is usually leave all the dialogue until the end and try not to think about it; to try not to constipate the dialogue. I find that if I get preconceived speeches in my head, then I start refining them and pretty soon they sound like people.

So I let that go as sort of that final coat, which is that three- or four-week period when I actually put it into the proper format in the word processor. That's working from notes and whatever else, little thoughts and ideas. I have a portable tape recorder in my car. And I'll just jot things. This has probably evolved through convenience, because I just want more time with my family. I find that when I am in the final stage of writing I very often actually have to move out of the house. We have two houses, so I'm lucky that way. But if we're all in Florida, I'll just go and rent a joint on the beach and sit there and eat Spam until I'm finished.

WIATER: Do you keep making horror movies because you truly love the genre? Or do you keep making horror movies because it's a pretty safe bet it will keep you in Spam?

ROMERO: Well, it's a little deeper than that. I mean, I don't think anyone will hire me for other genres. My wife and I bought the rights to a novel, which is nonhorror, and I wrote the screenplay, which I really like a lot. I've gotten a lot of phone calls from people saying, "Gee, that's a wonderful screenplay," but that's about as far as it goes.

Now, there are a few groups that have faith in me and will give me a shot at other things. I'm hoping that one of these days we will make one of those projects into a film, rather than just a commissioned screenplay. But the answer to that is that people are not generally going to call me up unless it's horror related. Although, since *Monkeyshines*, they will now call me up with suspense stories or with real-life, nonsupernatural, nonhorror thrillers. Aside from that, I do love it. I really *do* love it! [Laughs.] It's been my ticket to ride. And with horror, you can tell parables, and that's a lot harder to do with a straight thriller.

It's much harder to take a parable and squeeze it into a real-life story. Whereas with supernatural material you can make anything happen so as to fit in the notion that you want to fit between the lines. You can go back and forth between the text and subtext much more freely! It's a bonus in this genre, which I rather freely have done over the years.

WIATER: Wes Craven has also stated that he finds it all but impossible to get a project underway unless it's more or less directly horror-related. He also would like to stretch his talents, but he's stereotyped by the industry.

ROMERO: It's pretty frustrating. I do find myself pretty angry and much less civil than I used to be when faced with those situations. It's just not worth it anymore.

WIATER: But overall, are you satisfied with your work? You've pretty much thumbed your nose at the Hollywood establishment and, like Frank Sinatra, been able to say "I did it my way," haven't you?

ROMERO: Every week you get some new understanding about how some part of this business works. I'm sort of happy with my view of things, of the business side of it. I'm very unhappy with some of my work. I don't think that I have yet made a film where I've had the money or time to execute it exactly the way I would want to execute it. I'd like to do that sometime.

WIATER: Any film that still stands out as perhaps coming closest to your initial vision?

ROMERO: Strangely, a little film I made called *Martin*, which was a $275,000 production, comes closest in terms of the finished product to what my conception was going in. That's because all of us were working on that out of dedication. It was one of those little films that we went out with nine people and made a movie. It didn't matter if we had to shoot at night, we shot at night. We were just there to get the movie done. I had the most freedom on that film that I've had on any of the other ones.

WIATER: Yet you've had some fairly decent budgets on a few of your projects, haven't you?

ROMERO: *Creepshow* was the most expensive film that I've made to date. Actually, I guess *Monkeyshines* was a little more expensive. But in both of those, there were external factors that kept me from being able to do exactly what I wanted to do. In the case of *Creepshow*, we could have used a lot more money, and even though it had a very long production schedule, it needed more time to do optical effects.

It wasn't quite there; we came close, but it wasn't one hundred percent. In *Monkeyshines*, it was mostly the monkeys, and again the time to execute it properly. *Monkeyshines* is pretty successful in terms of what it was supposed to be. But we lost so much time and energy to the monkeys, and to other external factors such as disagreements amongst the producers; none of it was bad intentioned, but it got in the way.

And when you lose time, you lose time and never get it back again.
WIATER: How would you describe your style as a director?
ROMERO: I haven't been able to define my style yet, and I think that in my mind I'm always experimenting. In every film that I make there are sequences in them that are different, where I'll try something new. I think I'm a stylist more than anything else. You can recognize Alfred Hitchcock's style the way you can recognize Bach, you know. He probably *is* the Bach of filmmakers! To me, Hitchcock wrote the textbook on suspense cinema. Everyone says that my style is a lot like Hitchcock's, and it's funny because I don't think it is. I think it's more like Orson Welles's, and I don't mean to elevate myself to that level. I'm not saying that I'm not good, but if there is anybody that I try consciously to emulate, it would be Orson Welles more than Hitchcock.
WIATER: Why Welles over Hitchcock, the acknowledged master of suspense?
ROMERO: I find it hard to watch Hitchcock movies. I find them slow, tedious, and yet they're great exercises. I enjoy watching them from an investigative point of view. But I never get involved with a Hitchcock character; they never bring a tear to my eye. So I find that his films are just not emotional in any way; they are very, very cold. My work, I think, is more emotional.

I can't tell you: "Here's a classic sequence." The only thing I can point to is humor. It's really hard for me to take things seriously sometimes and I can't resist a joke. So I will very often shuffle in humor, particularly with the shock material. Even if I went in with a vision, with something that was completely plotted out, I'd wind up just having to work within the budget. And to some extent, everybody does that. So it's rare when you have such control over the pages you have to get done that day, and the circumstances under which you have to do them allow you to shoot alternates or fool around. Or even just do what you planned in the first place.
WIATER: Some of your films have been quite explicit in their gore and violence. What kind of battles have you had over the years with the MPAA?
ROMERO: Personally, the rating system hasn't had a tremendous effect

on me because all of the times that I did really graphic stuff, we had a distributor who was willing—and in fact wanted to—go out unrated. The only time I had to make physical cuts in something because of the MPAA was in *Martin*, and it only amounted to twelve frames across the course of the whole movie. I have had a lot worse problems overseas, and in other countries. In Ontario, I think they cut thirteen or seventeen minutes out of *Dawn of the Dead*, which is really major.

It's all so gray and pliable. There are appeals to the ratings so if you have just made *All the President's Men* and you want someone to say "fuck," the MPAA will let you do it because you just made *All the President's Men* and not *Dawn of the Dead*. You can appeal, but those kinds of gray areas are always going to be there.

WIATER: Do you get the sense that the MPAA will always be prejudiced against horror movies, that they simply can't perceive them as worthy of any serious or artistic consideration?

ROMERO: There is a real prejudice by the *world*, I think.

WIATER: Please don't say it's always going to be "us against them."

ROMERO: I think so. There is definitely a prejudice against horror films. They are considered to be on the low totem, maybe one step up from chop-sockie movies, maybe not. Unless it's a major production, like *Aliens*, and the fact that the studio put $40 million into it, we are not supposed to take this genre seriously. I don't think people by and large in the mainstream take them very seriously.

WIATER: Recently a network news program did an interview with Roger Corman. To make a long story short, they presented Corman as if he was some kind of freak, making movies with crazy titles about ridiculous subjects, movies that the mainstream public were never supposed to have heard of before.

ROMERO: Sure! "Here's this curiosity." I've been there. I take my daughter to school, and someone will say, "Hey, I hear you make movies. What kind of movies do you make?" I'll say, "Well, horror movies, mostly." "Oh, I don't go to those." I mean, just flat, gone, no more interest! I probably would get more sparks if I was doing hard-core porn.

WIATER: The flip side of that, there are also people who love horror movies more than any other kind of film. Period. Doesn't that bring some kind of energy to your beleaguered creative soul?

ROMERO: You have to understand, there is a fandom, which is more dedicated probably than most other fandoms. But even that is sort of underground. Most people walking by the Sheraton when one of those horror conventions were on would probably steer a few blocks clear of it when they got a load of some of the people going in. Yet there are those rewards that come back because there is this incredibly dedicated fandom.

WIATER: Unlike perhaps any other genre, there are people who will faithfully line up to see a Cronenberg film or a Craven film or a Carpenter film or a Romero film. . . .

ROMERO: And it is true. I have a hard-core bunch of fans that will go see a beer commercial if I made it.

So it's rewarding in that way. There are times that you just wish that you could be one of the players. The people are saying, "How do you keep surviving? Why do you stay in Pittsburgh?," those kind of questions. Man, I'm making good money, people know who I am, I can call almost anyone in the business and at least get somebody's ear. But I don't want to play for bigger stakes. I like standing at the $2 window. I figure I can stand here longer.

WIATER: And not see your career halted by a major studio disaster?

ROMERO: Exactly! That has always been my philosophy, and I do much prefer it. My biggest frustration is I would like sometime to have a comfortable budget where I could just once say, "This is really exactly what I intended," just to see if there is a style and identify it.

WIATER: You've had books written about you, and there have been major retrospectives of your films. Any thoughts about where George Romero will eventually wind up in the history of the cinema?

ROMERO: I don't know. I think it might look something like that Roger Corman profile: "You might not know about this guy, but there was once this strange guy . . ." [Chuckle.] I'll be in the chapter about Earl Owensby and John Waters, if there is ever a definitive Britannica on this. At least I've earned that much. [Pauses.] I hope that someday one of my other films may buy me another inch of space in that book, and it doesn't just continue to remain to be for *Night of the Living Dead*.

WIATER: But with twenty years of hindsight, do you have any major regrets about where your career has taken you?

ROMERO: No, I don't have a regret in the world. I'm doing exactly what I wanted to do, I've done it all my life. I've never had a another job, I've never even had to wait a table. How can I be pissed off about anything?

WIATER: Yet some people in the horror business seem to be somehow embarrassed to be so closely associated with it. I can never understand how someone can first embrace a genre, and then try to distance themselves from it after they become successful.

ROMERO: A lot of people are sensitive about it because it's one of those things that you don't want to admit. I can't think of a good analogy, but it's like having herpes and not wanting to say right away that you've got herpes.

WIATER: No, that's pretty apt—some critics contend that fans of this genre must be "sick" to enjoy it. Are you ever concerned that you might, in some small way, be bringing harm, not entertainment or art, to the public?

ROMERO: No. I've really looked for it, because I worry about it obviously. If you have a conscience, you examine it a lot. But I really don't believe that it's true. If the pop culture has contributed to the desensitization of America's youth, it does it in all sorts of insidious ways. And horror movies are only a part of it. As is rock 'n' roll. But also as is the National Football League and everything else—it's this barrage of advertising and electronic media. I think the lack of ethics, the breaking up of families, the destruction of the planet—all of those things are bigger factors. *That's* what makes you apathetic.

WIATER: Do you have an argument against those who feel that to display horror and gore in the movies serves no useful purpose in our society?

ROMERO: I still think most of the data indicates that, in fact, it acts as a defusing element, the same way that porn does. Based on the things that I've read about it, and the people that I've talked to about it, that's what I believe. Yeah, maybe I'm just building my own case, but that is what I believe. Fantasy is fantasy—it's no worse than dreams. If you read Joseph Campbell, he says we need this stuff, and I believe him, too. We need *some* kind of heroes, and I think that putting them in the context of another world is safer than *Beverly Hills Cop* for that matter.

WIATER: In other words, when in doubt about figuring out this world, shoot somebody?

ROMERO: Yeah, shoot somebody or put them through a plate glass window. Those actions are acceptable to these kids on the streets. You can behave that way, and you don't need a laser blaster or anything else. I'm very comfortable with my conscience; all the blood I've spilled has been spilled by zombies. Always in the fantasy context, except for *Martin*. In fact, *Martin* is about a kid who in my mind was affected by everything from the pop culture on. What I mean is, it's the only one of my movies where the central character is a human being doing violent things to other humans.

WIATER: Since you're considered one of the kings of independent filmmaking, what practical advice can you give to someone wishing to follow in your footsteps? That is, making movies without making the move automatically to Hollywood?

ROMERO: I always say the same thing: you have to get around a film production, somehow. The best way is to work your way through the ranks, unless you get real lucky like me and go make an independent movie and it becomes a hit. Then you'll get a blank check. So I'll never discourage anybody from going out and trying to make a little movie. That's cool.

But if you can't do that, if you don't have an uncle who will give you a couple of grand, you have to get around somebody else's production. That means getting to a city where there is state-of-the-art production activity. Now, that doesn't necessarily mean that they are making features, but somewhere there's an active PBS station, like Boston or Pittsburgh. Some place where you can meet the working professionals, get on the set, work for free if you have to, make relationships. That's exactly the way it works. It's all grapevine, and anyone who has the instinct and the talent and the dedication will come and find work.

It comes down to those old values. One thing about a film production is that it must run efficiently; there is no room for dead wood. So somebody that hangs around by the coffee wagon won't get hired again, but somebody who is dedicated and works hard and really puts out will get noticed by the people that matter around there, and will get asked to come back again. I've never seen it fail, it's almost automatic. If you have that spark, if you've got what it takes, you'll work.

It's as simple as that—there's nothing mysterious about it.

Tom
Savini

Tom Savini

When one considers how the history of motion pictures can still be changed by an individual, one usually thinks of a director, producer, or an actor. However, this is not always the case, especially in the horror genre. For in the summer of 1980, a low-budget, independently produced film entitled *Friday the 13th* was released. Not only was it a surprise hit, it spawned a continuing series of sequels (seven to date) and a television series. (Aptly called "Friday the 13th: The Series.") More important, this extremely gory tale of multiple murders by a masked, unstoppable killer spawned dozens, if not hundreds, of imitators. It was one of the first of the notorious "splatter" films, so termed because they were produced primarily to show every grisly death as explicitly as possible: shotgun blasts to the head, arrows through the eye, throats cut, heads exploding. Yet the man most responsible for *Friday the 13th* being such a huge success was not the first-time screenwriter nor the director nor any of the unknown actors.

It was special makeup effects master Tom Savini.

Savini's credits go well beyond *Friday the 13th*. They include such acknowledged "splatter" classics as *Deranged*, *Maniac*, and *The Prowler*. More recognized still is his work with director George Romero, for whom he has done *Dawn of the Dead*, *Martin*, *Creepshow*, and *Day of the Dead*, among others. Savini has made his mark in the cinema of the fantastic as being one of the first "special makeup effects artist" who can fully realize just about any gory demise or hideous monster that a director's or screenwriter's imagination can devise.

Like his colleague Dick Smith, Savini has always been candid with telling the amazed moviegoer just how he has engineered his most incredible effects. In fact, in 1983 Savini wrote a book called *Bizarro! The Art and Technique of Special Makeup Effects* where he details his highly unusual career as a technical creator of dark visions.

Though less known in these areas, Savini is also an accomplished actor, fight choreographer, and stuntman. His acting credits include Romero's *Knightriders* and as the title character in the little-seen *The Ripper*. Further expanding his range, Savini has also made the move into directing, with several episodes of television's "Tales from the Darkside" to his credit.

At the time of our conversation, Savini had just finished work on a film called *The Awakening*, and was preparing to announce that he had been given the opportunity to direct his first feature film: a remake of *Night of the Living Dead*, with a screenplay by George Romero.

SELECTED FILMOGRAPHY

Martin (1976)

Dawn of the Dead (1979)

Friday the 13th (1980)

Eyes of a Stranger (1981)

The Burning (1982)

Creepshow (1982)

Day of the Dead (1985)

Monkeyshines (1988)

Red Scorpion (1989)

Night of the Living Dead (1990) (director only)

WIATER: Your love for movies and makeup began when, as a child in Pittsburgh in 1957, you saw Lon Chaney's life story, *Man of a Thousand Faces*, correct?

SAVINI: Yes, in the same movie theater where I was going to see *Creature from the Black Lagoon* and those kind of things. [Laughs.] I had no idea then what the movie was going to be about. At the time I went to see practically every movie that came out; I lived in the movie theater. But it was the movie that made me realize, "A-ha! Makeup! That's how they do those monsters." And for me, that was the day that the Creature, and the Frankenstein monster, and all the other monsters I believed in, died. Because I suddenly realized, at twelve years old, that they were all created by makeup people. I'm still living in the same neighborhood, but back then I was a poor little Italian kid, loafing around the street corners. This was the movie that gave me a purpose.

WIATER: Your talents go beyond makeup. You had one of the lead roles in *The Awakening*, besides your responsibility for the special makeup effects. What amount of creative energy does that take away from accomplishing your effects?

SAVINI: None! In fact, acting gives me energy. I played a part, staged the fights, and did the effects! It was the most fun I have had in a long time doing a film. It was like *Dawn of the Dead* again, when every day was Halloween.

WIATER: In terms of doing such effects, to what degree do you confer with the screenwriter or the director about how explicit the final result should be?

SAVINI: I work most closely with the director, of course. In *The Awakening*, the director was John Russo, who also wrote the book and did the screenplay. So we had a lot of conversations before we even started production. I always ask: "What do you want to see?" And the director tells me, and we'll see if we can do it or if it's impossible. In fact, nothing's impossible; it's just a matter of working it up. I tell them what I need in order to make the shot work. Like in a magic trick, but on film.

WIATER: Could you give me an example of your magic?

SAVINI: In *Friday the 13th*, there's the scene where the person is hit in the face by an ax, but in fact it's a fake one. I like to have a shot of the real ax hitting something like a wall or some object, so we establish that the real ax has some power and is deadly. When the rubber ax actually hits the actor, the audience still believes it has the power of a real ax.

WIATER: Which type of effect gives you the greater personal satisfaction—totally outrageous as in the zombies of *Dawn of the Dead*, or totally realistic, as in the operating sequences for *Monkeyshines*?

SAVINI: Well, you didn't give me a third choice—directing! [Laughs.] That's my ultimate goal. Because as a director, I could continue to be doing the effects, and I could still be acting. I could still do everything—but have control over it all. Of course, if it's bad, then it's my fault. So far, I can look back at a couple of my movies and say it's bad because of the way the editor cut it, or the way the director shot it, or whatever. This would be a way of alleviating some of those frustrations. Second, it's emotionally intoxicating. And third, it's the most rewarding. As the director you do *everything*. It's ridiculous the way people think directors just say "Action" and "Cut!" You shoot the whole movie on paper before you even begin anything else; you cut pieces to a puzzle, and when you're done, you put the puzzle together.

WIATER: Some of the movies you've worked on have been panned by the critics as purely exploitative, to say the least. More often than not, however, your contributions have been singled out as the only item worthy of praise in otherwise forgettable films. In a sense, your effects were the true stars.

SAVINI: I think you've hit it there. I read the reviews and they're always kind to me. "No matter where the movie failed, at least Savini's effects delivered," that sort of thing. I used to hear that Sean Cunningham, the man who directed *Friday the 13th*, had said: "I made Tom Savini's career. I made him famous." Depending on who it was said to, they would come back with, "Well, Savini didn't do too bad for your career, either. He made you famous, too." Do you understand what I'm saying?

After a while, I began to realize that my effects were the star of that particular film, just as the reviews said. But lately I've seen some films where the effects were *wonderful*, but the film itself stank. I mean, in *Phantasm II* the effects were great, but I fell asleep so many times! . . . Good effects do not necessarily a good movie make. You can have a clunker that's still full of good effects.

WIATER: How close are you to directing your first feature?

SAVINI: *Very* close. I'm very close to doing a remake of a film which at this time I'm not at liberty to tell you the title. But the script is brilliant. The script is the most unique handling of a remake that I've ever read. So, we'll see.

WIATER: As I'm sure you're well aware, there's intense censorship of horror films around the world, including England. What are your thoughts on the subject?

SAVINI: It's pretty strange about censorship and England. When I was growing up, we used to see the Hammer films with whole chunks missing—like when Dracula decomposed at the end of *Horror of Dracula*. I understand that those scenes would of course be intact in England, and they would censor it *here*! But now it seems to have gone into reverse, with them censoring scenes in England and leaving them intact here.

Censorship is pretty strange to me anywhere. One of the films I did, *Maniac*, was untouched everywhere except in Miami, Florida! Why? Maybe because at the time there was more violence in Miami? I don't know. But I really don't believe in censorship. It's really illogical when you think about it, because the films released in the video stores can get away with pretty much anything, while they attempt to censor the films that play in the theaters. Now I realize there's a lot of films that shouldn't be seen by children. I wouldn't let my own young daughter see any of my films until it's explained who these imaginary people like Elvira and Freddy Krueger and Jason are. But in a theater, anyone who really wants to get in to see an R-rated film will get in. So do these ratings really work? Who knows?

WIATER: Actually, you and your colleagues are the very first victims of censorship, as in a horror film the gory special makeup effects are always the first to be excised.

SAVINI: Well, I could say I hate the censors because they cut all the effects out of certain films. But what I really believe is the less you show, the better off you are. The better the audience should like it, too. Except, lately, the audience would be disappointed if you didn't show them everything. Like in *Fright Night* for example. The effects were so wonderful I had to go back and see it a second time. But then I realized how the first forty-five minutes were so boring until the effects came on the screen.

WIATER: Yet the infamous *Maniac*, which even you have disowned, seems to have been designed only to present disgusting scenes of murder and dismemberment. So how can you claim "less is more?"

SAVINI: It was the grossest splatter film that my name has ever been associated with. Yet I can logically say that's okay, because it *was* just a showcase for splatter. When you sit down in a theater, and you don't know what's coming, and then the effects come—that's glorious! That's great. But when you're getting effects from the very beginning of the film, and it's just splatter, just excuses to show blood . . . that's when it becomes real close to porno films. When an effect happens, and the camera goes right up close to it in graphic, clinical detail, that's pornography to me. That's why I hate porno films, because to me it's like watching people go to the bathroom. I have no interest in seeing a clinical study of somebody do that.

WIATER: But you've built your reputation on breaking down the barriers on graphic gore and violence. How can you say it doesn't interest you?

SAVINI: I agree wholeheartedly that's where my initial reputation was made. But we're leading to a point here. The point being, even though I've done that kind of effect before, it doesn't mean I didn't realize it was "splatter pornography." Because that's the way the filmmakers did shoot them: "Let's get some teenagers together, and when we kill them, let's go in real close and be really graphic about how we show them being killed."

This is all going back to the less you show, the better or more dramatic is. Nobody has been able recently to handle this premise, with the exception of *Alien* and its sequel, *Aliens*. Kubrick can. Romero—with the exception of *Dawn of the Dead*—can do it. Polanski can do it. And William Friedkin. But you don't see their names on the dozens of *Nightmare on Elm Street* and other splatter films. You never see their names associated with these kinds of films. Can you imagine if Kubrick did a Freddy Krueger movie? And Hitchcock, of course, who was a master at putting himself in the position of the audience, and figuring out how best to entertain them. The best way is *not* to show them everything.

Unfortunately, today's audiences are looking for the "instant high." They're not patient enough—because we've spoiled them—to wait for the film to present itself in a way that will give them the greatest level of entertainment. It's our fault, because now the greatest level to the audience is the "cum shot"—the instant porno high. We all know that the main moviegoing audience is between thirteen and twenty-one, so how do you go about reconditioning these young people to appreciate the way suspense and violence was done by these masters?

WIATER: Yet the critics still damn you by saying that because of filmmakers like yourself, today's audiences not only have to see someone being shot, but witness the bullet blowing the head apart and then splattering the wall behind it.

SAVINI: But wait, there *is* a difference here. What most critics do is to put the blame on me. But I don't personally like that stuff. And I'm not saying there's something wrong with those filmmakers who do; there's a reason for everything. But my job, when someone presents a script to me, is to make this scene as realistic as possible. Obviously, my notoriety comes from how well I do that. As an artist, when someone comes to me with a script and wants me to do something, I go in and do the best that's possible. But only when I'm the *director*, can I do it in the way I've been talking about. I'm like everyone else who has to make a living, pay the light bills. So I did these films.

At one point I even said I wasn't going to do any more splatter films, because I wanted to make the transition to creatures and monsters. I was lucky enough to be able to do that for a while, with films like *Creepshow* and the film I did in Hong Kong, *Scared to Death*. But then *Friday the 13th, The Final Chapter* came along, and I did that because I wanted to kill off Jason, who I had created in the original. How did I know they were going to keep making more? And *Day of the Dead* for George Romero. There was no way I was going to turn down that film after *Dawn of the Dead* and my long association with George. So it's not me as a creator of these films saying I won't do any more splatter, it's me as someone who makes a living doing these effects who takes the work as it comes.

WIATER: You've described yourself in the past as a "paid assassin." You go where you're hired, and cinematically kill who you're ordered to kill. Are there any motion pictures you refused to be associated with?

SAVINI: Listen, I have passed up so many splatter films you can't imagine! Like a movie where the whole premise revolved around a Swiss army knife and the killer using different instruments on it to kill his victims. I remember another film where the murder instrument was a Cuisinart! I turned down *Neon Maniacs*. I turned down *It's Alive III: Island of the Alive*. I turned down *Return to 'Salem's Lot*. And *The Stuff*. I mean, my résumé should be the projects I turned down! [Laughs.] And I was right to do so, because those films didn't last very long in the theaters.

But I've also done films that aren't splatter, including *Monkeyshines* and the Chuck Norris picture, *Invasion U.S.A.* That had some variety in it, with bullet hits to the head and a knife in the hand. . . . Or the torture scene in the new Dolf Lundgren film, *Red Scorpion*. Those aren't splatter films. But you have to remember, I don't write these pictures, and I don't direct them.

I still feel less is more. But I think just about everybody misses the boat on suspense. No matter what my effects can do, it's the director who creates the suspense, and it's created before you shoot one frame of the damn movie. So even if I do these films because I have to make a living, I can still feel that they haven't been done correctly. And that all leads back to why I want to direct.

WIATER: Since it appears inevitable this dream will come true, what kind of goals have you set for yourself as a director, when your reputation clearly rests on your special makeup effects?

SAVINI: I realize I have to have *some* effects in my films, or I will disappoint an audience. They'll say, "I went to see a Tom Savini film, and there wasn't a single effect in that goddamned thing!" Okay? But my goal is for somebody to say, "I went to see a Tom Savini film, there wasn't one effect in the damn thing, but it was fabulous! It was great! It scared the piss out of me!" To me, that's the highest compliment.

WIATER: So you're interested in exploring psychological horror, not just capitalizing on the more popular gore?

SAVINI: One of the scariest movies I've seen didn't have one monster in it, or have one makeup effect. It was called *The Haunting*. It scared the fuck out of me, but it was psychological. Okay, that was made before every movie that came out had a thousand effects in it. Which is why I'm saying that if a movie came out with my name on it, there are going to have to be effects in it. But they are *not* going to be pornographic.

Hopefully, they are going to have a purpose behind them; they are going to lead to something, and they are going to be shot in such a way that you have never seen before. So that when the effect happens, it's going to be at the peak of some dramatic moment. And not just be instant gratification for you because you're sitting there, eating popcorn, simply because you paid your money to get in.

Dick Smith

Dick Smith

I t may only be a coincidence, but the fact that Dick Smith has worked on all three productions of *The Godfather* is one of the reasons why he is considered "the godfather" of special makeup effects.

The list of movies that Smith has been involved with range from such popular and critical successes as *Little Big Man* to *Taxi Driver* to *Marathon Man*. In 1984, he won an Academy Award for his work on *Amadeus*. Within a career spanning some forty-five years, he has also been responsible for some of the most imaginative and frightening makeups ever created. Period. These include such classics as *The Exorcist* and *Altered States*, as well as David Cronenberg's *Scanners*. A partial listing of some of his more memorable effects in genre films includes *The Sentinel*, *Exorcist II: The Heretic*, and *Ghost Story*.

Born in Larchmont, New York, in 1922, Smith still works

in his hometown, making the basement of his house the place where most of his fantastic creations are born. (Or at least constructed or molded.) Smith tells me that the workshop downstairs has become so crowded that he has to hang new projects from the ceiling for lack of any other space to put them.

It's impossible in this brief introduction to address fully the impact Smith has had on the entire motion picture industry, but just in terms of dark visions, it can be stated with some confidence that because of a booklet published in 1965 called *Dick Smith's Do-It-Yourself Monster Makeup Handbook*, he appears to have had a major influence on many of today's biggest stars of special makeup effects, including Rick Baker, Craig Reardon, and Kevin Yagher.

As was amply demonstrated in that handbook (revised and reprinted in 1985), another secret to Dick Smith's nearly legendary success is that he keeps no secrets. That is to say, throughout his career Smith has always been forthcoming with his knowledge of the art of makeup so as to draw more people toward the field—not keep the curious away from it. Simply put, when this soft-spoken and modest man finishes his last assignment, there will be no one who has pioneered as many new makeup techniques and applications and designs as Dick Smith.

I spoke with Dick Smith just after he had returned from Europe and the production of *The Godfather, Part III*.

SELECTED FILMOGRAPHY

The Exorcist (1973)

The Stepford Wives (1974)

Taxi Driver (1974)

Burnt Offerings (1976)

The Fury (1977)

Altered States (1979)

Spasms (1982)

The Hunger (1983)

WIATER: Is the fact that you just may be breaking new ground the main reason you may or may not decide to take on a project?

SMITH: No, it's more complicated than that. And at this point, frankly, I'm not keen about breaking new ground. I usually do in small ways, but I'm not looking for challenges. Frankly, I'm tired of challenges. I'm sixty-seven, I expect that I will be active only a couple more years, and so I'm trying not to work so hard. In the last couple of years my attitude about this has really turned around quite a bit.

WIATER: What would be your interest in doing *Godfather III*, other than the fact that you were associated with the other two?

SMITH: What I am looking for today usually has to be something that I'm happy with and I don't feel too much stress about tackling it. So obviously old age makeup, which is something I've dealt with all my life, is an area that I feel comfortable with. The *Godfather III* involved exactly that. Also it didn't seem to me that it was something for which I would need a large crew. In fact I only used one assistant. The most fun I've had in recent years was doing the single aging makeup in *Amadeus*, which I did all by myself. So repeating that kind of job is really my ideal.

Godfather III seemed to be somewhat that. It turned out to be a fiasco. I started off thinking this would be kind of a fun job. It mainly involved aging Al Pacino and a couple of other people from *Godfather* and *Godfather II*. This particular part is supposed to take place twenty-five years after *Godfather II*. This would make Al Pacino around sixty. In the script he was described as sort of bulldoglike in appearance with thinning gray hair, etc., actually not entirely dissimilar from the image of Brando himself. Al is actually forty-nine, though he looks younger than that. I prepared a number of different appliances, I made a number of different tests. The problems with this production were several.

First of all, Al Pacino couldn't really give me adequate time to do tests. I would go to his house and start work, and Al would announce that he had a meeting in New York and he would have to leave. This meant that I had to rush through a partial test, et cetera. But nevertheless, over a period of about a month I managed to do a number of tests of different appliances and old age stipple. That's the technique of applying a liquid latex formulation, stretching the skin while you dry it, and making it form into natural wrinkles. This is the same technique used on Brando in the first *Godfather*. I tried this assortment

of things, took pictures of them, and sent them over to Rome because
that's where Coppola was. An additional problem was the fact that
Al hates to cut his hair. It was very long, almost black, very thick,
and his hairline was very youthful and dense. Al felt that he couldn't
cut or do anything with his hair until Coppola was present in order
to say, "Yes, this is the way we will do it." Normally on such a
film that is budgeted at a minimum of $40 million, you do extensive
preparations. You definitely do screen tests of an appliance makeup
at least a month before you start filming.

On *Amadeus*, for instance, I was flown all the way to Czechoslova-
kia to do a test a month beforehand. This did not take place. Without
having the hair done, the makeup was only half completed. I said to
the production that we must have at least two weeks prior to filming
to be in Rome and work on Al to solve all the problems that would
add up to giving him the proper characterization. We got five *days*.
We started on Monday, and on Friday we were assembled to hear
what Coppola's decision was on what to do with Al's hair. Nothing
had been done up to that time except putting in some gray streaks by
bleaching it. Against my recommendation, he was given a haircut that
I was opposed to. That was on the Friday preceding the Monday that
we were to start filming. My associate, who was to stay on and apply
the makeup every day of the filming, had not been given the opportunity to rehearse the makeup. You don't just put on a two-hour appliance makeup job without practicing it at least a couple of times.

We started shooting on Monday a fairly large, complicated scene
on location in Rome that involved sixty or seventy extras as well as
some speaking principles, one of them being George Hamilton. So,
the makeup didn't work out well, not badly, but certainly not A-1
on the first couple of days. The point is that they found themselves
in the middle of filming an important scene, with incomplete, unsatis-
factory makeup, and they dumped it. They turned it over to the local
Italian makeup artist, who was a very fine makeup artist, and said
just give him a coat of stipple and let's see if we can film that.

So that was it. My associate and I said, "Good luck to you," and
we went home. All that work went down the drain through, in my
opinion, very sloppy production.

WIATER: To what extent do you have artistic control over your
makeup and props once they have been approved by a director? Do
you recall any instances where it was your suggestion that saved a
particular scene or sequence that otherwise might have been botched
by the director or actors involved?

SMITH: This question really relates to one of the most difficult areas
for a makeup artist. In general fact, you have very little control over

what happens to your creations. We are pretty much in the same boat as a screenwriter. You know how screenwriters' parts get picked apart and rewritten time and again. In a sense, the same thing can happen in makeup. You can fulfill to the best of your ability all the wishes of the directors, producers, actors, etc., and you can come up with the best work that you think you've ever done and it can all go down the drain for one reason or another. A perfect example is my experience with *Godfather III*. Or, it may be that you've done a beautiful special effect and the director may shoot it wrong. It is either badly edited or something is done to it so that it just ruins the effect, or the angle could be wrong, or the photography can be lousy, or it can simply be cut right out of the script. I haven't found any way to assure myself that I have that kind of control before I go into a production. You can't write it into your contract because you can't say, "I can tell the director what to do." He is the boss and makes the final decision, and there is no way of you vetoing his final decision. So you are at his mercy. Of all the leading makeup artists that I know who get into these complicated things, there's not one that hasn't suffered from this. That is the one aspect of being a makeup artist I don't like. I love everything else about the business.

Actually for this reason, there are a lot of makeup artists who are getting out of the makeup business and trying their hand at directing.

WIATER: That brings me to Tom Savini. He was tired of his work being botched by incompetent directors.

SMITH: There you have it! The same thing has happened to other people, for instance Stan Winston, Tom Berman, and Rob Bottin. Frankly I would never want to be a director, so this is not an option for me, so I've been stuck with it.

WIATER: Tom Savini said that he sometimes felt like a "paid assassin" because his job was to find more creative ways of killing people. Thinking back to *Godfather* and *Taxi Driver*, did you ever feel like that was the case, that you were getting paid to kill people realistically?

SMITH: Well I wouldn't put it quite that way. Though it is true that blood and gore play a big part in special effects makeup. The goriest that I ever did was *The Sentinel* and also *Taxi Driver*. I went through an agonizing internal struggle on the *Godfather*. When I got into it and realized what I was doing I really wondered if I was doing a moral thing to work on this film, which I felt was glamorizing and glorifying the Mafia as well as the graphic bloodshed. This is something many makeup artists go through, wondering whether you should be doing this or not and whether you are responsible or not. In articles many times we makeup artists are taken to task on this.

WIATER: Yet would directors present such vivid nightmares on the screen if it were not for the fact that the special effects makeup people could deliver those nightmares into reality?

SMITH: There is a vicious cycle here in that, as makeup artists demonstrate ever-increasing skills of pulling off these horrible effects, it gives the writers and directors increased incentive to top the ones that someone else did.

WIATER: Who has the ultimate moral responsibility for these outrageous effects?

SMITH: I think categorically as a result of my agonizing that it certainly is not the makeup artist primarily, it is the writer and director who order these effects. You must remember that most blood and gore is done in low-budget films, certainly not the big elaborate ones. Most are done by makeup artists starting out in the field who are poor, unknown, and trying to make a career for themselves. It's pretty hypocritical to expect that a young person who is trying to make a living is going to say, "No, I won't do your blood and gore because it's a nasty and immoral thing to do." They would laugh him out of the county and someone else would jump in and do the job. In a slight way you might say it's like the drug problem, that even the director and writer are not entirely responsible in the sense that there is a market out there. The audience eats it up. In the last ten years I have not seen any decrease in the appetite to see the most horrible mayhem. It keeps getting worse and worse. If the market were saturated, then that type of film would start dying out, but I see no sign of it.

WIATER: A large part of it is the video explosion. People who wouldn't necessarily go out to see a movie at a local cinema now can rent that low-budget splatter movie at their video store, so it won't stop for some time to come.

SMITH: I think the explanation for this social phenomenon would take a whole battery of psychiatrists to try to unravel. There is something going on in our society that perpetrates this kind of horror. It's certainly unhealthy, in my thinking.

WIATER: Do you hold any more to the catharsis theory? Or are we just being saturated with violence in society?

SMITH: I agree with that. It has certainly gone too far.

WIATER: From the stills in your book on monster makeup it is clear you always had a great fondness for the classic movie monsters such as the Phantom and Frankenstein's monster. What made you become fascinated with the dark side of human nature at such a young age?

SMITH: I'm not saying that any personal feelings for the allure of monsters has affected my work. That doesn't relate. The creation of a monster tends to be an intellectual, artistic creation just as much as creating old age. There are certain steps that you go through to create this sort of thing from your knowledge and research. The fascination that strikes many young males—girls don't seem to be affected much by this—there comes a time in their life that they become truly aware that they are going to die someday, that they are mortal. At the same time they realize that they are vulnerable, living organisms that can be terribly hurt. This universal fear, the fear of death, we become aware of early in life and we never lose it, really. But we have to deal with it emotionally in some way. There are many ways that people handle this.

I think getting involved with monsters is one of them. "If you can't beat 'em, join 'em." Making yourself up as a monster is a wonderful experience because now you're the big guy that no one can touch, your parents, your teachers, and all the authority figures. No bully can touch you, you are now superhuman. So now your fear of a monster has that sort of flip side to it. I remember when I first put on monster makeup as a freshman in college, it was a great thrill. I was a shy, introverted kid, and I felt like a big extravert when this happened.

Years later I discovered something else: When we were brought up we were taught to hide our aggressive feelings. In my time we were taught you had to be good, you couldn't get angry, you certainly never could say nasty things to your parents or teachers. All this had to be kept inside to be a gentleman. Self-control was terribly important in the way I was brought up. So, I was never allowed to let out any aggressive feelings. Well, as a monster you are acting out your most aggressive feelings in a most wonderful way. So the putting on of monster makeup, for me, served as a marvelous release of aggressive feelings. I could act them out harmlessly by putting on this makeup. And even more convenient was the fact that I never lost control. That was really good therapy. Putting on the makeup and acting out the monster is much more complete than just watching the movie, where you just get a sort of mental empathy.

WIATER: Do you think there are any unique attributes one has to have to become a special effects makeup artist? Is there any special temperament or personality you have found is unique?

SMITH: I don't think one can categorize makeup artists as being in the same mold. Let me tell you the characteristics of one's nature. One has to be an artistic, creative person, with an imagination, with artistic talent, an ability to sculpt naturally, use color naturally, those sorts of things. But those are certainly common with anyone in an arts field, whether the person is an artist or possibly a dental technician, anything in relation to visual art. So, those things are nothing really special. I think other things that are not really special are an ambition, a drive, a passion for doing the job right, a love of dealing with problems so you keep searching for an answer, those qualities that make you strive to go to the top for one reason or another. Those are not uncommon things.

I think the only unique thing is that fascination with makeup. Many people are interested in makeup but it is the true makeup artist who has the lifelong passion or love of makeup. Why they do, I don't know. It may be the emotional need that I've expressed. What makes ballet dancers devote their lives to dancing?

WIATER: To me there are two ways of looking at the art of makeup. One is that because of people like you, everything that can be done to the human form has been done. Then, on the other hand, because of the increased technology of the materials and visual effects, there's now a whole new horizon of ideas of creations that makeup people can come up with. Is that true?

SMITH: Yes, pretty much so. Let me tell you what I see that has changed. It is an incredible change in the last fifteen years. It is the birth of special effects makeup. Special makeup effects have become so sensational, so attractive, they have been noted so much and have gotten so much publicity. Very few young people in my day and age turned to makeup. They didn't even notice it. The first truly gifted makeup artist that I ever met was Rick Baker when he was about seventeen or eighteen, who came to visit me. Up until that time I had never encountered someone who was such an obvious genius. Since Rick came along and the special effects era has burst upon us, the image of being a makeup artist has been so glorified that there are now a hundred times the number of young people interested in makeup. What's happened then is that instead of saying that one Rick Baker turns up in a year, there are now ten Rick Bakers simply because of the numbers. If ten percent of young people are artistically talented, well, the more people that turn to makeup obviously the more truly creative people are going to be available.

And there's another thing, because special effects makeup seems to be a wonderful, creative field with far horizons, a higher caliber of creative person is turning to makeup. Whereas before someone who had quite extraordinary artistic talents might want to go in for fine arts or some other field that seemed to him more demanding. Now they can look at special effects makeup and say, "Wow, that's a field where I could really go crazy." Because of these two general things I am seeing a tremendous increase in the number of highly talented people trying to get into makeup. I get people coming to me who are incredible and they are only thirteen to fifteen years old. I tell you that I when started getting into the makeup profession when I did (I wasn't half as good as these people), I wouldn't want to compete with these young people today.

WIATER: You mentioned Rick Baker before. Would you tell me some of the other special effects makeup men who directly credit you for being a major influence on their own careers or becoming makeup artists?

SMITH: The only other person I've known for most of his life is Craig Reardon. Craig contacted me at about the same age as Rick Baker. He wrote me a seven-page, single-spaced, typewritten letter. It blew my mind. He was a very intelligent, versatile young man. For so many years he had so many irons in the fire that it took him a long time to settle into makeup. He didn't concentrate on it as Rick did, but he was a very creative guy. But I don't know any others who had the kind of close relationship to me that Rick had. I guess there are others that say they were influenced simply by reading the book or looking at my work.

WIATER: Can you tell me about your relationship with the syndicated television program "Monsters"?

SMITH: There's not a lot to tell, really. They approached me to be a consultant. It's a very low-budget series. This is their main problem. In fact it's been the main help that I've been able to provide in these two seasons. They'll come up with a script that has no holds barred. Yet here we are with an extremely low budget and are asked to create some monster, not just a mask, but the *whole body*! Often it is something quite elaborate. I've had very little to do with designing the makeup, but generally I have turned it over to the artist who is actually doing the work. He has put his own imprint on it. Most of the work has been done by John Dodd, who has done a super job.

WIATER: It was an honor on their part that they could get your services.

SMITH: Yes, I think they felt that having my name on the thing was an asset and that's okay. [Chuckles.]

WIATER: Because of the low budget I look at the series and say, "Well if only this had been a little bit better," and then I see your name on it and I kind of wonder to what extent your work was involved.

SMITH: You mean am I ashamed because of lousy work?

WIATER: Well no, that's too strong a point and I really don't mean to imply that. It's just that sometimes you wonder what was your exact input for that particular monster.

SMITH: I am brought in as a consultant only on the scripts where they feel there is a problem that their regular makeup artist can't handle. So I am not involved on every script by any means. I am only involved on a minority number of the scripts.

WIATER: Some critics say that today's movies rely too much on special effects and many motion pictures try to compensate for a poor story line with some great special effects. Do you think that special makeup effects have become an "artistic crutch" that filmmakers now rely on in place of a good story line and good acting?

SMITH: I certainly think it happens, but I don't think it is intentional in most cases. It happens most often with low-budget horror effects.

WIATER: What would be your most satisfying experience on a project in the horror, science fiction genre?

SMITH: I think *The Exorcist*. At the time that also was a very traumatic experience. During *The Exorcist* at one point I quit. I had a fight with Bill Friedkin. Since then when we contact each other, it's been with great friendship, so it all worked out in the end. But, there was a point on that film where I was so exhausted from working seven days a week that I was on the verge of collapse and just blew. Looking back on it, I love it for three things. I'm very happy with the makeup on Linda, I'm happy with the few effects I did, and I'm very happy with Max Von Sydow's appliance makeup, because most of the audience never knew he was made up even when they got tight close-ups.

WIATER: There are two extremes that I would think a makeup artist could be satisfied with. One is having an inanimate object, a body prop, that looked like a living human being. And then you have someone like Max Von Sydow who you say, "No, of course that's not makeup, he's really a seventy-year-old man." It's the other end of the spectrum where you think the person *isn't* made up.

SMITH: That's why I am proud of the film. And also, what's always wonderful is if you've got good work that ends up in a film that lasts, that's a blessing no makeup artist can be sure of. The same is true of *Amadeus*, in that there's a film that will always be a classic. I did a nice job on *Everybody's All American*. The film died at the box office. Everyone who has seen it liked it, but of course it will never be remembered.

WIATER: Would you relate the story about Karen Black's breasts from *Carnal Knowledge* becoming Katherine Ross's breasts in *Stepford Wives*?

SMITH: Mike Nichols in casting originally chose Karen Black for the part that Ann Margaret eventually played. He asked if it was possible to make breasts that were believable. I was happy to try, so I cast her chest, came home, and set up the cast in my lab. I went and borrowed all my son's *Playboy* magazines, found the best pictures, and mounted them all up in front of my work table for reference. I'm deeply immersed in this intense sculptural quest, and my wife called down that the plumber was here about the furnace. I told her to send him down, and this plumber, who was new to us, came down saying "Mr. Smith, Mr. Smith." I said, "I'm in here." He turned into my little room here and said, "I'm here to fix . . ." and his mouth fell open as he took in this scene. I could read his mind and I let him stew for a minute, and then I said, "You're probably wondering what I'm doing." He nodded, so I explained the situation, and of course he was fascinated. He eventually went and fixed the furnace. His interest must have continued because he stopped by more than once to make sure the furnace was working.

So anyway, when the appliances where finished, they were sent out to Hollywood where another makeup artist applied them to Karen Black. They were vetoed by Mike Nichols. It may have had something to do with the way they were applied, but I think he would have vetoed them anyway because now he was concerned about what would happen when she lay down on her back, whether they would flatten out as a normal female breast would do in that position, and of course they won't. So hence, she lost the job and it went to Ann Margaret. The only use then I had for them was that my wife brought down some of her bowling chums to show them these artistic marvels and they took turns visualizing what they would do for them. [Chuckles.]

They sat there until the job of *Stepford Wives* came along. I did intend to sculpt them all over again, but I found that what I already had was of the proper size and shape for Katherine Ross. So that's where they were used. Since that time there have been many instances where breasts, and even whole chests have been done. Now it's a routine thing for both men and women.

WIATER: Since you are acknowledged as the dean of makeup artists, what advice do you have for someone who is thinking of entering your profession or any creative artistic profession?

SMITH: Well, I'll tell you what I tell young people who come to me and say, "I love makeup and want to be a makeup artist, how do I get in?" The first thing they have to do is work on their own studying the handful of books on the subject. He has to go through a trial period. I mean starting off with basic makeup books, *Stage Make-up* by Richard Corson is the first one I recommend. They need to practice on themselves and friends the techniques there and then go on to the three-dimensional aspects of makeup. I would recommend *The Techniques of Three Dimensional Make-up* by Lee Bagin. That book teaches how to make life masks, molds, how to sculpt models for appliances, how to make foam latex, and how to put these things on. I suggest going through these books and practicing until they can turn out a decent three-dimensional makeup, hopefully an appliance makeup with foam latex. I feel this does a couple of things. It determines if the person has the inner resources and intelligence and creativity to learn by themselves. It teaches them a certain amount of self-reliance, which is absolutely essential in this profession. Makeup is not handed to someone on a platter. You don't just go to school and have the teacher lecture to you and you learn makeup. It is something where you are so dependent on yourself, on your own creativity and ingenuity. So if you can't master the fundamentals on your own by reading a couple of decent books, then you're not going to make it.

The other thing that it does is tell that individual whether they're cut out to be a makeup artist because it puts them through a hell of a lot. It puts them through just the discomfort of applying a lot of sticky, gooey makeup and cleaning it off. That stuff is fun. It determines whether or not they have the real love of makeup to persist, to make hundreds of mistakes and not get discouraged, to keep on striving to get better. They need to keep learning about how to correct what they've done wrong. It's a testing period for them. If they get discouraged and can't get through that trial period, then they shouldn't want to be a makeup artist.

In fact, many people that I put this test to drop out. They never bother again. There is no way for me to determine whether they really have it in them. Just talking about makeup doesn't mean you have it in you, that passion and drive.

Joseph Stefano

A ll things considered, it should be enough of an accomplishment for a screenwriter to be associated with one classic film in his career. Joseph Stefano, however, has a double dose of acclaim in the horror and science fiction fields. For not only is he the screenwriter for perhaps the most frightening film of all time—*Psycho* (1960)—he was also the primary talent behind the greatest science fiction series of the 1960s: "The Outer Limits." (Stephen King has called it "perhaps the best program of its type ever to run on network television.")

Strangely enough, Stefano never thought he'd be so closely associated with either horror or science fiction when he began his career first as a songwriter, then as a composer of musical comedies. Born May 5, 1922, Stefano's first screen credit was for an original screenplay with the appropriately dark title *The Black Orchard* (1958).

The fateful turn in Stefano's career as far as the genre's fans are concerned came when he adapted Robert Bloch's novel to the screen for director Alfred Hitchcock, resulting in that masterpiece of terror, *Psycho*. He has also written three acclaimed horror and suspense films: *Eye of the Cat* (1969), *The Kindred* (1986), and *Blackout* (1988). He has also written several made-for-television movies in various genres, including *Snowbeast* (1977). His most recent work in the genre, not too surprisingly, is the original cable television production for Showtime, *Psycho IV: The Beginning*. He has also written the pilot for, and is now currently producing, a new cable television series based on the popular comic book character "Swamp Thing."

On the other hand, even if he never wrote a single movie, Stefano would always be revered by science fiction fans for being the creator, producer (with Leslie Stevens) and principal writer for the now classic television series "The Outer Limits." This show, which ran for only a season and a half in the early sixties, is still seen in syndication around the world. It has in fact started a whole new life cycle with individual episodes now being released on videotape.

I spoke with Joseph Stefano shortly after he had visited the production for *Psycho IV*.

SELECTED FILMOGRAPHY

Psycho (1960)

Eye of the Cat (1969)

The Kindred (1986)

Blackout (1989)

Psycho IV (1990)

WIATER: Let's begin with an obvious question: What enticed you to write *Psycho IV—the Beginning*?
STEFANO: The fact that it *was* a prequel. I was not interested in any

of the sequels to *Psycho*, either in a writer's sense or in a viewer's sense. I just was not interested in what would or could happen to Norman Bates twenty or twenty-five years after the *Psycho* that I wrote. But I had always been fascinated by the fact that there had always been an enormous story in the Norman Bates character that I had invented in order to write the script for the original *Psycho*, but that could never be told because the movie simply couldn't support any background history of the kind that I'm talking about. So you were always left wondering what would turn this sort of young man into a killer. And so when I was contacted about *Psycho IV*, my first comment was I would be interested in it if it were a prequel. It just so happened that was also what the producers wanted as well.

WIATER: In terms of research, did you ever view *Psycho II or Psycho III*? Or did you purposely avoid them?

STEFANO: I saw *Psycho II* on television a few years after it was released. I missed *Psycho III*. But when I was about to do *Psycho IV*, I decided to see that. But the producers and the studio had already told me that I wouldn't be hemmed in in any way by anything that had been said in *Psycho II or Psycho III*. The studio felt that the audience for *Psycho III* had been small anyway, so that anything portrayed in it wasn't necessary to continue on.

WIATER: Much of the movie is about the tormented childhood of Norman Bates. It's clearly a departure from what the reader is able to learn about the character from reading Robert Bloch's original novel.

STEFANO: Since this was a character I invented, it is not the same character as the one in the book that Robert Bloch wrote. The one in the movie that you saw was very different from the one in the book. I invented a history for Norman Bates because it was just something that I needed to know to write the scenes that I wrote. I'll have a history for any character that I write about, and can talk for hours about a character you'll see for maybe ten minutes on the screen. As a matter of fact, I discussed one sequence with Hitchcock, telling him how I was building up the life that had turned Norman into a youth who could kill his mother, and Hitch was very fascinated by it and sorry that we weren't able to shoot it.

WIATER: When you wrote the screenplay for *Psycho*, the elements of sex and violence, to put a blunt point on it, were considered very daring for the time. Nowadays of course the levels of explicit sex and violence that can be shown in a horror film have almost no limit. Did you approach *Psycho IV* any differently knowing that you could truly "tell it like is" in terms of the abnormal subject matter?

STEFANO: No. But after the film was in production, the producers decided to make one sequence in my script much more sexual than I had allowed. But there's really nothing you can do on the screen today that I would do with *Psycho* to make it any better. It was never intended to be what later became "slasher movies." It was always a psychological study of a very strange case, and I always dealt with it that way. I don't feel that adding a lot of very explicit violence or sex changes the movie very much. I don't know what you could add to *Psycho* that would increase the intensity of it.

WIATER: How do you respond to the critical charge that there wouldn't be any "slasher movies" today if *Psycho* hadn't laid the groundwork for them in terms of the perverse sex and explicit scenes of violence?

STEFANO: But it was much more meaningful in *Psycho* than it was in the films that followed! I think *Psycho* handled those scenes at the precise time in history that it was necessary to handle them that way. Unfortunately, the sequels that followed simply did not take enough time to get you to really care about who is getting killed. And when you get into movies where there are seven or eight young people at a mountain cabin, and one by one they're getting killed, it almost becomes a sport. And it no longer has anything to do with character— or caring.

WIATER: The body counts were starting to get pretty ludicrous if you consider the people dispatched in the two sequels to *Psycho*.

STEFANO: I think it would have been futile to do a *Psycho IV* simply where *Psycho III* left off. It becomes a game. You're not being moved by death anymore—or loss or grief—you're kind of fascinated by how they came up with that new idea. [Chuckles.] I felt that the reprises of killing in *Psycho II* and *Psycho III* were the least interesting parts of each film! They might have been better movies if they hadn't gone for that.

WIATER: Critics always applaud the fact that this is "Hitchcock's *Psycho*." I'm curious to know if the movie would have been as effective if some other director had used your screenplay?

STEFANO:I really can't say. There were certainly directors at that time who could have made almost exactly the same movie—because Hitchcock shot the script that I wrote. With ultimately few changes. Another director might have done it differently, but I still believe it would have had the same impact. But with another director, I don't think the audience would have been as "geared" for what was about to happen. I mean, in those days a "Hitchcock movie" meant certain things. I think a lot of the success of *Psycho* was that Hitch had gotten back to something that he had kind of given up in his later Hollywood years. He had been doing big, glamorous kind of wedding cake pictures—*To Catch a Thief* and *North by Northwest*. And with

Psycho, Hitch went back to that particular vein in himself, where his films had tension, such as *The Lady Vanishes*.

WIATER: As everyone knows, Anthony Perkins is the one and only Norman Bates. Did he have any input into your script when you were writing *Psycho IV*?

STEFANO: Yes, in the sense that he had script approval over the project. So when I went and told him the story I had in mind, his response was very favorable; he liked everything about it.

WIATER: One of your most recent screenplays was for a film called *Blackout*. It in many ways seemed definitely set in *Psycho* territory.

STEFANO: I guess it was, in that I was reaching into the past. *Psycho* had so much to do with the past. The interesting thing about *Blackout* is that it never shows you the past, but has a lot to do with it. The thing I like best about my screenplay is that the present-day story isn't nearly as important as what I'm not telling you about the past. Although the director did it differently from the way Hitchcock would have done it, *Blackout* was really much more about incest. Which again was a very small part of what you saw on the screen—you didn't know until the very end that the brother and sister had had a sexual relationship. In the same sense you don't know Norman Bates's mother is dead until the end of *Psycho*.

My need in writing a script is to have it be about something—but never make that the story. In other words, to do a story about incest, I wouldn't know where to begin. But to do a story about a girl who returns home under the impression that her father needs her, and to have all the events that follow happen because two people had had an incestuous relationship, and the dangers of that, and the consequences of that, make for a very different kind of movie.

WIATER: Does it take a special talent to write suspense?

STEFANO: I'm not sure that it's much different from writing non-horrific drama. It's something I've always felt as a storyteller—to keep you in suspense. Mainly, to keep your interest! I've never thought of it as writing in a "suspenseful way." It's just that I need to keep you in suspense in order to take you down this road. In any movie that I've ever written, I've always felt that I had an element of suspense, because I think that's my style of telling a story. I always make clear-cut decisions about when I'm going to tell you something I want you to know—or when I'm not going to tell the audience—or when to let you in on something that the character hasn't been let in on. I think the reason Hitch and I worked so well together was that all his career as a director he had been using the same technique. This is the way I've always gone—to keep you interested as long as possible with suspense, and then in a way reward you for having remained interested.

WIATER: Tell us about your script for the film *The Kindred*. How did you get involved in what is unashamedly a full-blown, mad scientist–monster movie?

STEFANO: I became involved in it primarily because of the producer, Ed Feldman, whose work I admired very much. He was going to do the movie based on the reel that the two young directors had shown him. They had a script, but Feldman knew the script could not be shot. So he wanted to know if I wanted to do a new script, and I knew what it was that had fascinated him. There was nothing in the script that really fascinated me, except what you were talking about—with DNA, gene splicing, genetic engineering, and all this, we could really tell *Frankenstein* all over again.

It would have been fascinating to do one of those kind of stories. But as the movie ultimately progressed, a lot of the mysterious suspense element that I liked and had written into it was dropped in favor of a kind of breakneck speed that I felt the movie shouldn't have had. I wasn't terribly pleased with it, but it was still something I originally felt would be fun to do. The way I had written it was what had interested Rod Steiger and Kim Hunter, who ordinarily would not have done a science fiction type of movie. The directors ultimately went back to what they knew best, and I felt the movie suffered for it. I think my version would have been just a little more eerie.

WIATER: Tell us about "The Outer Limits"? I watched it as a youngster and am thrilled to see a whole new generation of fans discovering it on videotape.

STEFANO: It's not just the people buying the videotapes, which is tremendous. It's the fans who write to me, and who are just discovering the series and can't believe something like this was ever on television! There's a real sense of continuing awe about that series. I'm not sure exactly why, except that generally it was just a very good show. Certainly the first season, which I produced and wrote quite a few of the episodes, they were just good old plain knock-'em-down gothic horror movies. We shot them just like an hour-long movie. And the science fiction element didn't get in the way of the drama.

You see, I just wasn't that interested in science fiction at that point in my life. But I sure as hell was interested in doing scary shows on television!

WIATER: As you know, there was a *Twilight Zone: The Movie*. Are you ever approached to a similar *Outer Limits: The Movie* project?

STEFANO: Well, we have talked about it from time to time, and have in fact come very close to doing a movie version. But my feeling on the subject has always been that you've got to get it down to one single story—not two or three, like in most anthology-based movies. And it would have to be an incredibly good science fiction story to succeed. The problems we've had in getting that to happen unfortunately have to do much more with the state of the film business today, MGM and United Artists in particular, rather than with anything from the creative end.

Because anybody who's ever wanted to do *Outer Limits: The Movie* has wanted to do it as a good film; they don't want to make it different from the series. But MGM and UA, which is one of three owners of the series, can't seem to get their act together for the last ten years. So no film company's been able to get it off the ground. If we can just get all the lawyers together to settle on a deal, it still may happen someday.

WIATER: You've had considerable experience as a writer and a producer? Never any interest as a director?

STEFANO: I directed once, a pilot I was going to do as a series for CBS. But I simply have never been as fascinated with that particular job. As a producer, I will spend all day long on the set and watch every shot and every scene. I'll confer with the director continually— but for some reason, I've never been interested in me being *him*, and him being *me*. I really feel the director doesn't have as much control as the producer does. The only time a director has the control he thinks he has is when he owns the movie. Or when he is also the producer.

For instance, in *Blackout* there were lots of things I wouldn't have allowed the director to do—except that the director owned the movie! He raised the money for it, and there were times in the decision-making process when I simply lost because there was not a third party, no studio. If I had a disagreement with the director, I had to talk it over with . . . the director!

My point is I was never really that attracted to directing, or I probably would have done more of it. From the moment you hear the word "Action" until you hear "Cut" the director is God on the set. But between those words, there's a lot about a director's life you may not like.

WIATER: I understand you've recently written your first novel, entitled *Lycanthorpe*. Can you tell me what made you want to write a horror novel, after such a long career as a screenwriter?

STEFANO: I kind of felt like I needed a new mountain to climb. I needed to do something I had not done before. I decided to do a novel because my career as a writer—aside from writing song lyrics—

my career began with writing screenplays. So I've never had a lot of the experiences most writers go through, writing short stories, essays, newspaper reporting—I've never done *anything* like that.

WIATER: In other words, you felt that you were basically an "unpublished writer" because you'd never had anything published in book form.

STEFANO: Exactly! I also felt that I had earned the time in my life to take five or six years off to write a novel. It hasn't been published yet. When I finished it, I worked on it for almost a year with an editor, who then decided to quit her job. But I needed an editor—I didn't want to finish it myself. The publisher still hasn't come up with a suitable editor, so that's something still to happen.

WIATER: Until it does appear, can you give me a sneak preview of the story?

STEFANO: I've taken everything known about the disease lycanthropy and written a very present-day story about a man who suffers from it. There's no werewolf, there's no hair, and there's no teeth—it's about a man who believes he's a wolf. My feeling is most myths spring from reality. I was interested therefore in finding out what goes on behind a myth, so I began to read about the myth of the werewolf. I discovered that at a certain point in history people had this disease— this mental disorder—and their behavior was so extreme, so outrageous, that their victims may have imagined they looked like wolves. This was back in the fourteenth, fifteenth centuries.

So I brushed away several centuries and came up with a story about a man who had this mental disorder, which could have been schizophrenia or anything else, but happened to be lycanthropy. And there's nothing in our literature like that—treating the myth as reality. So I think it's an interesting book.

WIATER: Considering you've written now for movies, television, and a novel, do you ever precensor your imagination depending on the medium you're working in? Do you ever concern yourself with your material be censored by others?

STEFANO: I tend to be my own censor, and with me, it all has to do with taste. There's a scene in *Psycho IV*, where Norman is sixteen or seventeen years old, after he has killed his mother, and is out tending to the motel. A young woman about his age drives over, and she apparently has the hots for him, and wants very much to go up to his room. And the sexual nature of this scene was incredibly important, because this is part of the problem of Norman Bates. Now, if they show the woman's breasts, where thirty years ago they wouldn't, that's okay. But it's important that the producers *don't change Norman.*

When she climbs into bed with him naked, and he touches her body under the sheet, it's supposed to be a moment of anguish, not sexuality. It's not supposed to turn you on, it's supposed to make you realize how tragic it is to have any kind of healthy sexual relationships. What I wanted to show was that Norman's mother, unconsciously or otherwise, had cheated her son of the ability to have a luscious roll in the hay with a pretty young girl. Whether that scene will come across that way, when you have the ability nowadays to just say, "Let's show some tits," I don't know.

WIATER: It certainly can be played either with pathos or can be grossly exploitive, depending on how it's shot and edited.

STEFANO: And it can lose what your original intention was, simply because when you're showing naked people on the screen, some people are going to look at just that. It's also very hard to make flashbacks work with today's audiences anymore.

WIATER: What keeps drawing you back to the dark side as a writer? From what I've researched on your career, it's apparent you never intended to be so closely identified with the horror genre, did you?

STEFANO: It seemed almost impossible to get away with after *Psycho*. Although, as you say, nothing I had done in my career previously indicated I would ever write anything like *Psycho*. Anything *remotely* like it. Which may have been the very thing that attracted Hitchcock to me—the fact that I was not a writer of "Hitchcockian-type" films. I approached everything simply as a dramatic writer; in fact Hitchcock was worried that I was a little too much a serious writer, like Paddy Chayefsky, to consent to writing the movie. But I think it was precisely that approach to the material that made the movie work as well as it did. Because I was really tremendously concerned with who these people were and how they got to where they were, and I think that shows in the development of the script. . . . After that, there weren't a lot of people interested in doing anything with me except try and come up with another *Psycho*.

WIATER: But if you hadn't done that particular movie, you'd always be remembered for "The Outer Limits."

STEFANO: I did the "The Outer Limits," and that kind of sealed my doom. [Laughs.] I've done a lot of other projects, and yet very few people know about them, or are really interested in them. You begin to finally . . . kind of go with it. But it's one of those eternal conflicts in a writer's life. After I tell myself that I will never, absolutely never, do one of those kind of movies again, then there are moments when I feel I don't want to do anything right now but one of *those* kind of movies. So it keeps something electric going on in my life.

WIATER: So it doesn't overly upset you to think that your *Variety* obituary will headline you as the man who wrote the movie version of *Psycho* and created "The Outer Limits"?

STEFANO: No, that's okay. [Laughs.] It really is. Sometimes, when I'm feeling a little overemotional about my career, my wife quietly reminds me of those very two things. Reminding me that there are a lot of Hollywood screenwriters who don't have anything outstanding that they can point to in their lives. So while it may have had an effect on my later output, I in no way regret having done them. I love the people who love them and who write to me still about "The Outer Limits." In fact, I have friends today who became friends through their love for that show and their willingness to write me a letter or pick up the phone.

The point of all this is to *communicate*. To reach people out there who are total strangers to me, to comprehend what I'm thinking—or to at least listen to it—and if I've done that in two such extraordinary instances, it would not be very elegant of me to complain about it!

Stan Winston

Already an Emmy Award–winning makeup artist for his work in such television productions such as "The Autobiography of Miss Jane Pittman" and "Gargoyles," Stan Winston has since moved on to become one of the most respected special makeup effects artists in the motion picture industry, having been nominated for three Academy Awards, and winning one (*Aliens*).

His speciality: monsters.

Starting from a relatively minor assignment on *Dracula's Dog* in 1977—where he designed the canine fangs—Winston has gone on to create or build full-fledged (and sometimes full-sized) monsters. These range from the acid-veined creatures in *Aliens*, to the title horror in *The Terminator* to the otherworldly hunter in the two *Predator* films. Not to mention effects for *Dead and Buried, Something Wicked This Way Comes, Invaders From Mars. . . .*

Besides designing creatures, the forty-year-old Winston has also moved into the director's chair. His first feature was the well-received *Pumpkinhead*, a relatively low-budget film where, fortunately, a great deal of attention and respect was spent on the loathsome creature of the title. It is a testament to his skill as both monster creator and director that Winston's Pump-kinhead creation was one of the most frightening, yet totally convincing, *things* ever presented on the screen.

In fact, Winston had already had experience with making monsters come to life because of his role as second unit direc-tor for James Cameron on both *The Terminator* and *Aliens*. Winston has his own makeup and effects company—Stan Winston Studios—which is large enough in its facilities to tackle any assignment he's offered. Although Winston still gladly takes on any number of projects—including some of the character designs for the Tim Burton film *Edward Scissor-hands*—he now believes his future lies in movies that he can direct as well as supply the effects and the monsters. For him, it's simply yet another way to convey his fantastic visions.

When I spoke with Stan Winston, he had just finished work on his second feature as a director, entitled *A Gnome Named Gnorm*. He describes it as a "buddy film, except where one of the two main characters happens to be a gnome."

SELECTED FILMOGRAPHY

The Terminator (1984)

Starman (1984)

Aliens (1985)

Pumpkinhead (1988)

Leviathan (1989)

Predator 2 (1990)

WIATER: My first formal question is that you started out working in mainstream television and films such as *Roots* and *W. C. Fields and*

Me, to name only two, what initially attracted you to work in the horror, science fiction genre, which I know goes all the way back to *Gargoyles* in 1972?

WINSTON: Actually it goes back to my childhood. I was a fantasy, horror, science fiction fan from the time I was a child, as I think were most people who are in this end of the business. Since I was a fan since I was a child all the historical characters and character makeups in that type of film were my background and my interest. When I graduated from college—the University of Virginia as a fine arts major and a drama minor—I went to the West Coast to become an actor.

I wanted to be a character actor. When I was in college I did character roles, and I'd do my own makeup. So when I came out here that's what I wanted to do, and while I was waiting to become a star, I applied for a makeup apprenticeship program because I wanted work in any aspect of the business while I was waiting for jobs as an actor. I got into the apprentice program for makeup because I was an artist, a painter, and a sculptor. I loved that aspect of it. From that, going into my apprenticeship at Disney, everything snowballed. The snowball kept going and my career kept going in that direction.

WIATER: So it wasn't an "accident" that you found yourself doing more science fiction and horror films? It was something you actively enjoyed doing all the way through?

WINSTON: I actively enjoyed them all the way from childhood.

WIATER: I'm curious to know, considering how today's audiences are so sophisticated, how do you manage to keep one step ahead of them? Is it more of a challenge or a frustration to keep ahead of us in terms of what we expect?

WINSTON: It's definitely not a frustration, it's definitely a challenge, and I think that is the thing that keeps you excited and alive in this business. In any creative field your challenge is to keep giving the audience something they haven't seen before. At the same time there's *nothing* they haven't seen before! I feel that if I have an edge it's because I totally understand what is most important film, be it science fiction, fantasy, horror, drama, complete love story, whatever. It has to do with story and character development. That's what films are about; they're good stories with wonderful characters. My feeling is that my job creatively, whether I'm doing effects or directing, is to create wonderful characters. And that is what is special about any film. I don't even like to consider that what we are doing is "special effects." I'm creating characters for film. As long as you can create a wonderful character, you're going to please the audience because whether they know it or not that's what they're coming to see.

WIATER: What is so memorable about the film *Pumpkinhead* is the monster itself. When you think of the Frankenstein monster, Dracula, and the Wolfman, these creations stand out because they have a full character behind their monstrosity. Pumpkinhead certainly does, and I'm wondering if you can tell me how that film came about?

WINSTON: The film came to me as a small film that they were interested in me just building the monster for. Considering my fortunate status in the motion picture industry, I was able to say that the only way I would consider doing the creature would be if I also directed the film. So, by whatever fate it was, everyone seemed very accepting to that particular scenario. By doing so I was able to reconstruct the screenplay that came to me to give this particular monster—which in its original form was just a killing machine—some personality and make him a character where we saw how totally evil he was. That it wasn't just an ugly killing creature, but that you saw the pleasure he was getting out of his killing. Where you saw he had a method to what he did. There was a torture in his killing that wasn't so much the torture to the victim, but the torture to the loved ones of the victim, which is the real pain. I searched for that.

I figure if you are going to create something that is evil, then create it as evilly as you can. It was a burden to me to a certain extent because I had to think very evil thoughts, and you have to allow yourself to think of the worst possible scenarios to let it happen on the screen. But fortunately it gets it out of your system if you're basically a good human being. I think all of us have those little seeds of darkness in us. It's a good escape, this type of film. Also to create good characters, characters that you empathize with, characters that you love. I mean, the only way you can totally hate something is if that thing that you hate has done away with something that you really love.

No matter how evil Pumpkinhead was, if he was just going around slapping mosquitoes, you really wouldn't think that he was that bad because you'd slap the mosquito yourself. But if he goes around slapping your mother, it's a different thought. So that's basically how it came to me. I wanted the audience to care about the people who died, and I wanted them to see the ultimate evil in Pumpkinhead. I also wanted to create around it a wonderful frame to give it some texture to have this backwoods-type atmosphere.

I love the witch that was in the original script. One of the things that really turned me on to doing it was the basic structure, which was there. I don't want to say that nothing came to me before I did this. The script that came to me was the same basic story as what you saw on screen. The things that I was able to do, for example:

for the ending I stole the premise from a classic science fiction film that I always loved called *Forbidden Planet*. The premise was that Walter Pigeon was in fact creating the monster that was killing everything. It was the monster from his Id. That was the premise that I added to *Pumpkinhead*, the reality that the creature was from the grieving father. It was his own inner devil that came up, and in order for him to kill the monster he had to kill the source, which was himself.

WIATER: Tom Savini told me that one of the reasons he wanted to become a director was because he only felt satisfied with his own particular scenes as a special effects and makeup person if he directed them himself. Only he could really make the effect work if he directed the entire sequence. And he felt for the rest of the film to be as effective as his sequences, he was better off directing the entire film. Was there any of this rationale in your desire to become a director?

WINSTON: Well, maybe I've been more fortunate than Tom Savini. I've worked with directors whom I find extremely talented and who have made entire movies, including my work, look wonderful. I naturally like what I've directed myself and like the aspect of movies that I've added to it. But I've also been fortunate enough to work with extremely talented, creative, visionary directors.

The first one that comes to mind, which I consider a boon to my career, was working with Jim Cameron. For me to say that no one could do my work as well as I can is an absurdity because Jim has done wonderful things with my work and has been a great inspiration to me as a director. Because of his background as an artist, he understands the genre. He understands the creativity, and I've learned from watching him in my own directing style. Although I have a great deal of respect for myself as a creative artist, I have fortunately worked for people for whom I have a great deal of respect for their vision. When I am not directing I realize that it is my job to help that director come forth with his vision, because that's what I expect when I direct. Maybe I'm just older than Tom.

WIATER: This leads to the question of the relationship with the director and screenwriter. To what extent do you actually start conceptualizing your monster? For example, *Leviathan*. At what point were you conceptualizing the monster?

WINSTON: I read the script, I talked to the director, and I started to conceptualize once I was asked if I would consider doing it. There was a great deal of work in the conceptualization of the character. Again the problematic situation is, whether you liked *Leviathan* or hated it, that there's a reality that goes along with anything you create in this business. You *do* create according to what is envisioned in the screenplay. You give it as much as you can within certain parameters. If you create a wonderful creature that has nothing to do with the movie—but you've served yourself—then you've done a disservice to the movie and to yourself. There's nothing more wasted than good effects in a bad movie. Again, the job that we have is to make the movie as good as we can by enhancing it with our characters and our creatures, not distracting from it and having them stand out as their own separate entities. They should fit fully within the entity of the movie.

Now we are strapped to certain screenplays. If you don't like the screenplay or if you don't get along with the director and you feel that your vision is entirely different from theirs, then first of all it is your responsibility to voice that opinion, to say, "I understand what you're saying here but what if you went in this direction?" Then, if in fact that doesn't fit within the director's concept or whatever, then it is also your responsibility, which is very difficult at times, to say either okay, I'll do what you want, I may not be one hundred percent thrilled with it, but I will do the best that I can. I will put every bit of my artistic energy into trying to create your vision and put it on screen, and if it's bad, it's bad, if it's good it's to your credit and to my credit as an artist that I've done as good as I could do with your vision, or bow out of the movie.

We can't always bow out. Every human being has a responsibility to ourselves and our families to work. We don't always have the option to do just the projects that we want to do because this particular script is not the best script or this director is not someone I like or I don't know if this is the best thing to do, but I need the job. Therefore I am going to take the job, and now that I have taken the job, what is my job? My job is to serve the film the best I can.

WIATER: Are there any certain projects that you just automatically say this is not right for Stan Winston?

WINSTON: Absolutely. I've never done a slasher film and I won't. I definitely have a strong moral conviction. I do films where people get slaughtered and decapitated, but it's always by fantasy characters. It is by big alien creatures. For me it's fun, I want to scare the poop out of the audience, and I want them to say "Ooh, gross, oh no, not that, it's horrible." I don't do *Friday the 13th* kind of films, and I don't plan to. Things that people take home with realistic nightmares, I personally have nothing against people who do them, but they're not for me. I do fantasy films. The last film I directed is a nice family film. It's PG. Yes, I do draw the line at the type of film that I will be involved with. But the line is drawn at how real is it. I don't want to disturb someone unnecessarily.

WIATER: What is it about the Stan Winston Studios that makes it unique, that producers say, "This is a job for Stan Winston and nobody can do it better?"

WINSTON: There are people that I have a great deal of respect for that I think can do things as well as we can. Basically I look at Rick Baker and I have a great deal of respect for Rick. I'm always looking to see what he does so that I can know that there's something there nipping at my heels and I can't stop for a second.

The thing that I believe allows Stan Winston Studio to do as good as can be done is that I have a great deal of faith in my judgment and my taste in making the right choices and understanding character and genre and being able to look at a picture and being able to say what's wrong with this picture. I am also surrounded by some of the finest artists in the business and have what I consider to be an unsurpassed team support system.

And a gift, that if nothing else, I was born with. Because it doesn't have to do with modesty, it has to do with being lucky that I enjoy working with people, therefore I feel that people possibly enjoy working with *me*. We can as a team get the job done. I work well with people that I work for, and I work well with people that work for me. I don't have any bad feelings on anything throughout my career. I have a great deal of respect for the people that I work for, and I have a great deal of respect for the people who work for me. I think that combination allows you to do the best job.

WIATER: Can you honestly say in your career that there have been only up moments, and not any down moments?

WINSTON: There are a lot of jobs that maybe the final look at the movie is not what you had hoped for, but that's life. That's not anything to whine about. I'm fortunate that I had the job and we did the best that we could. The times when you feel the best is when your work is within the scope of a body of work that is well received. That was my point earlier. In order to be proud of your work, you need to be proud of the vehicle that your work is within, which is the whole movie. This means that your job is beyond the scope of just what am I doing, but how am I helping this film? How am I making this whole film better? It's taken me years to learn that.

It's very easy to look back on my career and say, "What great work I did, but what a crummy movie." But then, did I help that movie or how much was I the rebel who said, "I'm wonderful and I'm gonna do my job this way and I'm gonna look good and you guys are going to look like crud because I'm better than you?" In the final analysis my work may look great, but the movie is a piece of shit. What good was that? If anything I was a thorn to the movie because I had an attitude. It's much too easy to criticize. I have been at the helm, I know what it takes to make a movie, and I also know what it takes to make a makeup. I know that it takes a coordination between the people at the top and the people under them. That is what people lack in the world, is working together.

WIATER: I am wondering is there a special camaraderie between a Rick Baker and Dick Smith and a Kevin Yagher and Stan Winston where very few people can grasp how complex and marvelous your careers really are?

WINSTON: Absolutely! But I think that is universal. It would be absurd to say if someone totally understands my work that I don't have an affinity for that person. There is a camaraderie between me and the people that you just mentioned, as there should be and is camaraderie between certain actors, directors, and stuntmen. Where it becomes unfortunate is people who, instead of this mutual respect, find it necessary to talk down to people who do the same thing. You hear so much of that. That's a major bother. I'm totally inspired by good work done by anybody, and I think that anybody is in our craft. Yes, there's definitely a camaraderie because we understand the details and the amount of work that goes into it.

I am fortunate, I also have a camaraderie with the director, because I have directed. So therefore it's difficult to chose sides, there is no "This is my job and that is your job." Making the film is *our* job, doing whatever we can to make that thing happen together. And that's the only problem with that camaraderie. If there is something that I can add to the camaraderie I have with the makeup effects people in the industry right now, it is a further understanding of what the film-making process is and how we all need to work toward the right goal. To make a *film* that people are going to come in and enjoy, and not making an *effect* that people are going to come in and enjoy. It never works.

WIATER: Are there still any projects where you are in a sense "hands-on" applying the makeup and effects?

WINSTON: I still do. I will occasionally dabble in it behind the scenes when no one is looking. Once in a while it's a joy to "get my hands dirty." Can't do it too often, because you don't have any time. You must set priorities.

WIATER: What do you tell someone who you've encountered at a screening when they say I really love films and I'm considering special effects and makeup as a career?

WINSTON: I would never persuade anyone. I would always say that if someone really wants something that they could achieve it. Really wanting something and thinking it would be neat are two different things. If people are really inspired and they want it more than anything, they'll do what is necessary. It is *extremely* competitive. They have to work on their artistic skills, school themselves in every aspect of the arts, drawing, painting, sculpting, study the work that has been done, other artists, artistic work, and understand characters from all times, do a lot of research, use all that research for the work that they prepare for themselves, and be prepared to show what they've done on their own. For someone to come in and say I really want to do this but I haven't done anything yet, with the competition that's out there right now, that just won't cut it.

You have to be able to show your wares and show that you've improved. If you come in and show your wares and they're not so good, then go out, continue working, and get better. If they want to work on an apprenticeship level to be around it, that's always a possibility. To sweep floors, to do whatever they can for next to nothing because they have to realize that at that point in their career, they're really not worth anything. They're trying to get to the point where they are of value to someone else. To do that you must on your own school yourself, educate to a certain extent, work yourself to a point where you can get in and then be working on jobs. Then once you're on the job, you continue to work to get better and continue to be inspired by people around you. I'm constantly learning every day from the people who are around me. Wonderful talent, it's all there.

WIATER: Dick Smith is one of the masters, and he says there's no idea of retirement because every day is a new, fun day. You wake up and say there's something that I'm going to learn today.

WINSTON: Absolutely.

WIATER: Do you think that your area of expertise has become truly vital to the Hollywood industry because the audiences now always expect state-of-the-art special effects and makeup?

WINSTON: Just as poor quality film won't do, you must stay up with the state of the art. But definitely technique, special effects, and fantasy characters are not vital to motion pictures. They're only vital to the *type* of motion picture that requires them. If a picture requires a special fantasy effect or anything like that, then yes you must stay up with state of the art. As in any other art form, you must be up to date. You can't fall back on it and let it be sloppy or be less than state of the art. At the same time to say from a Hollywood standpoint that a movie is dependent on good special effects is an absurdity. A movie is dependent on a good story and good performances, period. Everything else is icing.

WIATER: What has been the most challenging project you've worked on to date?

WINSTON: The next one. Each one must be more challenging than the last one. You do that to yourself. The last one was more challenging from an effects standpoint than the one before it. You continue to make each one more challenging because you keep stretching. The answer is the next one.

Kevin Yagher

At the ripe old age of twenty-eight, Kevin Yagher is already a seasoned veteran in the world of dark visions. In spite of a humble start running a Halloween mask business in his hometown of Dayton, Yagher always knew his destiny had something to do with monsters and horror movies. Corresponding with makeup master Dick Smith while still in his teens, he was advised by Smith that if he had the courage of his convictions, he had to move to either New York or Hollywood to try and make his mark.

Convinced that the young Yagher had genuine talent, Smith supplied him with the names of several Los Angeles–based special makeup and effects artists. He broke into the field by working on several projects with such recognized effects masters as Rick Baker and Stan Winston, including episodes of the television series "Amazing Stories" and "Beauty and the Beast." Some of his early work in features is on view with the alien creatures in *Cocoon* and the title creature in the Walt Disney production, *Fuzzbucket*.

However, his major break came when he was asked to redesign the makeup for Freddy Krueger in the first sequel to the phenomenal series, *A Nightmare on Elm Street, Part II*. He worked on *Part III* and *Part IV* as well. If that wasn't enough to make a name for himself, Yagher created the incredibly lifelike "animatronic" puppet known as "Chucky" for the very successful *Child's Play* and its first sequel, *Child's Play 2*.

In spite of these ongoing series of successes, my initial impression of Yagher is that the only dirty word in his vocabulary is *vacation*. A certified workaholic, Yagher is a man who has accomplished so much because to him it's not work, it's simply fun and a joy to do.

I talked with Kevin Yagher at a time when he was stretching his talents to include a stint as a director for the HBO cable series "Tales from the Crypt." His production company was also involved in a number of ongoing projects, and *Child's Play 2* was about to be released in a matter of weeks. As usual, Yagher was up to his eyeballs in work and couldn't have been happier.

SELECTED FILMOGRAPHY

Trick or Treat (1986)

The Hidden (1987)

A Nightmare on Elm Street, Part II (1985)

A Nightmare on Elm Street, Part III (1987)

Child's Play (1988)

A Nightmare on Elm Street, Part IV (1988)

Bill and Ted's Excellent Adventure (1989)

Child's Play 2 (1990)

WIATER: There's talk already of doing a *Child's Play 3*, even though the first sequel has yet to open nationwide. It's nice to be that confident on a project.

YAGHER: Well, they know they have a hit for *Child's Play 2*. It tested *really* well—much better than they expected. We'll see. But I'm sure it will make all the money the producers want it to make—and more! [Chuckles.]

WIATER: More and more of your colleagues, such as Tom Savini and Stan Winston, are going into directing. What's your interest there, since you already have a remarkable career in special makeup effects?

YAGHER: As you know, I grew up in Ohio and was a monster freak. Well, a lot of young people come out here to Hollywood because of an interest in animation and wanting to be another Ray Harryhausen. My brother and I fooled around with animation for a while, but you get discouraged because it takes too long to get your film back, and they *always* ruin it. The first three feet is always screwed up or they'll expose it wrong or something. Anyway, my brother went off to be an actor, and I stayed in Ohio and made monsters and masks.

WIATER: I still don't see the connection between making monsters and being a movie director.

YAGHER: I didn't set out to become a director, because when I first came out here to Hollywood, so many people wanted to be directors, too, that I thought I'd never have the chance. When I first came out here, I wanted to be a makeup effects artist, and that was all I wanted to do. But when you're out here after a while, and you see so many bad scripts come across your desk and so many not really talented people that you're working for—including directors—then you start thinking along those lines that you can do it better.

Although my first introduction to film was through such creatures as Wolfman and Frankenstein, since that time I've become a big fan of *all* kinds of films. So eventually I'd like to do a movie that has nothing to do with creatures. I did an article for a film magazine once where I said I would like to do a film where people just talk to one another. But right in the middle of it I'd probably go crazy and have to throw in a gargoyle or demon that comes in and kills everybody and then leaves. [Laughs.] So I really would like to do something that's a love story someday. I'm meeting with Richard Donner's development people right now about a science fiction story, and hopefully something will come of that. But it took some time for me to decide to become a director. I just didn't wake up one morning and say, "You know, this director's a jerk—this is how *I'm* going to do it!"

WIATER: But do you have any intention of giving up your present career to pursue one in directing?

YAGHER: I truly do love my work. My wife says I could stay in my shop twenty-four hours a day, which really isn't true, but I do enjoy this. I mean, working with your hands, there's nothing else like it! To sit down like you do when you're writing, and physically create something that didn't exist before is amazing. It's great fun. Now with directing, you really have to have a lot of money. And time. But when I get bored, or just want to get away, I get a lump of clay or something to draw and make something out of it. Even if I never finish it, I get the high out of creating.

WIATER: Because of you're specializing in horror and fantasy films, I imagine you've had some encounters with the MPAA by now?

YAGHER: It's such a ridiculous situation! The filmmakers will always put in more explicit scenes, because they *know* the sequence will eventually be hacked up by the MPAA. And you're left wondering, "Is that gag I'm doing one they're going to purposely cut anyway, and the producers already know it?" So it's kind of frustrating when things are cut, and it's just for timing. It's a hurtful lesson, but you learn it quick, and try not to take it personally.

But the first time it happens—when you've been working months on something and you really want to show people what you can do and you're real excited about seeing this effect of yours on the screen—and then you go to a screening. And it's either cut *completely* out, which is unbelievably devastating, or it's shown so fast you really don't have a chance to focus on it.

But after learning more about the medium, sometimes that's all you need. The imagination is always stronger than what you can see on the screen. I learned about that and also learned how much effort too put into certain things—such as not to put eyelashes and every little pore on a monster that the camera isn't going to get that close to or hold on. Well, I will anyway [laughs], but I won't put my heart and soul into it when I know now that fifty percent of my work will be cut out anyway. So that's how I go into it; it's the only way I can survive. I'll still put everything into it as an artist, but as far as getting emotionally involved—I try not to.

WIATER: Yet if your heart and soul isn't in it, how can you achieve any satisfaction from your efforts?

YAGHER: Well, a lot of times I end up making things just for myself. Or I'll tell myself, "What a great shop display piece this will make." Or you go, "Yeah, I'll get some great video on this one, or I'll put it on my [résumé] reel when they get done." Because you do it just for the film. You really do. You just have to go into the project with that attitude. Or you'll get devastated and you wouldn't want to do anything. Some people get bitter, but I don't think that's a good idea either. But then again, this is one of the reasons you think, I'm going to do a film and I'm going to direct it and I'm going to put this creature in it and really highlight it.

Without overdoing it, of course. You don't want to be masturbating and showing off all your effects to people—that's ultimately boring. The bottom line is, you have to have a story, and everything else is secondary.

WIATER: What are your feelings on film ratings and censorship?

YAGHER: Once you've rated the movie, as far as cutting scenes out of it, I think it's a shame. You should leave that up to the filmmaker. If he's a good filmmaker he can determine how long to hold a shot of a bloodied head or whatever. Just to get the desired effect, and then move on. There's no reason to dwell on it, because as I said, the imagination can do so much more. But I think it's a shame the way the MPAA goes about hacking up films, and the filmmakers have to bring their films back three and four times before the board. And at the end of it, there's nothing left.

WIATER: There's been some backlash against the character of Freddy Krueger in the *Nightmare on Elm Street* films. What are your feelings about why he's become so popular with young people?

YAGHER: He is essentially the boogey man. That's the way I see it. Everyone has their version of the boogeyman, and when Wes Craven made him a child killer, well, the threat of being killed is what every child fears, so what else is there? So I have no problem with that, because they've made Freddy the boogeyman and able to travel in your dreams, which is a great idea. I like him better than I do Jason or Michael Meyers from the *Friday the 13th* and *Halloween* films, because they're just basically killing machines. They have no personality, and I love the fact that Robert Englund gave Freddy his own personality.

That's the one thing about all characters—including Chucky and the Crypt Keeper—I think their popularity stems from having a personality. Freddy is not just a child killer; he's a personality with a sense of humor, as opposed to something that is just a blatant horror. Like in *Alien*, where the monster is just a survivor trying to kill everyone. I prefer something with a personality; something you can laugh at. And as far as the backlash, if parents don't want their kids to watch them, then they shouldn't let them watch them. These films *are* rated.

WIATER: Could you tell me about your relationship with actor Robert Englund, whom you've worked with on several major projects?

YAGHER: I've put the Freddy Krueger makeup on Robert, over the years before I stopped working on the *Nightmare on Elm Street* series, more than a 150 times. Now I've had makeup on many times, but I couldn't do what he does. The skin takes a tremendous beating. I know he hates the smell of the glue, and it takes a while for him to get into it. And who knows what the long-term effects of these chemicals are doing to his skin?

But when we were working together, I think I knew him better than his wife did! [Chuckles.] I was looking in his ear every day, and we were smelling each other's breath; you get to be together so much you know everything about each other, hear his every thought. You see what he goes through in prepping for the part of Freddy, too. It's funny, because as the makeup goes on, he would literally transform. You put so many pieces of makeup and he's still Robert. Then that one little piece goes on, like the nose, and once that final piece is on, toward the end, he's really starting to get nasty. I mean that in a fun way, with humor. But by the time we're through he's this cold Freddy. I don't think he was even conscious of what he was doing. It's just his way of getting into the character.

WIATER: Do you have a favorite monster or special makeup effect of your own?

YAGHER: I guess the most fun for me so far is the Crypt Keeper for "Tales from the Crypt." Basically they just left me alone and told me "Do whatever you want to do." I even had to cast the Crypt Keeper's voice. I was then able to direct the wraparound sequence that are part of every episode, and then a complete episode. So I had the most fun I think doing that.

WIATER: Your killer doll Chucky is also a pretty memorable creation.

YAGHER: It's really great fun to create something that you do entirely on your own. If you're putting makeup on an actor, you're still working with that actor and his personality. Robert Englund gets credit for being Freddy, but every time I see a poster, I'm thinking, "Hey, I had something to do with that. That was my sculpture, or that was my paint job." It was my creativity that makes him look the way he does, and then Robert brings out the character's personality in combination with a writer and a director.

WIATER: Yes, but after reading the script, how Chucky came into existence was totally reliant on your skills and imagination, not the interpretation of an actor.

YAGHER: Yes, it's nice when it's your creation, and nobody else's but yours. But it's true, I'm like Chucky's agent [in mannered voice]: "Yeah, babe—want Chucky on the set for fifty days? Sure, babe, sure." [Laughs.] Because on these films, along with the actors, Chucky's on the set *every day*. And along with him come eight or nine puppeteers. It's a major undertaking, but he is the star. Everyone else can be phased out, but he is going to be the one sticking around.

It's the same thing with Freddy; you can have different casts and crew, but they always have to bring back the monster. It's nice to have a part of that, when the producers always have to go to you.

Sure, they own the copyright on the film and can always go to someone else for the special effects. But they're usually a little afraid of doing that; they don't want to change a good thing. They go for another actor to play Freddy, but that would be foolish. I don't think anybody is out to rob anybody, and the audience wouldn't like it if they were to change actors now, this late in the series. And Robert should get a considerable amount of money, because he's coming back for the four, fifth, and sixth time to do this character.

WIATER: You've done an amazing amount of work in a relatively short amount of time. Why are you working so hard—you haven't hit thirty yet, and you've done more work than some people have with another decade of experience behind them.

YAGHER: I don't know, have I? I guess I'm in fear of that one effect getting out there that won't be good enough. I don't turn down that much work. I always try to take on work that will challenge me, to see how much I can take on and still deliver a good product. I don't want to see any part of it suffer; I try to put my all into everything I do.

But I do love to work. I know there's people who do a lot of work and then go on a long vacation, or they love to take on only a certain amount of work. I think I'm trying to work a lot now so I can get to the point where I can pick and choose my projects. I'm using my youth to work as hard as I can, until I'm too tired. I *am* resting; I'm married now and my wife makes sure that I do that. But people are always telling me to "take some time off."

Well, I think there's always going to be time for that later, and I want to have a good time now and have the finances to say later, "Okay, I'm going to take a year off and develop this project." Nobody really "stops working." We're all workaholics—we love what we do, and nobody really wants ever to completely stop. But I'm trying to get as much experience as I can now so I can have choices later on.

WIATER: What do you do to fuel your imagination?

YAGHER: Anybody can get rusty. I always try to look at other people's art, in whatever form, whether it's art for art's sake, or in a film or in a story. You also always try to keep up with what everybody else is doing. When you start out, the imagination is flowing, and you have so many ideas. But when you get done with those ideas, you say, "Now what?" You tell yourself you have to do something bigger and better. So it gets more difficult to be constantly creative as time goes on.

WIATER: True—then how do you do it?

YAGHER: You have to keep feeding that imagination. You have to keep from getting jaded. You have to not let show business bring you down, because out here you can get literally burned out. You can get tired and not want to work anymore. And let your imagination just die on you. After working on some project for six months and not being able to sit down and draw for a long time, it can be tough. Then you come home with a script and sit down at the drawing table and say, "Okay, I've got to come up with a monster." And you're sitting there, and there's *nothing*! And what I found out about myself is that it takes three days of "nothingness" before anything new comes to me.

What I like to do is look at different people's artwork and different people's style. And not try to mimic it but take from it what I can. To do my take on it, to try and keep my style changing. When I look back at my own work and see similar styles in the sculptures, I especially want to keep doing it differently. You only have one life to live, so I'm saying do what you can, but enjoy it also. You won't burn out if you regulate yourself. Try and do a little bit of everything.

Sometimes I'll come back after a long time away and I'll do great things, because I haven't drawn or sculpted for a while. It's so easy to go back and do what you know. The most difficult thing is to keep trying for something new.

WIATER: Again, it's still noteworthy how you've come such a long way in a relatively short amount of time. Any idea how you did it?

YAGHER: I haven't really looked back at what I've done and said, "Well I did that wrong." All I can tell you is what impresses me when young people come to me for advice. I have a couple of new guys in the shop, and I can tell right away which are the ones who are eager to work. Not work in the sense of throwing their lives away and doing nothing else, but who are willing to spend that little extra time. I mean, I didn't give up my high school prom or dances, but I was always trying to create new things rather than just sit in front of the television when I got home.

Because you really have to *love* it! People come in here and it's clear they don't really love it. They did something else before this or found out they could do this type of work and make some money or they just love the *idea* of working in this business. You can usually tell that, because first of all their work reflects it. You can tell how much time they really put into it. And if they're the lucky ones, and can sit down and do great work and don't have to work at it because

God blessed them with this amazing talent, you can still see it in their attitude. The best people are the ones who really care.

Back when I was in Ohio, I remember thinking, "I want to make things look real to the eye." So that maybe in a slightly dim light you could fool somebody. My biggest thrill was putting makeup on and fooling somebody in a dimly lit hallway—even if it was only for a moment. It was such a *thrill*! That was the clincher for me. That's when I knew I had to do this for a living.

So keep experimenting, and read everything you can get ahold of. You'll know you're ready to come out here when you look at a magazine and say "Hey, my stuff is better than that." Or "Half of my work is better than these quickie slasher films effects." Be confident in yourself, and don't be afraid of success. Your parents tell you when you go out in the world, you've got to be ready or they'll chew you up and spit you out. And they're right! Especially here—there are people who will eat you up. But you can't let that get in your way of doing what you want to do.

But most important, if you love what you're doing, you'll succeed no matter what. You won't let anything stand in your way. I recognized that in myself when I was eighteen. I wasn't going to let anybody else's fears get in my way.

Brian Yuzna

The Guyver Productions, Inc.

As has been shown repeatedly, the most creative film-makers in the horror field are those who, for lack of a more intellectual analysis, were simply *born* to view life as a series of dark visions.

One of the most exciting producers to appear on the scene in some time is beginning to make his mark as a director as well. The name: Brian Yuzna. One of the reasons his name is going to be familiar is, of course, due to his association with director Stuart Gordon. Acting as a creative team, they were responsible for several fine horror movies in the late eighties, the most noteworthy—of course—was 1985's *The Re-Animator*. If Yuzna was never to produce another film in his career, he would still be able to correctly say he had made his footnote in horror cinema with that motion picture alone.

But as he freely confesses, Yuzna has always been an unabashed fan of horror and science fiction movies. Growing up mostly in South America, he lived with his parents on a military base and had very little exposure to television as a child. However, he did have the opportunity to go to the movies every Sunday, where he saw "maybe a double feature and serials like *Captain Marvel, Rocket Man*, and *Dick Tracy*." Not too surprisingly, he can vividly remember his very first horror movie, 1955's *Creature with the Atom Brain.*

Although the movie gave him nightmares, Yuzna, like so many others in the business of giving other people nightmares, was hooked for life: "It's kind of like a drug; you keep going back for more. I used to see about six movies in a weekend once I was able to go out on my own. I loved to see anything with a monster."

It was clearly a natural progression for Yuzna to find his life's work making horror and fantasy movies. Recently he has begun to direct as well as produce, with two noteworthy films: *Bride of Re-Animator* and *Society*. Although the former movie may prove to be the more commercially successful, it's the truly unsettling *Society* that gives the first indication that he may become as formidable a director as he is a producer.

I spoke with Brian Yuzna as he was preparing to get underway with a number of projects, such as a thriller entitled *Animus* and a live action version of a popular Japanese science fiction series.

SELECTED FILMOGRAPHY

The Re-Animator (1985) (producer)

From Beyond (1986) (producer)

Honey, I Shrunk the Kids (1989) (producer)

Society (1990) (director)

Bride of Re-Animator (1990) (director)

WIATER: Which is the greater turn-on, producing or directing? I've talked to both producers and directors and each seems to think that the other role is the less challenging one.

YUZNA: I like doing both. What I like the best is to produce *and* direct. Directing has a great amount of arbitrary creative decision making, and a director gets to invent a lot of things. A producer has to deal with the reality of engineering these things. I've always been a very creative producer. I like to produce things that I originate. I like to build the script and production. But I think the fun is in directing. It's more intense work during the period and is more challenging. If things are going well, a producer doesn't have much to do. But the other part of it is that a director is off the show once he has finished directing it, and a producer's job keeps on going.

I think every movie has different dynamics as far as control. With Sylvester Stallone there isn't much argument about who has the control, the producer or director. Sylvester Stallone has the control. Some producers have a lot of weight and they have the control, but some directors have a lot of weight and they have control. Many producers do nothing more than work for a director. So, I really think it depends on the individual. I have found that if I just do one or the other, I am frustrated in one way or another. The times that I have been very satisfied have been when I have directed *and* produced, so that's my aim.

WIATER: To my knowledge, the only film you have directed and produced was *Bride of Re-Animator*. Is that true?

YUZNA: Yes, that's the only one. Although I have to say that what you do isn't necessarily credited.

WIATER: What about *Initiation*? Didn't you direct and produce that?

YUZNA: I just directed that. It was a much smaller-budgeted movie than *The Re-Animator*. It was very tough. It was what I call a "psycho-fiction." The key phrase for psycho-fiction is that fears and phobias are real but entertaining. It's just fun. A lot of people will say that there are scenes that are disgusting and not fun at all, but I don't agree.

WIATER: In your dark visions, is there anything you would consider disgusting, beyond your boundaries of "good taste"?

YUZNA: I guess, but I usually try not to think of things that way. There's things that I wouldn't do that bother me. It's your own personal quirks. For example what disgusts me are things like Debra Winger dying of cancer in *Terms of Endearment*. I hate movies where people are dying from disease. If there is some element of fantasy in a movie, then the very twisted and strange things can be dealt with. It gives you a way to distance yourself from it. I have a problem with movies that exploit that kind of stuff. I am also not crazy about seeing a movie that graphically depicts rape, realistically. It's not entertaining to me to look at real terrible things. When you get into horror and science fiction, you're basically dealing with entertainment. It's pretty hard to confuse it with something that is real.

WIATER: Then why do the censors prefer to pounce on horror films more so than mainstream films? If it is "only" fantasy and "just" entertainment, why does the MPAA jump down your throats when you try to deal with issues via a fantasy element?

YUZNA: I think you are really asking two questions. One is why are they acting like censors, and the other is why do they think this stuff needs to be censored? I think the reason they are acting like censors is because they *are* censors. It seems like a stupid thing to say but I remember seeing a TV show about behaviorism where an experiment was done on a college campus. They used psychology students and took half of them and put them in jail for a week, and the other half were their jailers. They studied their behavior, and as the days went by the jailers acted like jailers; they were being sort of sadistic to them. They were treating them in a certain way. And I have certainly noticed that for myself as far as my appearance, what clothes I wear, what car I drive, et cetera, that affects how people treat me.

If you are in the role of the censor, after a while you just become the censor. There is a really twisted meddling power thing that goes on with that, and I think that's what's happening to a certain degree with the MPAA. I've dealt with them and you have to play a real game with them. The more you give them, the more they twist you. You have to be very careful.

It's like politicians. Sometimes people say that the only rational political stand to take is to throw the rascals out. Because if you really believe that power corrupts, then anyone you give power to is going to become corrupted by it. If a person gets elected to office, they turn into a politician. If someone is made a censor, they turn into a censor.

WIATER: Why do you think they jump on horror films in particular? Their meddling is almost taken for granted nowadays.

YUZNA: I don't know. Why is it that people are offended by them? I bet if you had a bunch of teenagers on the board, they wouldn't be! It could be because horror films bring up issues that they don't want to deal with. My own opinion is that horror as a genre is kind of an adolescent genre. I'm not saying this in a negative way because I'm a fan of horror. I don't do it because it's just a way to make money and go through life. I like the fact that something that I was such a fan of years ago, now I get to make. But I also know that they don't mean to me what they used to when I was a kid. I think they mean something to teenagers that they don't mean to adults. When I look at something like *Dead Ringers* I think now there's an *adult* horror movie. No kid would like that movie. I can also see why no one went to see it. I think it was probably the best movie of the year, but nobody wants to walk out of a theater feeling like that—it had everything that a horror movie has without any of the escape.

I think with teenagers horror movies operate the way that fairy tales do for children. This isn't my idea; I've basically borrowed this from other people who have written about this stuff. I do think that they work for kids by instructing them in puberty and sexuality, what's proper and what's not. With kids, the fairy tales are dealing with parental separation anxiety. I think with horror movies, it's easy for a teenager to see a movie that deals with metamorphosis, which would fall under the werewolf, Dr. Jekyll, Mr. Hyde categories.

WIATER: But if you're a guy, you're gonna end up like the two fellows in *Bride of Re-Animator* One character loses his love and instead of saying, "Well I've got this new babe in my life," he's still hung up on reanimating the other girl's *heart*. Talk about carrying a torch!

YUZNA: Obviously, *Bride of Re-Animator* deals with all those issues very clearly. That was my concern in that movie with Mary Shelley. What I like about her is the existential conundrum of the creator rejecting the created. It's what makes that story always so fresh.

WIATER: I would like to ask you about the two versions of *The Re-Animator*—was it necessary to have two versions of that film? Why wasn't there one "pure" version, so to speak?

YUZNA: Well there is—the original version. I didn't have anything to do with the second one, which is the R-rated one. The unrated, eighty-seven-minute version that played in the theaters was my version. We were in Italy and I made the mistake of letting Charlie Band get a hold of that movie. Charlie Band had nothing to do with it except that he owed me money. I used his postproduction facilities, and I made the mistake of letting him distribute it. As a matter of fact, just last month I finished a three-year lawsuit to get that picture back. I certainly disavowed the R-rated version. I would have been happy to cut an R-rated version but I don't think I would have done it that way. Whole scenes were cut out of the movie.

WIATER: It's my understanding that when it was sold to cable television it was your unrated version that appeared in some areas and in other areas it was the R-rated version. Why?

YUZNA: I presume, but I have to tell you that one of the things that I learned about the movie business is just because you produce, direct, write, act that doesn't give you any more insight into the business of selling a movie than someone who doesn't. So when someone owns the distribution rights to your movie, they do whatever they want whenever they want, and they have no obligation to tell you about it.

So your sources are as good as mine on that. I could find out because I have finally won my legal battle and everything comes back to me. I do believe they showed different versions different places. The reason there was an R-rated version is the same reason that we have to get R ratings on other movies. That is that certain parts of the country will not accept it, so you have to provide them with something they can use.

I know that the business of movies pays for movies, and I personally have no problem making an R-rated version, especially because the unrated version has had enough viewership with the people who want to see that to satisfy me. The one exception that I would like to make is that I would like to be in control of that R-rated version. I'm happy to cut it, because I believe in my own abilities to keep what is important. Obviously there's some things that would be very difficult to hang on to, but let *me* make that choice.

WIATER: Do you still have a working relationship or friendship with Stuart Gordon?

YUZNA: Not actively now, he's in Rome doing *The Pit and the Pendulum*. I think it's a natural progression that we went through. *The Re-Animator* was the first movie for both of us. Stuart had never directed a movie and I had never really produced a big movie like this. We were very fortunate that it worked out real well. After that we made two or three more movies. We made *Dolls* and *From Beyond* and then basically what happened is that I started having problems with Charlie Band on a business level. I produced *Robot Jox* for the first six months or so and finally it was necessary for me to sever any business with Charlie in order to go forward with getting redress for what I perceived to be trespasses that were done on a business level for *The Re-Animator*. Stuart continued to work on *Robot Jox*, so at that point we quit working together.

We did have other projects together, and I had spoken to him about doing a film that our kids could watch. I had had an idea that I had when I was a child about kids riding an ant and a bee. I mentioned to Stuart that we should do something about kids who shrink down real tiny and can't get out of their backyard. He immediately got excited about that and we started inventing the story. This became *Honey, I Shrunk the Kids*. I produced the movie for about a year and built all the sets. Of course, Stuart got very ill right before we were going to shoot. He got high blood pressure and his doctor suggested that he should leave the film. When that happened, they got a new director who wanted a new writer and producer. So ultimately I ended up with a writing credit and a co-producing credit. But I didn't follow through on the picture. After that we tried to work together on a couple of other projects, but I think after that we had kind of "ridden the wave." At that point I started directing, so if I'm gonna direct then what is Stuart going to do? [Laughs.]

WIATER: In terms of *Bride of Re-Animator*, that was apparently something that you had in mind to begin with, that there would be a sequel.

YUZNA: Yes, we always talked about it, and the title came first. I had always expected that he would direct it.

WIATER: Was there any attempt to emulate the style that Stuart brought to *The Re-Animator* because that was kind of the magic, that wild style?

YUZNA: There was *definitely* the attempt to do that. If I could have imitated it exactly, I would have done it. I was basically trying to satisfy the fans, that was my biggest concern. Obviously, *The Re-Animator* is a much tighter picture than *Bride of Re-Animator*. *Bride* is a sequel for one thing. Second, I tend to put a lot of stuff in movies, and I think you can see that in *From Beyond*. I know that Stuart has told me that in *From Beyond* we had a couple of movies in there. I tend to overload these things with ideas sometimes. I can't help it, that's the way I am. [Chuckles.] I think with *Bride*, if I could have done it in the same style and had the same effects that *The Re-Animator* had, I would have done it in a flash. To a certain degree in *From Beyond* we were trying to emulate *The Re-Animator*. We were trying to play to an audience.

I think what is going on at the time you make a movie has an effect on it. Also Stuart and I have different strengths and weaknesses. Stuart is really terrific at story telling and is really good with actors. To me that's always been my standard answer to what I think is really terrific about Stuart. I'm not as good with actors, because Stuart had spent his life before *The Re-Animator* working with actors in the theater. I never did. I had to kind of learn about actors, acting, and directing on a soundstage. Stuart learned it on a stage. He knows how to tell a story with very little. When I get on a soundstage I am making a movie based on my experience of going to movies. When Stuart gets on a soundstage a lot of what he is bringing to it is his experience of entertaining people on a stage. I admire that.

WIATER: Was *Bride of Re-Animator* your first film as director or was it *Society*?

YUZNA: It was *Society*. Looking at the two movies, I think that *Bride of Re-Animator* is much better directed than *Society*. I learned a lot. I think that if I directed ten or fifteen movies I would learn a lot more. The way that I go forward is by trying stuff and building on what I know.

As far as strengths go, I am pretty good at story. I think my weakness is that I tend to overload a story. Sometimes I don't have confidence in the simpler things. Most of what I bring to a movie is that I like to experiment and I like to try for looks and learn things with the movie. My general thrust is to have a lot of ideas in a movie and then simplify so it becomes just pure entertainment. My ideal is to have a film that is nine-tenths below the water, so on the surface it's just a very simple, straightforward, highly entertaining piece of business. But if you dig down you will find all the ideas that I find fascinating.

For example on *Initiation*, that was a contract job and it was basically to make yet another unwanted sequel to *Silent Night, Deadly Night*, which nobody wants to see. What led me to do it was that I liked the producer, Richard Polaski. Basically his opinion was that it didn't have to have anything to do with the other ones. He wanted it to be about witches. So my feeling was that as long as it didn't have to be like the other ones and as long as the witches didn't have to wear robes and shams, I was interested. We did the script in probably ten days. What was exciting for me about that movie was that I was able to indulge in other big interests of mine. When I was in college I studied religion and art. What was great about *Initiation* was that I got into the goddess mythology. The story was built based on these myths. That to me was a great deal of fun and I think people tend to respond to that sometimes.

WIATER: As in *The Re-Animator*, you seem to have gone to the edge again with *Society*.

YUZNA: A lot of distributors that saw this movie were personally offended by it. I just thought of it as a burlesque. I thought it would be a lot of fun. I was disturbed when I found this reaction. I started questioning myself a little bit, thinking I was really "out to lunch." Then in Britain it did tremendously well. It played there for about four months and got great reviews. I realized that the British don't have a hard time realizing that there are classes. Americans, it's like messing with their mythology; you're threatening their whole world. American world view is predicated on this idea that those who have more really deserve it. It's not a matter of just placement. If we have just a little bit of luck and work a little harder, we will be there. One of the points of *Society* is that not only do a very small number of people control the world, but just having money doesn't put you in there. Whatever class you are born in is the class you will grow up in.

WIATER: Did you have any censorship problems with the MPAA over *Society*? I can't imagine that you didn't.

YUZNA: It just went over there, it hasn't been released domestically.

The British producer that bought it got it through the censors without a frame being cut. We were very careful, we didn't include the color red. The one thing that really puts people off is blood, so one of the things I said going in was that we would have no red in there, just slime. When we turned people inside out and popped their eyeballs out, we didn't do it realistically. If we had done it realistically I think it would have really taken away from the movie. As it was, it kept it on a more fun level. The argument for that was if they could metamorphasize like that, why should their interiors be the same? They are full of slugs anyway, they don't have hearts and lungs or anything like that. They need the underclass to invigorate the line. It's kind of like a purebred dog, you have to mate them with a mongrel every so often because they get all these weird diseases.

WIATER: Do you see *Society* as a more dangerous film than *Bride of Re-Animator* or even *The Re-Animator*?

YUZNA: Oh sure, *The Re-Animator* was just a good old-time horror movie. *It was just the horror movie you've always wanted to see.* I think the reason it worked was that Stuart and I were really big horror fans. Since I was paying for everything there wasn't anybody else saying what we should or shouldn't do. My biggest concern was that we didn't make a movie that failed due to weak heart on our part.

I know the part that really tickles people is the head giving head. I've always been a big fan of characters carrying around their heads for one reason or another. The villain is always after the girl, and when you have a villain that's just a head, what good can he do with the girl? When people are delighted by that scene, it's not because they are perverted. I think they love the contradiction in terms, it's such a delightful development. It's so appropriate and yet nobody's ever done it. That makes it a whole lot of fun. And of course we always backed it up with a joke anytime there was something that was real outrageous or possibly disgusting. As soon as that happens we have Herbert come in and make a joke about getting a job in a side show. As soon as he cuts off the head he pops it onto that letter holder to hold it up. Why? Because I'm a real fan of these head movies and these heads are always cut off so even.

When we talked about it I said, "What are we going to do with this head? How can we stand it up on the table?" Everybody knows how it's done, we're not going to fool anybody. They know the guy is under the table. If you put a head down it would naturally fall over. It's not going to balance on its neck! We always watch these movies and accept that outrageous stuff. Of course we did it ourselves. How could Dr. Hill talk if he didn't have any lungs? As long as he rasps his voice then poetically people would accept that he's just a head.

WIATER: Do you think there is a special talent that a person needs to make a horror film? A truly frightening picture?

YUZNA: I know for myself that it was a great interest in what scares me. I think now when I go to horror movies I'm always trying to recapture that fear. I can't anymore. There's a nostalgia going on here and a feeling of wanting to contribute to it. I love it when people are affected, scared, or grossed out! I don't actually know what it takes to make a movie frightening; why some people do it and some people don't. In a way you just sort of have to be a very irresponsible person to do it. There's no guarantees.

WIATER: There are certain films that stand out as being breakthrough films when they were released and certainly *The Re-Animator* was that type of film. Are there going to be more breakthrough films in this genre? Any darker visions?

YUZNA: I think that there *will* be new breakthrough films and there will always be new audiences to be surprised and delighted. You can still work on the old audience too. Horror really gets a bad rap. People are much more comfortable with *The Terminator*, with getting their rough stuff out in an action, sci-fi way. There's something about horror that really bothers people, it's too psychological. One thing is that horror deals with sex, and people are still very uncomfortable with sex. I personally find it fascinating.

Paul M. Sammon

Deana Newcomb

I n the course of compiling *Dark Visions*, all the professionals I spoke with had easily recognizable roles and occupa-
tions within the industry. One of the more unusual job
titles I was to come across was that of "special promotional
consultant." What that title actually means is that about a
decade ago, the Hollywood studios realized there was a large
group of hard-core fans of horror and science fiction films. A
group that in fact numbered in the millions.

One way of letting that number of potential ticket buyers
know what genre films were in production, or were about to
be released, was to hire someone who was already an expert
on horror and science fiction films. Not to mention being a
dedicated, lifelong fan of the movies.

Among the very first people to wear that particular hat in
the promotional end of the industry was Paul M. Sammon.
Born in 1949, Sammon began his career (which now overlaps

to include journalist-editor-author-publicist-filmmaker) writing for every major movie publication, including *Starlog*, *Omni*, *Cinefex*, and most important, *Cinefantastique*. From the late seventies through the early eighties, Sammon consistently delivered the most comprehensive production articles ever attempted on several of the most important genre films being made at the time.

Due to his extensive coverage of *Conan the Barbarian* for *Cinefantastique*, Sammon's journalistic talents were noticed by the publicity departments of the major studios, which allowed him to have a concurrent career as a publicist for such movies as *Dune*, *F/X*, *Return of the Living Dead*, and *Blue Velvet*. He was able to travel to numerous horror/science fiction conventions (which was where I first met him a decade ago) to preach the gospel and basically be paid for what most of us fans would gladly do for free.

Since then, Sammon continues to expand his horizons. He has become a documentary filmmaker (examining the production of such movies as *Robocop* and *Platoon*), and continues to develop as a writer, both as author (*Blood and Rockets: The 500 Best Horror and Science Fiction Films on Videotape*) and editor (*Splatterpunks: Extreme Horror*).

At the time of our conversation, Sammon's own promotion and production company, Awesome Productions, Inc., has optioned Joe R. Lansdale's novel *The Drive-in*. Not too surprisingly, he had already written the screenplay and hoped to be directing the picture by the time *Dark Visions* saw publication.

Since Paul M. Sammon is also, finally, one of the most reputable *cineteratolgists* around, it seemed only fitting to conclude this volume by talking to a fellow movie-watching fan who is steadily evolving into a moviemaking pro. (Coincidentally, writer-director Mick Garris [*Psycho IV*] also got his break into the industry as a special promotions consultant.) The lesson to be ultimately learned here is that no matter what road one takes—writer, director, actor, special effects makeup, producer—anyone can reach the magical land of Hollywood if they just remember never to give up their dark dreams.

Or dark visions.

WIATER: Do you recall your earliest exposure to the cinema of the fantastic? You once said it was an experience that changed your life forever—the "child shaping the man."

SAMMON: Well, when I was about three years old, my family was on a military base in Japan. My mother took me out shopping, and we then went to a Japanese movie theater—my mother has always been a big movie fan. I found out later it was a double bill of *Them!* and *Riders to the Stars*. I had no problem with *Them!*, but strangely enough one little segment of *Riders to the Stars* absolutely traumatized me. There is an accident, and an astronaut is propelled out into space. His helmet is shattered, and he's immediately killed. Another astronaut watches his corpse float by through a periscope—this is a science fiction state-of-the-art visual device for 1953!—and he sees the helmet is shattered, and inside the helmet is a skull.

Well, today you could probably see that in a breakfast commercial and not be upset. But back in 1953 I was a blank slate. I thought I was watching a documentary! That skull made me literally run out of the theater into the middle of Yokohama. Somehow my mother tracked me down, hours later, to a police station.

That little incident has always remained with me. But who knows what would have happened if I had been exposed to an MGM musical? Or a John Wayne Western?

WIATER: When you began your career as a film journalist, did you ever imagine it would offer you so many opportunities in the film industry itself? You've been quite the pioneer, actually.

SAMMON: Well, my filmic career really breaks down to two broad areas. One is writing about it. The other has to do with the fact that I've been involved, directly or indirectly, on a large number of films that have turned out to be among the greatest genre films of their time. Consequently, I had the opportunity to penetrate the film industry in a manner that assured a great deal of autonomy and an incredibly vertical freedom of movement within the industry itself. And that was mostly through the realm of being a special promotional consultant.

WIATER: Your articles are often considered the definitive examinations of the production. It's obvious that these assignments were tackled by someone who had an incredible passion for the movies in general.

SAMMON: I really like to think of myself more as a film historian than a film critic because I *have* a genuine passion and love for films. Everything I do flows from that. From the beginning, my desire was that, if I could not be involved in the actual creation of a film, at least I could chronicle it. Put the experience down on paper so that maybe years from now people could read it and say I was accurate and enthusiastic about what I was reporting on.

WIATER: There are still only a handful of journalists carrying on this role of promoting horror and science fiction films at the various conventions. When you were actively pursuing it, you were virtually alone, weren't you?

SAMMON: More or less. I basically embarked on an eight-year career in which I worked on dozens of films with dozens of different directors. As you know, the perception in Hollywood of who you are is pretty much limited to what your last project was. If you worked on what is perceived as a B Western, then that's where they expect you to remain. But if you are seen to work consistently with major A productions—and I started with *Conan the Barbarian*—well, because of that initial good fortune I found myself working on a lot of other major productions. Like *Blue Velvet* and *Dune* and *Blade Runner* and *Robocop*. . . . The list goes on and on.

WIATER: Do you believe that your promotional work served to change the studio's perception of the genre audience?

SAMMON: If there has been an effect, I'm sure it's been minuscule. I think it isn't any great secret that the bottom line for any film is economic. So when I was initially involved in this sort of marketing and promotion, one of the first things I tried to work up was an idea of what are we exactly talking about in raw numbers of genre fans? I realized there was a lot of overlap in genres, science fiction with thrillers, thrillers with horror. But, we still did a nationwide marketing survey. And when the numbers came back, way back in 1981, we found out we had at least *seven million* people out there interested in seeing films in these kind of genres! That's a significant number of tickets.

So if anything has had an impact on the studios over the past few years, it's the notion that the sheer number of genre fans are important to the studios in terms of being a core audience. And the studios know that there is competition from other studios to get that ticket dollar away from them and into their own pockets.

But in terms of actually altering the product or changing scripts to make them more meaningful or significant to the fans, I don't think that has ever occurred. Or ever will occur. One of the misconceptions that the fans—and the general public—have is that Hollywood is composed of a lot of know-nothing ignoramuses, who are out there simply for the buck and have no sense of who their audience is or what their product is. *Nothing* could be further from the truth. Although this industry does have more than its share of slackers, goof-offs, and know-nothings, there is also a very significant number of artistically aware and caring people. People who very much know what they're doing.

But *it's a crap shoot every time*. Another thing most people don't realize is that every film production is *completely* different from the one that came before it. Sure there is a certain structure and pattern to the physical making of films, but there is also always a different *deal* to put together; a different mix of ideology and esthetics among the people who are working there, the script is different, the actors are different . . . and ultimately it's a crap shoot as to whether it will be a hit or a bomb.

WIATER: Sometimes, as with *Dune*, everyone expects a masterpiece before it's even finished. In cases like this, it's almost impossible for a movie to live up to it's prerelease hype.

SAMMON: And sometimes films turn out good when you least expect them to—*Robocop* is a prime example of that. Orion Pictures had little faith in the original *Robocop*. The title alone was enough to turn off most people. And it was a very rough shoot, because of limited budget, weather constraints, and a lot of other problems among the filmmakers themselves. But what eventually transpired was this wonderful gestalt of energies, and it transformed what could have been a very superficial and forgettable film into a fine piece of science fiction. So you never know.

WIATER: This goes back to my original point in the sense that because *Robocop* was an unexpected hit, the public perception was that the sequel would be even "bigger and better." Most critics—and the public—were ultimately disappointed by *Robocop 2*. Didn't the studio want to please the ticket buyers who made the first film a success?

SAMMON: Believe me, there was every intention on the part of the on-site makers of *Robocop 2* to make it equal to, if not better, than the first film. I know—I was there. It wasn't a cynical exercise to make a sequel as quickly as possible just to try to make a few bucks. What happened in that case was a number of negative factors. One of them was the fact that Orion had locked itself into a specific summer release date. Unfortunately there was then a screenwriter's strike, and the original director dropped out after working on the production for eight months.

What this then meant was that the new director, Irvin Kirshner, was forced to go into the production with only six weeks of preparation—and with a script that wasn't finished. The screenplay was being written as the film was shot. That the completed film had any kind of integrity or effectiveness at all is purely through the talents of Irvin Kirshner, writer Frank Miller, actor Peter Weller, and producer Jon Davison. All these negative factors mitigated against everybody's best intentions.

WIATER: You worked on a number of productions that were done under the aegis of Dino De Laurentis. Many of the leading talents involved in genre filmmaking have also dealt with him. What was your impression of his influence?

SAMMON: Talking about Dino is definitely a conflicting experience. [Chuckles.] I've always perceived Dino as being the last of an old-time breed, the producer-as-showman. Like P. T. Barnum. The ones that can thump the drum the loudest, and get the biggest elephants and the gaudiest horses and the loudest bands to play in the show. And Dino has a mastery of that. He also has a genuine enthusiasm and energy for films that just don't make it. I think that many times people get swept up in his absolute conviction that what he's doing is right. And perfect. He's *very* persuasive. He also always managed to find the money to be able to pay the people who worked for him very well.

But—when it comes to the completion of the film, Dino would always insist on having the final cut. And I think that contributed to Dino's downfall: he may not have had a clue, artistically speaking, of what he'd paid to have put up on the screen.

WIATER: How do you feel about the state of the industry today, in terms of bringing forth new fantastic or dark visions to the screen?

SAMMON: We are living in very good times as fans of film art, because there are any number of very distinctive, individualistic voices working in film today. There's Paul Verhooven, the director of *Robocop*, and *Total Recall*. His visual style has almost become a cliché in terms of the way he presents unsettling violence right in your face. There's John Milius, the director of *Conan the Barbarian*, who is a poet/warrior and has that thematic thread running through his work. He's also one of the best screenwriters working in Hollywood. A director who has brought himself up to the pinnacle of genre visibility is David Cronenberg. Here's a director who is quite familiar with great literature. You can see a novelist's attention to language, thematic layering and philosophical issues in all of his work.

WIATER: You're actively planning to embark on a career as a feature filmmaker yourself. Your way of introduction is due in part to making short promotional films, now referred to as "electronic press kits." How did that come about?

SAMMON: I saw an opportunity to do this when I worked on *Dune*. I was able to make my own short films—and direct them and write and produce and edit them—and as someone who has always admired the frugal artistry of Roger Corman, I insisted that I do it all myself. It's just been an ongoing evolutionary process. Learning one thing always leads to another, and so I ended up doing dozens of these documentary films, and commercials as well. I also did a very specialized featurette on an Academy Award–nominated makeup by Carl Fullerton for a film called *Remo Williams*. That featurette is still being shown on television stations around the world.

At this point in my career I'm co-producing a weekly Japanese television show, and so I'm very familiar with production techniques. It's called "Hello! Movies" and is basically a version of "Entertainment Tonight." It's the most successful entertainment show of its kind in Japan today.

Again, all of this just sort of happens! [Laughs.] A lot of people have diagrams laid out for their time on this earth. Me, I've always just been happy to learn something new. So I've recently written a screenplay, and hope to direct a low-budget feature film soon.

WIATER: You've been a chronicler of the genre film scene for some time now—what do you think the 1990s hold for horror films?

SAMMON: In one of his recent columns, Harlan Ellison stated his belief that the horror film is dead as a genre. That it has been recycled and redone to death, and no one cares about horror films anymore. As much as I dearly admire Harlan, what I think is really happening to the horror film is that it is going to become increasingly absorbed into the mainstream. For instance, when a movie like *Fatal Attraction* becomes one of the most successful films of all time, by simply using one of the most tired horror clichés of a mad person threatening a family with a knife, then that tells you something!

What is obviously happening is that themes of moral terror, of personal pain, of twisted emotions, of the darker conflicts within us; of films dealing with our own everyday reality rather than someone else's imagined reality are becoming so accepted that they are no longer instantly categorized as "horror" to the public consciousness. What I think may happen in the coming decade is a little less product. It will be harder to find as many horror, science fiction, and fantasy films. I think we're on the downswing of a cycle.

Conversely, I believe this is actually good for horror and fantasy fans, because when there isn't a lot to see out there, the fans will be hungry for more. And the way to get more is to make the films a little better than they were the last time, and have an infusion of more adult concerns, with more crossover genres.

WIATER: Explain what you mean by crossover genres.

SAMMON: There's a whole area that almost no one has yet come to terms with. Films like the *Mad Max* movies, which are a combination of science fiction, Western, thriller, ecological disasters, political statements. . . . Or David Lynch's films: *Wild at Heart* is a perfect example—what is *Wild at Heart*? [Laughs.] It's a road movie, it's a *noir* film, it's a horror movie, it's a sexual film. . . . So this blurring of genre values is to me very exciting, because it really means that literally *anything* can be done.

You can have films with broomstick genitals, as in the recent German *Nekromantik*, or the Spanish art film *In a Glass Cage*, which is about a former Nazi paralyzed in an iron lung who is sexually humiliated by one of his child victims now grown. What a horrifying concept. And yet that's an art film! So I'm very excited—I think this blurring of genres is going to be very good for all of us.

WIATER: On a personal level, wouldn't you agree that your own career could qualify as the ultimate example of a fan literally transforming himself into a pro through sheer love of the medium?

SAMMON: On one level, I suppose you could say that. I certainly don't want to be held up as an example for anyone to follow! [Laughs.] On another level, what you're seeing with me is sheer *passion*. I'm still a fan! I'm probably a bigger fan now than when I started out. I see more. And I know more, certainly, about the reality of filmmaking. It's all absolutely *fascinating*! So what really keeps me going, what makes me so enthusiastic, is that I love what I'm doing. Believe me, I love movies. And you'd better capitalize that—I LOVE movies! [Laughs.] Basically I just hope I can make a couple of decent ones myself before I close my eyes for the last time.

WIATER: So you have no hesitation about making your own dark visions appear before an audience someday?

SAMMON: Oh, no, not at all! My particular outlook on the universe is that it is infinite and apathetic. We basically live in an existential void, and whatever we project onto it is what we perceive. But I think it's a very hostile universe out there. A capillary can explode in your brain at any time. And where's the justice in Turkish prisons, where prisoners are systematically tortured? Existence is just an accident of geography as to where you are born, and an accident of states whether you're "politically correct." I think a lot of life depends on simple good fortune and circumstance. It's what you finally do with your reality that will be inked in the plus or minus column in that great big accounting ledger in the sky.

Biographical
Note

STANLEY WIATER is a widely published journalist, *cineteratologist*, and short story writer. He has interviewed more horror authors, filmmakers, and artists than any other writer, for such magazines as *Rod Serling's Twilight Zone Magazine, Prevue,* and *Writer's Digest.* He has been a contributing editor to *Fangoria* and *New Blood* and England's *Fear.* His first published short story was the winner of a competition judged by Stephen King. Several of his interviews with King were reprinted in *Bare Bones* and its companion volume, *Feast of Fear.* He has also contributed to the anthologies *Reign of Fear, Clive Barker's Shadows in Eden, Cut!, Stephen King and Clive Barker: The Masters of the Macabre, Fly in My Eye, James Herbert: By Horror Haunted,* and *The Shape Under the Sheet: the Complete Stephen King Encyclopedia.*

His short stories have appeared in *Rod Serling's Twilight Zone Magazine, Castle Rock, Cavalier, Mike Shayne;* anthologies such as J. N. Williamson's *Masques* series, Thomas Monteleone's *Borderlands* series, Gary Raisor's *Obsessions*, and have also been adapted for horror comic books. In 1989 he edited the anthology *Night Visions 7* and recently compiled another entitled *After the Darkness*. His first book of interviews, *Dark Dreamers: Conversations with the Masters of Horror* appeared in 1990 from Avon Books. (*Dark Dreamers* subsequently won the Bram Stoker Award for superior achievement in nonfiction from the Horror Writers of America.) He lives with wife Iris and daughter Tanya in rural western Massachusetts.